MW01025678

Genetic Joyce

The Florida James Joyce Series

UNIVERSITY PRESS OF FLORIDA

Florida A&M University, Tallahassee
Florida Atlantic University, Boca Raton
Florida Gulf Coast University, Ft. Myers
Florida International University, Miami
Florida State University, Tallahassee
New College of Florida, Sarasota
University of Central Florida, Orlando
University of Florida, Gainesville
University of North Florida, Jacksonville
University of South Florida, Tampa
University of West Florida, Pensacola

GENETIC JOYCE

Manuscripts and the Dynamics of Creation

Daniel Ferrer

Foreword by Sam Slote

UNIVERSITY PRESS OF FLORIDA

Gainesville / Tallahassee / Tampa / Boca Raton

Pensacola / Orlando / Miami / Jacksonville / Ft. Myers / Sarasota

28 27 26 25 24 23   6 5 4 3 2 1

Library of Congress Cataloging-in-Publication Data
Names: Ferrer, Daniel, author. | Slote, Sam, author of foreword.
Title: Genetic Joyce : manuscripts and the dynamics of creation / Daniel
  Ferrer ; foreword by Sam Slote.
Other titles: Florida James Joyce series.
Description: Gainesville : University Press of Florida, 2023. | Series: The
  Florida James Joyce series | Includes bibliographical references and
  index.
Identifiers: LCCN 2022050102 (print) | LCCN 2022050103 (ebook) | ISBN
  9780813069715 (hardback) | ISBN 9780813070476 (pdf)
Subjects: LCSH: Joyce, James, 1882–1941—Manuscripts. | Joyce, James,
  1882–1941—Criticism and interpretation. | BISAC: LITERARY CRITICISM /
  Modern / 20th Century | LITERARY CRITICISM / European / English, Irish,
  Scottish, Welsh
Classification: LCC PR6019.O9 Z5333775 2023 (print) | LCC PR6019.O9
  (ebook) | DDC 823/.912—dc23/eng/20230127
LC record available at https://lccn.loc.gov/2022050102
LC ebook record available at https://lccn.loc.gov/2022050103

The University Press of Florida is the scholarly publishing agency for the State University System of Florida, comprising Florida A&M University, Florida Atlantic University, Florida Gulf Coast University, Florida International University, Florida State University, New College of Florida, University of Central Florida, University of Florida, University of North Florida, University of South Florida, and University of West Florida.

University Press of Florida
2046 NE Waldo Road
Suite 2100
Gainesville, FL 32609
http://upress.ufl.edu

To Joachim, Alma and Cleo

Contents

Figures

Foreword

Texts change: texts are the products of change, changes inflicted over time. The archive of Joyce's works illustrates this phenomenon well. Joyce was a controlling, obsessive author who spent years working and reworking his books. His fundamental process of writing was addition and revision: his writings are accretive. With both *Ulysses* and *Finnegans Wake,* he did not begin writing from a fully fleshed-out plan; rather, to at least some extent, he learned what he was writing *as* he was writing it. Unlike Hitchcock, who fully envisioned his movies in his head before filming even began, Joyce's writing is not a linear development to some preordained goal; instead, the writing evolves, the creation is dynamic.

Daniel Ferrer has been one of the leading lights in what is called "genetic criticism": the investigation of a text's evolution across multiple documentary instantiations. Genetic criticism examines texts over time and across changes, which are recorded on various documents. Ferrer writes, "Every redrafting is, to some extent, a recontextualization of the material, implying a creative oblivion of the original context (the previous version). The final version somehow retains the memory of all the different contexts it has left behind, but the traces are normally too faint to be recovered from the printed text." Texts change and are laden with seams and strata of their changes.

Likewise, our understanding of Joyce is dynamic and continually evolves. We have come a long way from the pioneering work of A. Walton Litz and David Hayman. This has been especially true since the discovery of various manuscripts, previously unknown, in the first years of the twenty-first century. These manuscripts have cast new light on the collections that have been studied for decades. Literary criticism and scholarship are also always works in progress.

In this volume, Ferrer looks at the range of Joyce's writing and writing practices across his career, from the "Early Commonplace Notebook" of 1902/3 through to *Finnegans Wake*. These chapters are informed by many decades spent working on Joyce and are the result of the evolution of Ferrer's own understanding of Joyce and his manuscripts. By looking at specific moments within the archive, Ferrer elegantly educes the larger ramifications of subtle alterations, making this volume a role model of genetic criticism and essential reading for anyone interested in the full range of Joyce's writing practices.

Sam Slote
Series Editor

Acknowledgments

I express my sincere gratitude to Luca Crispi for his acute critical reading and to Geert Lernout for his encouraging reading of the drafts of this book. To Hans Walter Gabler for many fruitful exchanges over the years. To Michael Groden† for years of collaboration (he had offered to read this book in manuscript, but I was unfortunately too slow finishing it). To Jean-Michel Rabaté for his friendly impulse at the start. To Claude Jacquet† for launching me into notebook studies. To Hélène Cixous for encouraging me to look at Joyce's manuscripts at a time when it was not at all fashionable to do so and, before that, for teaching me how to *read*.

To ITEM (Institut des Textes et Manuscrits Modernes, CNRS/Ecole Normale Supérieure/PSL) for making this research possible; to the Royal Flemish Academy of Arts and Science for a fellowship in 2003–2004; to the Bogliasco Foundation for a fellowship in 2020.

The ideas in this book have been tried out in the following articles and chapters: "Hemingway aux sources de la Liffey," in *Genèses et métamorphoses du texte joycien,* ed. Claude Jacquet (Paris: Les Publications de la Sorbonne, 1985); "La scène primitive de l'écriture: Une lecture joycienne de Freud," in *Genèses de Babel: James Joyce et la création de Finnegans Wake,* ed. C. Jacquet (Paris: Editions du C.N.R.S, 1985); "Echo or Narcissus," in *James Joyce: The Centennial Symposium,* ed. M. Beja, Ph. Herring, M. Harmon and D. Norris (Urbana: University of Illinois Press, 1986); "Le texte sur sa réserve: D'un usage inouï de la citation chez Joyce," in *L'Ente et la Chimère, aspects de la citation dans la littérature anglaise,* ed. L. Le Bouille (Caen: Centre de Publications de l'Université de Caen, 1986); "Characters in *Ulysses:* 'The featureful perfection of imperfection,'" in *James Joyce: the Augmented Ninth,* ed. B. Benstock (Syracuse: Syracuse University Press, 1988); "Paragraphes en expansion" (with J.-M. Rabaté), in *De la lettre au livre: Sémiotique des manu-scrits littéraires*, ed. L. Hay (Paris: Éditions du CNRS, 1989); "Reflections on a Discarded Set of Proofs," in *Genetic Studies in Joyce: PROBES*, ed. David Hayman and Sam Slote (Amsterdam: Rodopi, 1995); "Les carnets de Joyce: Avant-textes limites d'une œuvre limite," *Genesis* 3 (1993); "Between *Inventio* and *Memoria*: Locations of 'Aeolus,'" in *Joyce in the Hibernian Metropolis*, ed. M. Beja and D. Norris (Columbus: Ohio State University Press, 1996); "The Open Space of the Draft Page: James Joyce and Modern Manuscripts," in *The Iconic Page in Manuscript, Print and Digital Culture*, ed. George Bornstein and Theresa Tinkle (Ann Arbor: University of Michigan Press, 1998); "'Prac-tise Preaching': Variantes pragmatiques et prédication suspendue dans un manuscrit des 'Sirènes,'" in *Writing Its Own Wrunes For Ever: Essais de géné-tique joycenne/ Essays in Joycean Genetics*, ed. C. Jacquet and D. Ferrer (Tus-son: Éditions du Lérot, 1998); "*Loci Memoriae*: Joyce and the Art of Mem-ory," in *Classic Joyce*, ed. Franca Ruggieri (Rome: Bulzoni Editore, 1999); "Les bibliothèques virtuelles de James Joyce et de Virginia Woolf," in *Bib-liothèques d'écrivains*, ed. P. D'Iorio and D. Ferrer (Paris: Editions du CNRS, 2001); "What song the Sirens sang . . . Is no Longer beyond All Conjecture: A Preliminary Description of the New 'Proteus' and 'Sirens' Manuscripts," *James Joyce Quarterly* 36–1, 2001; "'The Conversation Began Some Minutes before Anything Was Said . . . ': Textual Genesis as dialogue and confronta-tion (Woolf vs Joyce and Co)," *Études britanniques contemporaines* (Autumn 2004); "The Joyce of Manuscripts," in *The James Joyce Companion*, ed. Rich-ard Brown (Oxford: Blackwell's, 2008); "Writing Space," in *Making Space in the Works of James Joyce*, ed. Valérie Benejam and John Bishop (New York: Routledge, 2011); "A Mediated Plunge: From Joyce to Woolf through Rich-ardson through Sinclair," in *Parallaxes: Virginia Woolf Meets James Joyce*, ed. Marco Canani and Sara Sullam (Newcastle upon Tyne: Cambridge Scholar, 2013); "An Unwritten Chapter of Ulysses? Joyce's Notes for a 'Lacedemon' Episode," in *James Joyce: Whence, Whither and How; Studies in Honour of Carla Vaglio*, ed. Giuseppina Cortese, Giuliana Ferreccio, M. Teresa Giaveri and Teresa Prudente (Alessandria: Edizioni dell'Orso, 2015); "From Tristan to *Finnegan*: A Re-Telling," *Dublin James Joyce Journal* 8 (2015); "Libraries of Indistinction," in *New Quotatoes: Joycean Exogenesis in the Digital Age*, ed. R. Crowley and D. Van Hulle (The Hague: Brill, 2016); and "'L'oreille paradigmatique': Les listes dans les manuscrits de James Joyce," *Genesis* 47

(2018). Although they have been refashioned and recontextualized, a grateful "memory of the context" remains.

Before that, those ideas had been inflected by the expectations and reactions of audiences in Paris, Besançon, Orléans, Tour, Nancy, Toulouse, Pau, Montpellier, Valenciennes, Dublin, London, Cardiff, Leeds, Oxford, Antwerp, Ghent, Leuwen, Louvain la Neuve, Brussels, Geneva, Zurich, Pisa, Bologna, Milan, Turin, Padua, Venice, Perugia, Rome, Naples, Palermo, Trieste, Porto, Madrid, San Sebastian, Prague, Budapest, Oslo, Copenhagen, Moscow, Saint Petersburg, Ann Arbor, Buffalo, Evanston, Champaign, New Brunswick, New York, Baltimore, São Paulo, Salvador de Bahia, Taipei, Kaohsiung, Tokyo and Sydney.

I am grateful to the James Joyce Estate for graciously allowing the reproduction of the documents that are in copyright and to the Literary Estate of Virginia Woolf for graciously allowing the reproduction of a page from Woolf's notes on *Ulysses*. I am also grateful to the holding libraries for permission to reproduce the documents they own (see illustration credits).

Abbreviations

BL British Library (followed by the call number of the manuscripts).

Buffalo The Poetry/Rare Books Collection, The University of New York at Buffalo (followed by the call number of the manuscripts).

E *Exiles: A Play in Three Acts,* ed. Padraic Colum (London: Jonathan Cape, 1972).

FW James Joyce, *Finnegans Wake* (London: Faber, 1975); cited by page and line number.

JJA James Joyce, *The James Joyce Archive,* ed. Michael Groden et al. 63 volumes (New York: Garland, 1977–1978); cited by volume and page number.

Letters I James Joyce, *Letters of James Joyce,* vol. I, ed. Stuart Gilbert (New York: Viking, 1957).

Letters II, III James Joyce, *Letters of James Joyce,* vols. II and III, ed. Richard Ellmann (New York: Viking, 1966).

NLI National Library of Ireland (followed by the call number of the manuscripts).

SL James Joyce, *Selected Letters of James Joyce,* ed. Richard Ellmann (New York: Viking, 1975).

U James Joyce, *Ulysses: A Critical and Synoptic Edition,* ed. Hans Walter Gabler et al. (New York: Garland, 1984, 1986); cited by episode and line number.

Conventions of Transcription

Deletions are indicated by means of a crossing-out: ~~xxxxxxx~~.
Additions are indicated thus: ^+xxxxxx+^.
Nested additions: ^+yyyyy^+xxxx+^yyyyy+^.

Introduction

Writers Writing

The past assuredly implies a fluid succession of presents, the development
of an entity of which our actual present is a phase only.

"A Portrait of the Artist" (1904)

In 1973, Emile de Antonio directed a film called *Painters Painting,* a fascinating documentary about the New York postwar art scene. The meaning of
this title can be interpreted in two different (but not exclusive) ways. The
painting of artists such as Jackson Pollock, Franz Kline, Helen Frankenthaler
and some of the painters of the next generation is clearly oriented toward the
medium itself. It is a painting for the real connoisseurs—for those who care
for painting for its own sake, for other painters, for people who are interested
in the painterly medium and the problems it raises—more than for the general public, which tends to forget the medium and look for the subject matter. These artists could be called painters' painters, like Uccello, Chardin, or
Velázquez before them. In the same way, Joyce is an author for those who are
interested in the craft of writing: he is the supreme craftsman, with a concern
for his medium (the narrative medium and, ultimately, language itself) that
matches, at least, the passion for canvases and pigments that characterized
American Abstract Expressionists. In the same way as their paintings are
described as "painterly," Joyce's works can be called "writerly" in every sense
of the word.

The primary meaning of the film's title, however, is probably a different
one: *Painters Painting* shows painters *in the act of painting.* It is particularly

interesting, in the case of those artists who have been called "action painters," to see not only the result of the action, the trace of the painting gesture on the canvas, but also the gesture itself, the painter in action. Emile de Antonio's documentary quotes from Hans Namuth's photographs and film of Jackson Pollock dancing over his picture, dripping paint, flinging colors across the surface of a huge canvas on the ground. Now, the text of *Finnegans Wake* can readily be compared to the surface of a Pollock picture: the multiple layers, the intricacy of the intertwining strands of material, the all-over feeling, a sense that every known principle of composition is superseded by an overwhelming proliferation of local accidents at the heart of the medium. *Finnegans Wake* might be considered a kind of "action writing": the surface of the text bears the visible trace of the energies that went into its composition. Some of Joyce's manuscripts actually look somewhat like Pollock's canvases—but the superficial resemblance is misleading. The manuscripts of *Ulysses* or *Finnegans Wake* are not the result of an exuberant extemporization but suggest, on the contrary, a meticulous and protracted process of revision. It is manifest that the kinship between the finished works can hardly be the result of a similarity in the working process of the two artists.

We may feel that it is unfortunate that we do not have something comparable to the film recording Pollock in action: a documentary picturing Joyce in the act of writing. But perhaps we do have such a thing. The manuscripts (and a huge corpus of them has been preserved) could be the best possible record of Joyce's writerly performance, the best film that we have, if only we knew how to develop this film and how to interpret it. And this is precisely what genetic criticism proposes to do. It is a discipline that studies the traces left by the labor of writing—in notebooks, drafts, typescripts, proofs, correspondences, early printed versions, and all the available documents—in order to recover the process of *invention*.[1]

"Joyce" does not exist

For a discipline focused on invention, Joyce is an irresistible subject.[2] In the "Scylla and Charybdis" episode of *Ulysses,* John Eglinton affirms, "When all is said Dumas *fils* (or is it Dumas *père?*) is right. After God Shakespeare has created most." When all is said, we might come to the conclusion that Joyce, who claimed that he had no imagination, has invented more than anyone, and more radically, in terms of style, narrative technique and language (and that, in so doing, he has profoundly renewed our conception of our self as a multifaceted construction immersed in a flow of equivocal discourses).

After his statement about Shakespeare and God, Alexandre Dumas (the father!) goes on to say:

> It is *men* who invent, not one man alone. Each arrives in turn and in his own time, takes possession of the things that were known to his fathers, puts them to work in new combinations, and then dies, after having added something to the sum of human knowledge, which he bequeaths to his children. As to complete creation of something, I do not believe it possible. God himself, when he created man, could not or dared not invent him: he made him in his own image.[3]

For Dumas, then, individual invention is impossible, even for the Creator: invention is a purely accretive and collaborative process. One would perhaps expect genetic criticism, as a potential abettor in the kind of literary hero worship that surrounds Joyce (and other "major" writers), to strongly disagree with this opinion, which seems to run counter to what we have just said about the power of invention manifested by Joyce's work. Far from it—and not only because Joyce is not the mythical "solitary genius"[4] that we may suppose him to be (many collaborators were enlisted in the creation of the works that bear his name), but also, more fundamentally, because genetic criticism believes, and verifies in the manuscripts, that "Joyce" does not exist.

In the strong words of Paul Valéry, "The literary work is a lie," insofar as it pretends to be the production of a unified author. It is "the result of a collaboration of very different states, of unexpected incidents; a kind of combination of points of view originally independent from one another."[5] The figure of the author is thus a retrospective construction, deceptively based on the final resulting work. Most of the time, when we refer to "Joyce," we are not referring to the human being who created the works signed by this name but to a figure created *by* the works or, rather, inferentially derived from them.

It should be obvious to everyone that the Joyce who wrote *Stephen Hero* is not the same as the author of *Finnegans Wake*. Most people would also be ready to admit that the Joyce who began writing *Ulysses* in Trieste in 1914 is not the same as the Joyce who finished it in Paris in 1922, after a world war and several fundamental changes of project for the book, or that the Joyce who was taking notes at random for a hypothetical book in the autumn of 1922, or the Joyce who was writing a series of naïve vignettes in 1923, are not the same as the one who managed to integrate these elements into a book as complex as *Finnegans Wake* and to bring it to an end in 1939. In "Circe," Joyce stages the proverbial "Philip drunk" and "Philip sober" as two different characters. We do not know if Joyce sober ever corrected what he had written drunk, or vice versa, but genetic criticism believes (or rather observes) that the writer who starts a draft page is not quite the same as the one who completes it and even that the writer who strikes out a word currente calamo is not the same as the writer who inscribed the word a few seconds before: if the word that has just been selected is erased, it is because the writer's perspective has somewhat changed in the short interval. In the words of Bloom: "Or was that I? Or am I now I?" (*U* 8.608). What appeared to be, at least provisionally, the best choice no longer seems to be so once the word has been entered. The context has changed, ever so slightly, and the *evaluation* (of the appropriateness of the word) is modified. The genetic approach performs a kind of deconstruction[6] of the authorial figure that we hypostatize from the books published under a writer's name. Whereas the basic aim of traditional textual criticism is to establish texts, so as to publish "corrected" or "definitive" editions that comply with the author's intention, genetic criticism tends on the contrary to destabilize simultaneously the notions of text and of authorial intention by insisting on their mobility.

This is not to say that the genetic approach disregards the writer's identity. Writing involves a sequence of macro- and micro-decisions, and these decisions are not taken haphazardly. They certainly show a continuity of purpose, especially in the case of a writer as stubborn as Joyce (Eliot called him a fanatic).[7] Writers are (generally) not schizophrenic; their personality is relatively stable. They have been conditioned by their physiology, their background and their training so that they carry with them from their youth a number of habits, emotions and memories that leave a recognizable mark on all their productions (the habitus of Aquinas or Bourdieu). When studying their manuscripts, one can remark a number of typical procedures that remain stable during their whole lives. But if the original background, the innate faculties and the initial training play a decisive part in the writer's orientation, the background for each decision taken in the course of writing is a different one, and the training of a writer is a process that never stops.[8] Even if Joyce could have remained locked up in an ivory tower, immune from historical evolution, social and political upheavals, sentimental crises, viruses and health accidents, not to mention changes in the literary field around him, he would have been affected by the events occurring on the surface of his own manuscript pages. Even when it is not disrupted by the interference of external events of all kinds, the continuity of intent is constantly disrupted, because the implementation of each decision opens unforeseen possibilities and precludes others: it modifies the context in which the next decision has to be taken. Pierre Mac Orlan used to say that there are more adventures on a chessboard than on all the seas of the world. Some of Joyce's manuscripts are more eventful than many historical battlefields.[9]

"New" manuscripts

In 1919, after reading just a few pages of "Telemachus" in the *Little Review,* Virginia Woolf made this note: "Possibly one might write about the effect of reading something new, its queerness."[10] It is difficult for us to realize how strange, how queer, how shocking the first episodes of *Ulysses* were for the reader in 1919. It is difficult for scholars of modernist literature, who have read them so often and who have benefitted from so many works of exegesis, but it is difficult even for the first-time readers of today. It is hard for us to believe that, when he first received "Proteus," Ezra Pound (Ezra Pound!) should have found it "mostly incomprehensible."[11] Joyce's innovations (at least those displayed in the early part of *Ulysses*) have percolated through our culture, and even undergraduates are permeated by them. There is no longer the same sense of shock: to a large degree, the "queerness" has worn out or at least become attenuated. We might transpose what Pierre Bourdieu says about the perpetrator of another symbolic revolution, Manet:

> a symbolic revolution overturns cognitive, and sometimes social, structures, which become invisible the more they become generally recognized, widely known and incorporated by all the perceiving subjects in a social universe. Our own categories of perception and judgment—those we ordinarily use to understand the representations of the world and the world itself—were created by this successful symbolic revolution. The representation of the world created by this revolution is therefore self-evident—indeed, it is so self-evident that the scandal provoked by Manet's works itself is surprising if not scandalous.[12]

On the other hand, the more familiar we are with Joyce's text, the more we are liable to be shocked by a different kind of novelty, when we discover the work we know so well in a "new" form. The feeling of being confronted with different versions of the text that we are so familiar with and that suddenly appears unfamiliar can be truly *unheimlich*.

The more familiar we are with a literary text, the stranger it is to discover it in a different form in its other versions in the genetic archive, but the more we have acquainted ourselves with the archive, the more we have studied the manuscripts of an author, the more we are going to be surprised, thrilled, shocked, when we encounter unexpected manuscripts. It is one of the joys—and one of the dangers—of the geneticist's trade: as opposed to critics who work with a finite text, the genetic critic has to live with the fact that no archive is definitely circumscribed. We live in the hope that new material will be discovered but also under the constant threat that this new material will destroy the hypotheses that we have made on the basis of the existing materials.

The discovery can be quite small: just one word that we could not decipher becomes readable because someone has made a suggestion and suddenly it becomes clear to everyone. Or an accepted reading is contradicted by the discovery of a source or a previous draft. We all know that a single word, or even a punctuation mark, can make a significant difference. On the other hand, we are sometimes confronted with a massive transformation of the archival situation. In the case of Raymond Roussel, there were practically no extant manuscripts, and critics had to rely entirely on Roussel's own statements in his famous *Comment j'ai écrit certains de mes livres;* no real genetic study of his work was possible until 1989, when a trunk was discovered containing the almost complete drafts of his work. A whole new world opened up, fifty-five years after the author's death.[13] The case of Joyce is different. For many years, Joyce scholars had been blessed (or cursed) with a huge, accessible archive.[14] Most of it was reproduced in the two volumes of color facsimiles of the Rosenbach *Ulysses* manuscript[15] and the sixty-three volumes of the Garland edition of the *James Joyce Archive:* (eleven volumes for the early works, sixteen volumes for *Ulysses,* thirty-six volumes for *Finnegans Wake,* including the sixteen volumes representing the fourteen thousand pages of the Buffalo notebooks).[16] Nobody expected that anything substantial could still be discovered: a few letters and a few sheets of proofs might resurface from time to time, but not much more. The situation changed, however, with the new millennium when the "John Quinn draft" of "Circe" came out of hiding. Joyce had claimed that he had written eight versions of the episode, but we had only one draft (Buffalo V.B.19). In a letter accompanying the fair copy that he had sold to John Quinn, Joyce mentions that he is "throwing in" a rough draft. But it was only seventy-nine years later that Quinn's heirs decided to offer it for sale at auction.[17] The sale of the Quinn manuscript for a very substantial sum was the tremor that triggered a series of earthquakes. In the next few years, the landscape of Joyce studies was distinctly modified by the arrival of successive waves of new autographs: both manuscripts that were known to have existed, even if they were lost (e.g., missing parts of extant drafts), and manuscripts that were a complete surprise. First an unknown very early draft for the "Eumaeus" episode of *Ulysses* came on the market in 2001. Then a considerable number of fascinating manuscripts (notebooks, drafts for *Ulysses,* typescripts for *Finnegans Wake*) were discovered in the papers of the family of Joyce's private secretary, Paul Léon. And finally (?) the National Library of Ireland acquired half a dozen large sheets of papers that changed our idea of the transition period between *Ulysses* and *Finnegans Wake.*

It is easy to imagine the excitement of Joyce scholars—their wild surmise when these new planets swam into their ken—and also the traumatic effect caused by each of these revelations. We are far from having absorbed the shock. We will see, in the following chapters, how this massive new evidence forced us to reconsider some of our conclusions, but I would like to go further and suggest that every working manuscript, because it represents a field of virtual realities preceding the closure of the final text, has the same potential for subverting our understanding of the work as a "new" manuscript. The purpose of genetic criticism is to study manuscripts from this perspective: we have said that it is concerned with invention (or innovation), but invention is only a transition between phases of repetition, and it is possible to apprehend it only when it is stabilized through repetition, so that we have to make a deliberate effort to reanimate and reenergize it. In this respect, the unexpected emergence of new manuscripts is a useful reminder of this disruptive potential.

Homo geneticus

As Jon Elster has remarked, "One of the most persisting cleavages in the social sciences is the opposition between two lines of thought conveniently associated with Adam Smith and Emile Durkheim, between *homo economicus* and *homo sociologicus.*"[18] *Homo sociologicus* is "pushed" from behind by the quasi-inertial forces of social norms, while *homo economicus* is "pulled" by the prospect of future rewards, guided by instrumental rationality. Now, if there is such a thing as a *homo geneticus,* she or he is submitted to both these forces, pushed by preexisting determinations (unconscious drives, sociological dispositions, configuration of the professional field) and pulled by the perspective of the projected goal, a certain equilibrium of the different aesthetic choices. But the characteristic of *homo geneticus* is that she or he is moved by a nonlinear motion, which we could define as the dynamics of invention. *Homo geneticus* must constantly, and dialectically, adjust the goal, the means toward this goal, and the values according to which the result will be appreciated, in relation to varying external circumstances, but also in relation to the internal logic and the incidents and accidents occurring in the process of accomplishing the goal. So that apart from the two impulses, upstream and downstream, pushing and pulling, he or she is moved by a third category of impulses, issuing from within the creative process. It is this third category, this internal dynamics, that we can consider as specifically genetic.

To reveal these forces at work, I will start from an unusual set of documents: a batch of corrected proofs for *Ulysses* that arrived too late to be used by the printers. We will evaluate the consequences of this accident and see how Joyce used the unimplemented corrections at a later stage of the composition and how the postponement and the transposition (the deferral and the displacement) transformed the corrections and their environment.

In the second chapter, I will examine separately the effects of the superimposition of intentions in a single place, on the one hand, and the interference of contemporary acts of writing, on the other, and we will see how both phenomena contributed decisively to the shaping of *Ulysses* and *Finnegans Wake.* We will see that the accident of the stray proofs is only a special instance of the part played by chance in the genetic process and that the overdetermination of elements that is so much in evidence in Joyce's work is paradoxical from a genetic point of view. It necessarily relies on the connective propensity of textual matter, which is the best ally of writers in general and particularly of someone like Joyce, who knew how to take advantage of it and how to change the contingent into the necessary.

In the next chapter, we will look at some aspects of the transition between *Ulysses* and *Finnegans Wake* and see how the passage from one to the other was made possible by a process of decontextualization and recontextualization related to the procedures described in the first chapter. This will give us some insight into the genesis of chapter 4 of Book II of *Finnegans Wake*.

The fourth chapter deals with the spatial dimension of Joyce's writing. It shows how the layout of the manuscripts reflects the genetic process and also how it influences it.

The fifth chapter analyses two pages of a draft of "Sirens" and recapitulates what we know of the early development of this episode, highlighting what seem to be turning points in the development of the book.

The sixth and seventh chapters study Joyce's mysterious notebooks and his note-taking process. They consider the evolution of his intertextual relationship in the course of his career.

Finally, I will try to show how the genetic approach can move beyond the single-author perspective: we will look at Virginia Woolf's notes on the first episodes of *Ulysses* and see how they reveal a conversation between several voices, personal and institutional (Joyce and Woolf are obviously involved, but also May Sinclair, Dorothy Richardson, the *Little Review,* the *Times Literary Supplement* and many others). In comparison with Woolf's relatively transparent mode of taking notes and discussing her ideas, the singularity of Joyce's procedures and the difficulty of interpreting them stand out.

This book does not intend to serve as a manual of Joyce genetics: it would require a much larger volume simply to present the extent and diversity of the Joyce archive and to map the whole range of problems raised by Joyce's writing practices. Its aim rather is to make the readers of Joyce aware of the relevance of the domain that genetic criticism calls the *avant-texte,* give them an idea of the wealth of material that they can find there, and suggest ways of interpreting the complex mechanisms that rule this material.[19] Its main ambition, however, is to persuade readers of Joyce that they should consult the manuscripts for themselves, in the original when it is accessible, in the facsimile editions, or in the wonderful digital reproductions that are now available online for part of the corpus. Becoming personally acquainted with this fascinating universe should prove a transformative experience: it is likely to change their relation to Joyce and perhaps more generally to literature.

The book could also be used as a kind of introduction to genetic criticism, its purpose and its methods. Because of the nature of Joyce's writing, the creative impulse is more in evidence in his manuscripts than in practically any other writer's archive. The traces left by the writing process are extraordinarily numerous and diverse, but the problems raised by the interpretation of such traces also appear more distinctly.

1

Time-Bound Transactions
and Contextual Transgressions

Let us begin with an apparently unpromising document. It bears Joyce's hand and signature, but it is not one of those manuscripts that are generally sought by collectors. It is related to the genesis of *Ulysses*, and yet its content does not belong in the text or even in an apparatus, among the variants collected by textual criticism. I am referring to the document reproduced in figure 1.1 (the first page of a set of proofs[1] for a section of the "Circe" episode), and more specifically to the sentence written (in French) at the top of the page. It is addressed to Darantiere, the printer in Dijon who, in the last days of 1921, was desperately trying to finish *Ulysses* before the limit set by the author himself, February 2, 1922, Joyce's fortieth birthday.

Usually, on the final pulling of a gathering of proofs, the author writes the conventional formula, "*bon à tirer*" (passed for press, literally "good enough to be pulled") or "*bon à tirer avec les corrections*" (passed for press provided that these corrections are made). This time, the situation was different. The day before, or perhaps a few hours earlier, Joyce had sent a duplicate of this same gathering with the words "*bon à tirer avec les corrections / James Joyce,*" followed by the indispensable countersign of the publisher, Sylvia Beach, underwriting its passport to textual eternity. He knew, then, that if his previous instructions had been carried out promptly, this would arrive too late. The patience of Darantiere, who had already provided several pullings of galleys and proofs for this same passage, must not be tested too far. And the self-imposed deadline was drawing ever closer. So Joyce wrote, almost imploring (in his correspondence with the printers of *Dubliners* he had adopted a very different tone): "*Corrections supplémentaires si encore*

(*Excitedly.*) This is midsummer madness, some ghastly joke again. By heaven, I am guiltless as the unsunned snow! It was my brother Henry. He is my double. He lives in number 2 Dolphin's Barn. Slander, the viper, has wrongfully accused me. Fellowcountrymen, *sgeul inn ban bata coisde gan capall.* I call on my old friend, Dr Malachi Mulligan, sex specialist, to give medical testimony on my behalf.

DR MULLIGAN

(*In motor jerkin, green motorgoggles on his brow.*) Dr Bloom is bisexually abnormal. He has recently escaped from Dr Eustace's private asylum for demented gentlemen. Born out of bedlock hereditary epilepsy is present, the consequence of unbridled lust. Traces of elephantiasis have been discovered among his ascendants. There are marked symptoms of chronic exhibitionism. Ambidexterity is also latent. He is prematurely bald from selfabuse, perversely idealistic in consequence, a reformed rake, and has metal teeth. In consequence of a family complex he has temporarily lost his memory and I believe him to be more sinned against than sinning. I have made a pervaginal examination and, after application of the acid test to 5427 anal, axillary, pectoral and pubic hairs, I declare him to be *virgo intacta.*

(*Bloom holds his high grade hat over his genital organs.*)

DR MADDEN

Hypsospadia is also marked. In the interest of coming generations I suggest that the parts affected should be preserved in spirits of wine in the national teratological museum.

DR CROTTHERS

I have examined the patient's urine. It is albuminoid. Salivation is insufficient, the patellar reflex intermittent.

DR PUNCH COSTELLO

The *fetor judaicus* is most perceptible.

DR DIXON

(*Reads a bill of health.*) Professor Bloom is a finished example of the new womanly man. His moral nature is simple and lovable. Many have found

30

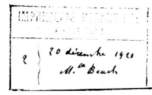

30 décembre 1921
Mon Beach

Figure 1.1. Proofs for "Circe," Gathering 30, second version. Buffalo V.C.5b (*JJA* 26:171).

possibles / James Joyce" (Supplementary corrections if still possible [signed] James Joyce).

The institution of the "Bon à tirer," the signed passed-for-press formula, has a great importance, because it marks, historically and symbolically, the simultaneous birth of the modern text and its counterpart, the authorial working manuscript.[2] It establishes a disjunction between the private sphere of creation and the public sphere of the printed text. Theoretically, beyond that point, the author relinquishes his creation and leaves it in the hands of the publisher and the general public, but here the sharpness of the divide is blurred by Joyce's irrepressible desire to *supplement* his work up to the last moment (and beyond the last moment) and his desperate attempt to keep open the *possibilities* of writing, begging for a reprieve of the closure inherent in the written text as a finished product. The stuttering of the author's official last word upon his text threatens the quasi-legal fiction of a unified authorial intention. Intention appears clearly as a fluctuating, time-bound transaction between a series of writing events and a series of external constraints.

An anecdote recalled by Eugene Jolas shows us that, ten years later, during the preparation of *Finnegans Wake,* Joyce's attitude had not changed:

> Once, I remember, I had just finished reading the last page of final proof and had given orders to go ahead with the printing. [. . .] As we settled back comfortably, the telephone rang. An excited voice announced that a heavy special-delivery letter from Paris had just arrived for us at the print-shop. Joyce wanted to make further additions, one of them probably the longest he had yet invented: an onomatopoeia of over fifty letters expressing collective coughing in a church during a sermon. It was included.[3]

Deferral and displacement

In the case of the belated "Circe" proofs, Joyce was not so lucky. Strictly speaking, his (conditional) instructions were ineffectual. The printer's stamp on the bottom of the page indicates that they were received on December 21, 1920, a few hours, perhaps, after the previous batch. By that time, it was too late. Darantiere had acted diligently on receiving the first "bon à tirer," and presumably the type had been broken up and reset, so the unimplemented supplementary batch of proofs was returned to the author on December 29.

This presents an interesting problem because it puts the corrections in a kind of textual limbo, belonging to a stage that is posterior to the completion of the passage but anterior to the completion of *Ulysses* as a whole. The context of this passage called for these corrections, but the end of the book was written in the context of their absence from the passage. It is an insoluble dilemma for an editor,[4] but it offers a very interesting field of observation for genetic criticism.

It appears that the proofs' circular journey from Paris to Dijon and back was not accomplished in vain. As a kind of empty sidestep in the efficient ballet of galleys and proofs between Joyce, Darantiere, and Beach, it resulted in a deferral and a displacement. Joyce accepted the impossibility of printing the passage as he wanted it (or as he had wanted it in the first days of December 1921), but he was understandably reluctant to waste the material that he had added there. Some of it is indeed very amusing. So he inserted at least two elements in another part of "Circe" on which he was working when the proofs were returned to him. As it could have been expected, the delay and the transfer to a different section of the episode did not leave these elements intact.

The first and most conspicuous case is the reimplantation (fig. 1.2 *a* and *b*) in the last pages of "Circe" of the following failed insertion:

DON EMILE PATRIZIO FRANZ RUPERT POPE HENNESSY
(*in medieval hauberk, two wild geese volant on his helm, appears and, with noble indignation, disowns Bloom*)
Put down your eyes to footboden, big grand pig of Jude all covered with gravy!
(*JJA* 26:175, simplified transcription)

as:

DON EMILE PATRIZIO FRANZ RUPERT POPE HENNESSY
(*in medieval hauberk, two wild geese volant on his helm, with noble indignation points a mailed hand against the privates*) Werf those eykes to footboden, big grand porcos of johnyellows todos covered of gravy!
(*JJA* 26: 316, simplified transcription, and *U* 15.4506–9)

The two passages are not quite identical. Some of the changes ("points a mailed hand against the privates" instead of "disowns Bloom," "johnyellows"

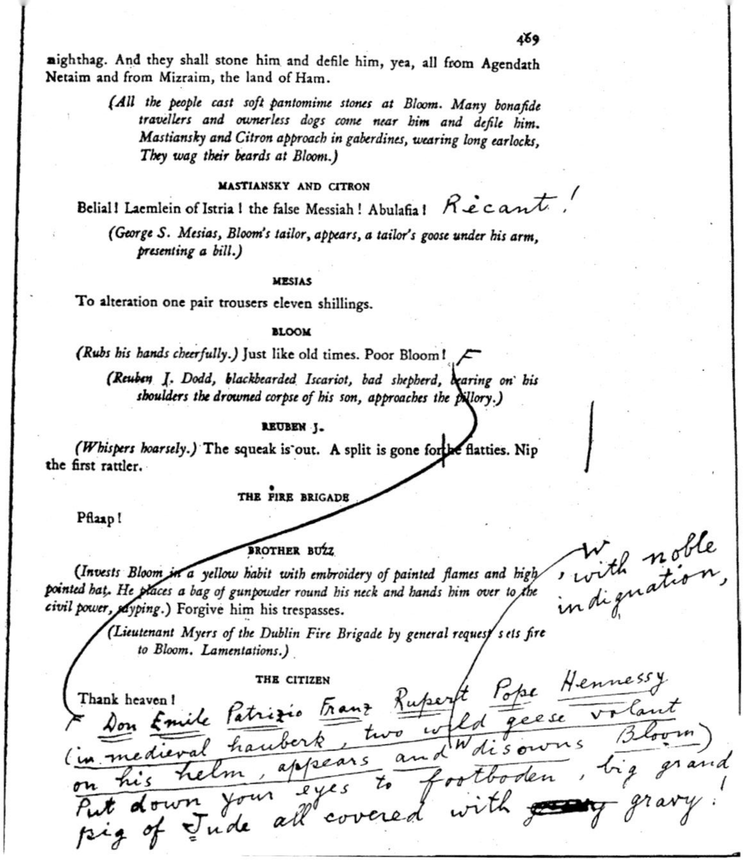

469

aighthag. And they shall stone him and defile him, yea, all from Agendath Netaim and from Mizraim, the land of Ham.

(All the people cast soft pantomime stones at Bloom. Many bonafide travellers and ownerless dogs come near him and defile him. Mastiansky and Citron approach in gaberdines, wearing long earlocks, They wag their beards at Bloom.)

MASTIANSKY AND CITRON

Belial! Laemlein of Istria! the false Messiah! Abulafia!

(George S. Mesias, Bloom's tailor, appears, a tailor's goose under his arm, presenting a bill.)

MESIAS

To alteration one pair trousers eleven shillings.

BLOOM

(Rubs his hands cheerfully.) Just like old times. Poor Bloom!

(Reuben J. Dodd, blackbearded Iscariot, bad shepherd, bearing on his shoulders the drowned corpse of his son, approaches the pillory.)

REUBEN J.

(Whispers hoarsely.) The squeak is out. A split is gone for the flatties. Nip the first rattler.

THE FIRE BRIGADE

Pflaap!

BROTHER BUZZ

(Invests Bloom in a yellow habit with embroidery of painted flames and high pointed hat. He places a bag of gunpowder round his neck and hands him over to the civil power, saying.) Forgive him his trespasses.

(Lieutenant Myers of the Dublin Fire Brigade by general request sets fire to Bloom. Lamentations.)

THE CITIZEN

Thank heaven!

Figure 1.2*a*. Proofs for "Circe," Gathering 30, second version. Buffalo V.C.5b (*JJA* 26:175). Unimplemented corrections.

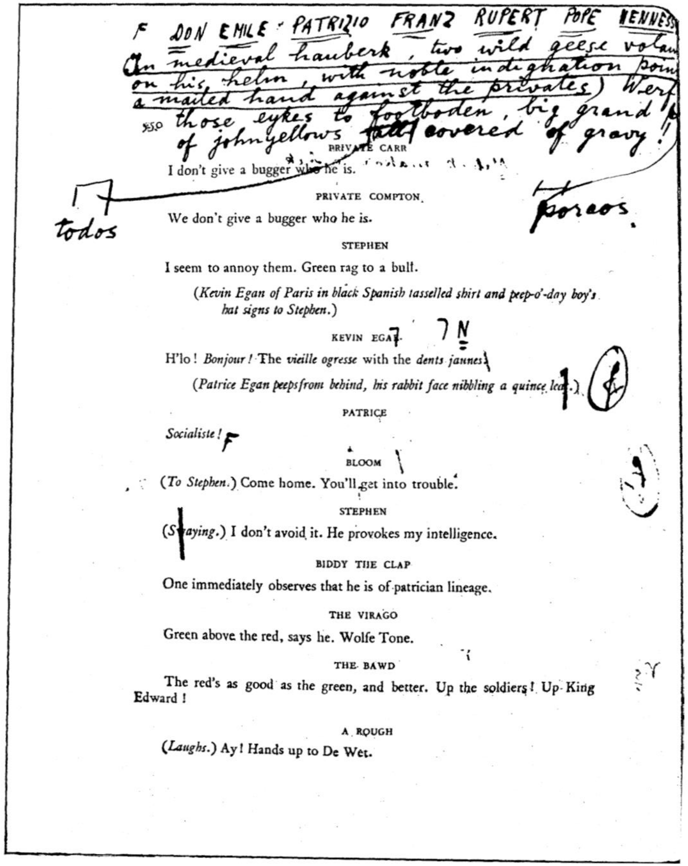

PRIVATE CARR

I don't give a bugger who he is.

PRIVATE COMPTON

We don't give a bugger who he is.

STEPHEN

I seem to annoy them. Green rag to a bull.

(Kevin Egan of Paris in black Spanish tasselled shirt and peep-o'-day boy's hat signs to Stephen.)

KEVIN EGAN

H'lo! *Bonjour!* The *vieille ogresse* with the *dents jaunes*.

(Patrice Egan peeps from behind, his rabbit face nibbling a quince leaf.)

PATRICE

Socialiste!

BLOOM

(To Stephen.) Come home. You'll get into trouble.

STEPHEN

(Swaying.) I don't avoid it. He provokes my intelligence.

BIDDY THE CLAP

One immediately observes that he is of patrician lineage.

THE VIRAGO

Green above the red, says he. Wolfe Tone.

THE BAWD

The red's as good as the green, and better. Up the soldiers! Up King Edward!

A ROUGH

(Laughs.) Ay! Hands up to De Wet.

Figure 1.2*b*. Proofs for "Circe," Gathering 35, second version. Texas (*JJA* 26:316). Corresponding to *U* 15.4506–4509.

instead of "Jude") are directly related to the new location: this composite archetypal incarnation of the Irish wild geese, who was adding his own very idiosyncratic voice to the general reprobation of Bloom, is now involved in the confrontation between Stephen and the British soldiers. The anti-Semitic outburst is thus converted, with the necessary adjustments, into anti-British insults. But the modifications are also connected with the contemporary (as opposed to the adjacent) context, with the genetic movement (as opposed to the narrative environment). The very fact that the insertion was deferred caused an evolution of the passage. The language of the cosmopolitan exile has become even more international and seems to have moved one step closer to the multilingualism of *Finnegans Wake*.

The rewriting indicates that an adjustment of purpose, perhaps even a stylistic evolution, has occurred within a few weeks. It is a process of interaction or transaction, for the influence is reciprocal. The new environment of the passage is modified by the insertion of the element from the earlier background: the end of the chapter acquires, through this insertion, something of the sheer exuberance characteristic of the Messianic episode from which it comes.[5]

The productivity of accidents

The process of interaction appears in a clearer form in another case of repurposing these wasted corrections. On the following page of the same set of proofs, Joyce had wanted to develop a brief reference to Handel's *Alleluia* (fig. 1.3).

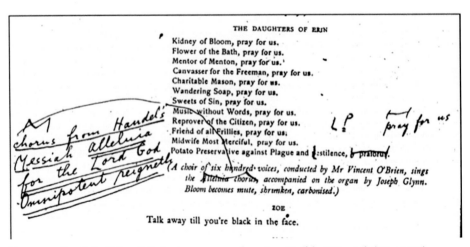

Figure 1.3. Proofs for "Circe," Gathering 30, second version. Buffalo V.C.1–30b (*JJA* 26:176). Unimplemented corrections

Again, when he found out that the correction had not been made, he re-circulated the material in a different context, but in a much transformed and amplified form. This time it was inserted in the Black Mass scene (fig. 1.4). What happened then demonstrates in the most graphic way the inertia of the signifier and the dynamics of writing. Because of the poor quality of the paper on which the proofs were printed, Joyce's corrections, marked with ink, seeped through the page, so that they are clearly readable, in inverted mirror form, on the verso (fig. 1.5 and 1.6). This *accident,* in the immediate context of the Black Mass (traditionally supposed to be celebrated as a literal inversion of the Holy Mass), triggered the following expansion of the scene on the next proofs (fig. 1.7):

THE VOICE OF ALL THE DAMNED
Htengier Tnetopinmo Dog Drol eht rof, Aiulella!

(*From on high the voice of Adonai calls*)

ADONAI
Dooooooooooog!

THE VOICE OF ALL THE BLESSED
Alleluia, for the Lord God Omnipotent reigneth!

(*From on high the voice of Adonai calls*)

ADONAI
Goooooooooooood! (*JJA* 26:322–33)

The published version of the scene looks so integrated that it seems difficult to believe that its elements belong to different strata of writing and that its present form is the result of a material accident. Is it possible, for instance, that Adonai's "Goooooooooooood" was not meant from the start to be an inverted echo of "Dooooooooooog"? Manuscripts show that the prolonged call was inscribed months before the writing accident.[6] This proves beyond any doubt that the canine echo, which is probably the most conspicuous element in the scene, is an afterthought, but this does not weaken the relationship established a posteriori between the two elements.

Other retrospective links are automatically established with the Protean *and appear to many. A chasm ● opens with a noiseless yawn. Tom Rockford, winner in athlete's singlet and breeches, arrives at the head of the hurdle handicap and leaps into the void. He is followed by a race of runners and leapers. In wild attitudes they spring from the brink. Their bodies plunge.* 555

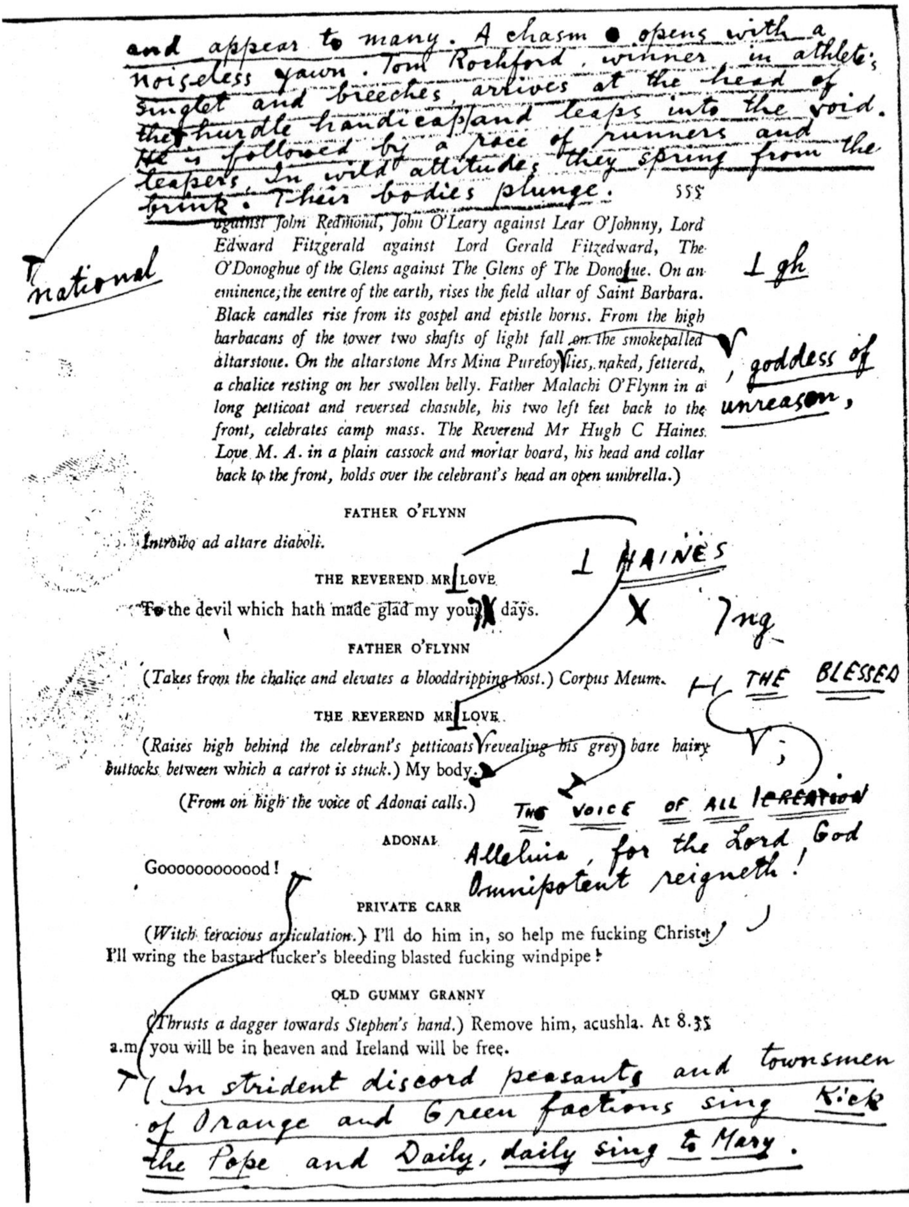

national

against John Redmond, John O'Leary against Lear O'Johnny, Lord Edward Fitzgerald against Lord Gerald Fitzedward, The O'Donoghue of the Glens against The Glens of The Donoghue. On an eminence, the centre of the earth, rises the field altar of Saint Barbara. Black candles rise from its gospel and epistle horns. From the high barbacans of the tower two shafts of light fall on the smokepalled altarstone. On the altarstone Mrs Mina Purefoy lies, naked, fettered, a chalice resting on her swollen belly. Father Malachi O'Flynn in a long petticoat and reversed chasuble, his two left feet back to the front, celebrates camp mass. The Reverend Mr Hugh C Haines Love M. A. in a plain cassock and mortar board, his head and collar back to the front, holds over the celebrant's head an open umbrella.)

⊥ gh

, goddess of unreason,

FATHER O'FLYNN

Introibo ad altare diaboli.

THE REVEREND MR LOVE

To the devil which hath made glad my young days.

⊥ HAINES

X Ing.

FATHER O'FLYNN

(Takes from the chalice and elevates a blooddripping host.) Corpus Meum.

H THE BLESSED

THE REVEREND MR LOVE

(Raises high behind the celebrant's petticoats revealing his grey bare hairy buttocks between which a carrot is stuck.) My body.

(From on high the voice of Adonai calls.)

THE VOICE OF ALL CREATION

ADONAI

Goooooooooood!

Alleluia, for the Lord God Omnipotent reigneth!

PRIVATE CARR

(With ferocious articulation.) I'll do him in, so help me fucking Christ! I'll wring the bastard fucker's bleeding blasted fucking windpipe!

OLD GUMMY GRANNY

(Thrusts a dagger towards Stephen's hand.) Remove him, acushla. At 8.35 a.m. you will be in heaven and Ireland will be free.

In strident discord peasants and townsmen of Orange and Green factions sing Kick the Pope and Daily, daily sing to Mary.

Figure 1.4. Proofs for "Circe," Gathering 35, first version. Buffalo V.C.1–35 (*JJA* 26:305).

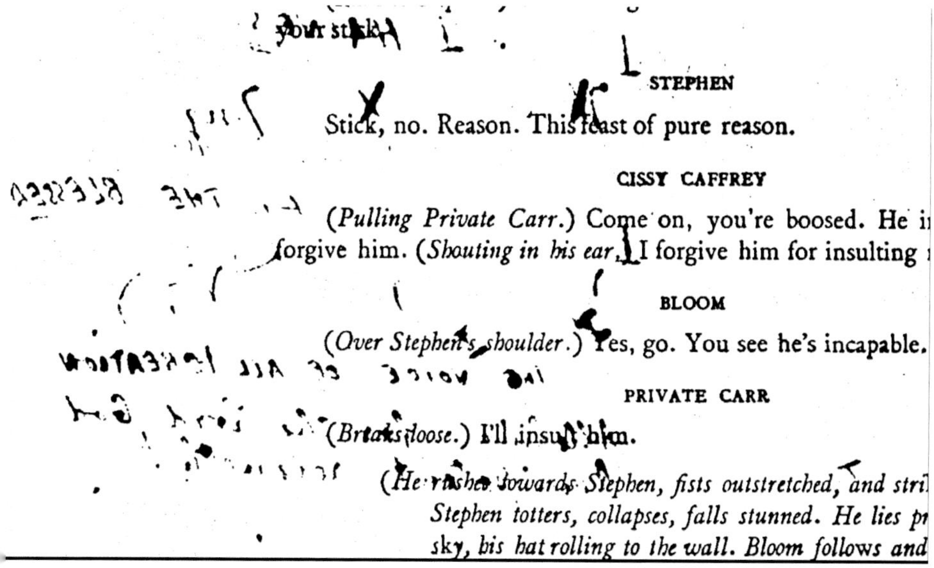

STEPHEN

Stick, no. Reason. This feast of pure reason.

CISSY CAFFREY

(Pulling Private Carr.) Come on, you're boosed. He i[
forgive him. (Shouting in his ear.) I forgive him for insulting [

BLOOM

(Over Stephen's shoulder.) Yes, go. You see he's incapable.

PRIVATE CARR

(Breaks loose.) I'll insult him.

(He rushes towards Stephen, fists outstretched, and stri[
Stephen totters, collapses, falls stunned. He lies p[
sky, his hat rolling to the wall. Bloom follows and[

Figure 1.5. Inkblots on the verso of the preceding page (JJA 26:306).

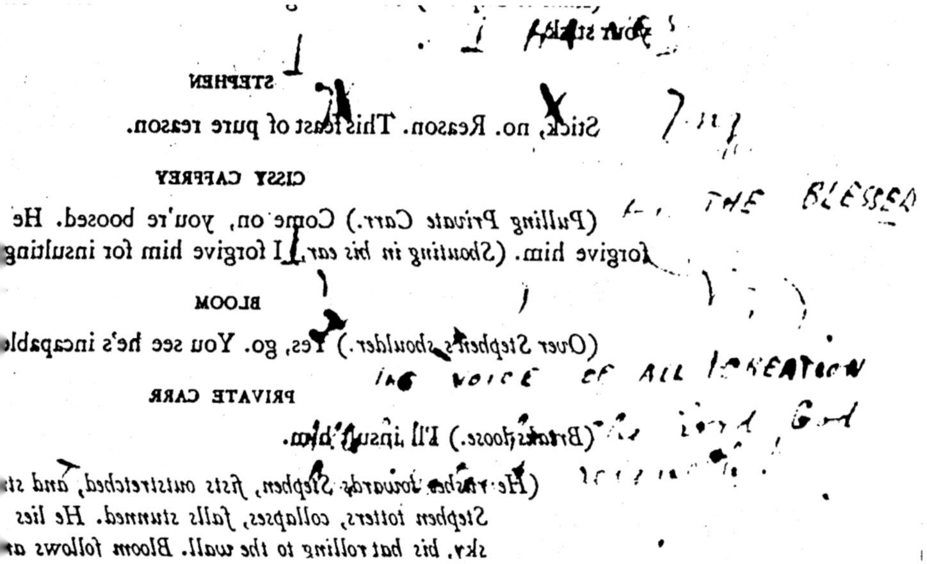

Figure 1.6. Inverted image of figure 1.5.

Introibo ad altare diaboli.

THE REVEREND MR HAINES LOVE

To the devil which hath made glad my young days.

FATHER O'FLYNN

(*Takes from the chalice and elevates a blooddripping host.*) Corpus Meum.

THE REVEREND MR HAINES LOVE

(*Raises high behind the celebrant's petticoats, revealing his grey bare hairy buttocks between which a carrot is stuck.*) My body.

THE VOICE OF ALL THE BLESSED

Alleluia, for the Lord God Omnipotent reigneth!

(*From on high the voice of Adonai calls.*)

ADONAI

Goooooooood!

PRIVATE CARR

(*In strident discord peasants and townsmen of Orange and Green factions sing Kick the Pope and Daily, daily sing to Mary.*)

(*With ferocious articulation.*) I'll do him in, so help me fucking Christ! I'll wring the bastard fucker's bleeding blasted fucking windpipe!

OLD GUMMY GRANNY

(*Thrusts a dagger towards Stephen's hand.*) Remove him, acushla. At 8.35 a.m. you will be in heaven and Ireland will be free. (*She prays.*) O good God, take him!

BLOOM

(*Runs to Lynch.*) Can't you get him away?

LYNCH

He likes dialectic, the universal language. Kitty! (*To Bloom.*) Get him away, you. He won't listen to me.

THE VOICE OF ALL THE DAMNED

Htengier Tnetopinmo Dog Drol eht rof, Aiulella!

(*From on high the voice of Adonai calls.*)

Dooooooooooo!

STEPHEN

(*Points.*) Exit Judas. Et laqueo se suspendit.

BLOOM

(*Runs to Stephen.*) Come along with me now before worse happens. Here's your stick.

STEPHEN

Stick, no. Reason. This feast of pure reason.

CISSY CAFFREY

(*Pulling Private Carr.*) Come on, you're boosed. He insulted me but I forgive him. (*Shouting in his ear.*) I forgive him for insulting me.

BLOOM

(*Over Stephen's shoulder.*) Yes, go. You see he's incapable.

PRIVATE CARR

(*Breaks loose.*) I'll insult him.

(*He rushes towards Stephen, fists outstretched, and strikes him in the face. Stephen totters, collapses, falls stunned. He lies prone, his face to the sky, his hat rolling to the wall. Bloom follows and picks it up.*)

MAJOR TWEEDY

(*Loudly.*) Carbine in bucket! Cease fire! Salute!

THE RETRIEVER

(*Barking furiously.*) Ute ute ute ute ute ute ute.

THE CROWD

Let him up! Don't strike him when he's down! Air! Who? The soldier hit him. He's a professor. Is he hurted? Don't manhandle him! he's fainted!

(*The retriever, nosing on the fringe of the crowd, barks noisily.*)

A HAG

What call had the redcoat to strike the gentleman and he under the influence. Let them go and fight the Boers!

dog roaming the episode, with Bloom's "Dog of a Christian" addressed to the Man in the Macintosh during the Messianic scene, with the mysterious answer (echo or dog whistle?) to Mulligan's call in the course of his initial blasphemous Mass, and so on.

The productivity of the accident does not stop there. A few days later, on another set of proofs, Joyce added the words "from right to left" to the description of the apparition of Bloom's son Rudy reading a book. This links the inversion of letters to Hebrew script and Bloom's memories of his father in "Aeolus" (*U* 7.206–7) and connects the Black Mass to a network of preexistent motives such as the Kabbalah.

On a small scale, but with widespread ramifications, this is a striking example of the constant interaction between the internal logic of writing and a flow of events that can be minute occurrences (coming to the end of the line or the page . . .) or portentous literary, biographical, social, or political circumstances.

In the next chapter, we will try to take stock of the lessons that these rather unusual examples suggest and to see to what extent they can be generalized, but first we should make two additional remarks inspired by the example of the stray proofs. Readers who are not particularly interested in the methodology of genetic criticism can skip the next two sections and go directly to the next chapter.

Acts of writing

The first remark is that our investigation into the genetic process is not directly concerned with texts but, on the one hand, with tangible documents that need to be considered in their full materiality (including characteristics such as the porousness of the paper or the fluidity of the ink) and, on the other, with actions: speech acts, or rather acts of writing. Although the sentence "*Corrections supplémentaires si encore possibles / James Joyce*" has no explicit verb, it is an instruction addressed to the printer. Joyce directs him to include in the final printed text the emendations marked on the subsequent pages. (Re)reading the proofs, marking them, penciling the directive on the first page prescribing a course of action for the printer and sending the package constitute a set of coordinated acts.

A genetic artifact should not be considered as an under-developed or abortive text but as a protocol for making a text, a set of implicit or explicit instructions, addressed by the writer to himself, to an amanuensis or to the printer.[7] The most elementary writing instruction is generally not formulated in so many words: any undeleted sentence normally implies the command "include this in the next version," as opposed to "don't include this," expressed by an erasure, a crossing out, or a *deleatur* in the margin. This universal instruction is the foundation of textual criticism. It is also extremely important from a genetic point of view, but, in addition, genetic criticism has to take account of much more intricate and ambiguous sets of instructions. How are we to understand a circle drawn around a word or a sentence? What are we to make of Joyce's use of an array of color crayons in his manuscripts? The Linati schema represents another case that is very difficult to interpret from a genetic point of view: it is based on a set of writing instructions that were at some stage converted into reading instructions. A note can be paraphrased as a self-instruction to "remember this" or "remember to use this in a certain context." But we usually do not know this postulated context, except retrospectively, from its finished state, which is doubly misleading: because the author might have changed his mind and used the note in a completely different place, and if he did not, the context as we know it is necessarily influenced by the insertion of the element from the notes, and we have no way of knowing exactly what it was like at the moment of note-taking.

Usually instructions that are not self-addressed are less ambiguous. But our *"Corrections supplémentaires si encore possibles / James Joyce"* proves that they are not necessarily a simple matter either. In a different order of difficulty, we can hardly conceive what would have been the instructions given by Joyce to James Stephens if he had pursued his idea to entrust him with the completion of *Finnegans Wake* ("If he consented to maintain three or four points which I consider essential and I showed him the threads he could finish the design").[8] If they were ever given and could be miraculously recovered, they would of course be an invaluable help for genetic criticism, but if we were naive enough to believe that they would supersede any other genetic investigation into *Finnegans Wake,* the vicissitudes of authorial intention that we have witnessed in the "Circe" proofs would be sufficient to convince us of the contrary.

Genetic paradigms

The example of the displaced "wild geese" insertion raises the problem of the interpretation of genetic paradigms. Substitution of one element for another can be considered as the basic genetic operation (provided that we consider an addition as a substitution of something to nothing and a deletion as a substitution of nothing to something). The fact that one item can be substituted for another implies not only that they belong to a common category but also that there is a difference between them that motivates the operation. To understand this motivation, the local substitution must be considered transversally in relation with other modifications introduced at the same time. This should reveal a coherent pattern of changes in the immediate vicinity or in long-range structural relationships, although we are not always able to understand the nature of this coherence.

The alteration must also be considered in the light of the historical development of the passage, which may or may not indicate a trend pointing toward the eventual substitution. For instance, on the revised set of proofs (fig. 2*b*), we can see that in the sentence "Werf those eykes to footboden, big grand pigs of johnyellows all covered of gravy!," Joyce deleted "all" and changed it to "todos." Here the similarity and the difference are clear: the two elements have the same meaning but are in different languages. The Spanish word is substituted for its English equivalent. The fact that "p[igs]" is also changed at the same stage into "porcos" confirms this pattern. And the earlier change (between the two versions) of "Put down your eyes to footboden" into "Werf those eykes to footboden" indicates a movement towards multilingualism.

When Joyce wrote "all" and then (probably a few moments later) changed his mind, crossed it out, and substituted "todos," it is clear that something of the original intention remained: the basic meaning is the same and an element of foreignness is added. But even when the change seems to reverse, deeply alter, or completely erase the original intention, something of the original state remains present: the paradigm that is the common ground between the two elements. For instance, in another "Circe" proof, corresponding to the "transformation scene" depicting the feminization of Bloom, Joyce changed the sentence "There's a good fellow now" into "There's a good girly now" (*JJA* 26:227). The word "fellow" belongs to the categories of English words, of words of Anglo-Saxon origin, of words of two syllables, of words beginning with "f," of gender-specific appellations, of patronizing terms when associated with "good," and so on. We can say that the local change, the *variant,* provides an interpretation of the passage by revealing which of these paradigms are relevant.[9]

If we consider the insertion of the whole passage rescued from the stray batch of proofs, we are not confronted with the usual change of an element in a given context. It is the inserted element that remains substantially constant, while the context is entirely different. The problem, however, remains the same: what is the relation between the original text and the new state of things? The substitution of contexts around the "Circe" insertion suggests (in connection with the "Cyclops" episode) an equivalence between Irish anti-British xenophobia and anti-Semitism. It also implies that the ordeals of Bloom, excluded as a foreign element even by the arch-cosmopolitan Don Emile Patrizio Franz Rupert Pope Hennessy, and of Stephen, integrated by force in a community of hatred from which he cannot escape, belong to the same paradigm.

The history of a passage can thus suggest new interpretations or tend to confirm existing ones, but, as we will see in the next chapter, it can never establish the *true* meaning and very rarely exclude any reading of the final text. The purpose of the following chapters is not to discuss possible interpretations suggested by the genetic documents but rather to explore the choices that they reveal and the evaluations implied by those choices.

2

Multiple Determinations

The changes on the "Circe" proofs that we studied in the previous chapter are remarkable because they combine in a spectacular way the effects of deferral *and* displacement, two forms of decontextualization and recontextualization. However, we must try to distinguish, at least heuristically, between two different things: the layering of changed intentions in a particular locus and the reciprocal influence of contemporary acts of writing.

Local interference of successive temporal strata

The superimposition of intentions in a single place is the most elementary observable genetic phenomenon. In the majority of cases, the writer's earlier intentions are more or less concealed under the later ones and can be retrieved only indirectly. Very often, however, Joyce prefers to let the original intention coexist visibly with the new one. His fondness for portmanteau words is emblematic of this tendency to prefer accumulation to replacement.

A portmanteau can be analyzed as a refusal to choose between different elements of the paradigm that are available to occupy the same position on the syntagmatic chain. If some of the portmanteau words appear fully formed in Joyce's notes or drafts (especially at the later stages of the writing of *Finnegans Wake*) and seem to have been sought out as such, very often they are the result of a gradual complexifying.

We can see this very clearly in this example from "Sirens." It all begins with an addition inscribed in the margin of the second extant draft (see chapter 5, this volume):

"a ray of hope is beaming. Lydia for Lidwell unsqueaked a cork."

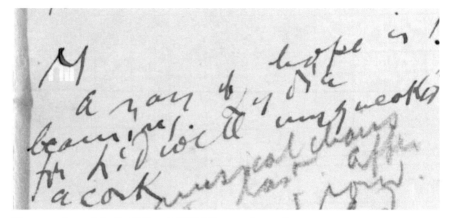

Figure 2.1. Second draft of "Sirens" (NLI MS 36,639/9, p. 19).

This is related to two of the "voices" that can be heard in the Ormond bar: Simon Dedalus singing an aria from Flotow's *Martha* and the flirtatious conversation between Lydia Douce, the barmaid, and her customer, George Lidwell. The first sentence is an (approximate) quotation from the tenor aria.[1] The second sentence, describing the action of the barmaid, includes a portmanteau (unscrew + squeak), expressive of the noise produced by the unscrewing of the cork. On the fair copy, Joyce changed this to:

—. . . . *ray of hope.* . . .
Beaming. Lydia for Lidwell squeak scarcely hear so ladylike the muse unsqueaked a cork.[2]

In this new context, "unsqueak" acquires an additional meaning (a suppression or attenuation of the squeaking), and the pseudo-genteel affectation ("so ladylike the muse") actually draws our attention to the sexual connotations of the unscrewing noise. (cf. *U* 15.1975; "Man and woman, love, what is it? A cork and bottle.") This version also emphasizes the interference between the song in the background and the narrative, with the separation of the word "beaming" from the italicized quotation and its integration in the authorial narration. The cacophony of the [k] sounds is emphasized.

In October 1921, in the margin of a galley proof for "Cyclops" (*JJA* 19:205) that he was revising simultaneously with the page proofs for "Sirens," Joyce tried out some verbal compounds. He experimented with a fusion of proper names that could express the identification of the listeners in the Ormond bar

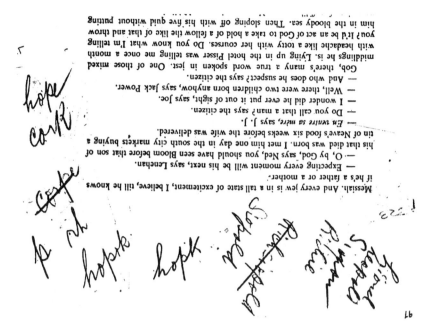

Figure 2.2. Material for "Sirens" on a galley proof for "Cyclops." Placards 37, first version. MS Eng 160.4, (96). Houghton Library, Harvard University (*JJA* 19:205).

with the singer and finally adopted the form "Siopold" (now *U* 11.751). He then turned the page upside down and tried out ways of combining "hope" and "cork." For obvious reasons, he rejected the simplest combination ("corpe") and then came up with "hopok," which he condensed as "hopk."

"Siopold" and "hopk" were inserted simultaneously on the "Sirens" page proofs. This is the new version of our passage:

—. . . . *ray of hope*. . . .
Beaming. Lydia for Lidwell squeak scarcely hear so ladylike the muse unsqueaked a ray of hopk.

(Gathering 17, pages 263, Rosenbach Foundation, not reproduced in the *JJA*. Now *U* 11.710–12)

The noisy cork being unscrewed is infiltrated with an echo from the singing, creating at the same time an onomatopoeic effect, imitative of the sound of the popping cork, with additional suggestions that the bottle being opened is a bottle of hock and that Lydia's behavior gives Lidwell some hope to get "better acquainted" (*U* 11.814). Whereas the first lexical creation ("unsqueaking") remained acceptable, as a well-formed hybrid, "hopk," the new portmanteau, appears as a disturbing linguistic chimera. It was so daring that it was considered as a complete impossibility by the proofreader of the 1926 edition, who saw it as a glaring typo and normalized it to "hope" (obviously without consulting Joyce), followed by all the subsequent editions until the 1984–1986 edition reinstated "hopk."

The final result is a rich and compact sentence, counterpointing noises and music; spoken, sung, or imagined voices; pretentious clichés and salacious innuendos. The history of the passage helps us to understand the sedimentation of intentions that pile up without concealing each other. Appropriately for this musical chapter, we are able to follow the entry of stratified voices and the gradual densification of the polyphony.

If we now switch from the micro-genetic to the macro-genetic level and look at the book as a whole, we will find evidence of a similar process of superimposition of large-scale temporal layers. Any work of art bears the scars of the process of its making, but these scars are usually almost invisible on the smooth surface of the finished product. In the case of *Ulysses,* they are quite plain: anyone can see that there is very little in common between, for instance, the "Telemachus" episode and "Cyclops" or "Ithaca." The difference is so great that it can only be explained by radical changes in the writing project, and any interpretation of the book that does not take into account the temporal dimension of its production is bound to run against insurmountable difficulties. Michael Groden has suggested that *Ulysses* as we know it is the result of the sedimentation (sedimentation, not juxtaposition) of three substantially different projects, corresponding to what he calls the early, middle, and last stages.[3] The early stage corresponds to what Joyce himself called the "initial style," a mixture, in various proportions, of monologues and third-person narration. The middle stage represents a shift away from realism and an emphasis on parodies and stylistic pyrotechnics. The late stage exacerbates some of the earlier tendencies toward symbolism and schematism, and the book seems to fold upon itself and to feed upon its own substance.

Although the three styles correspond primarily to the early, middle, and last chapters of the book, they are not merely juxtaposed in a linear sequence. The early chapters have been revised, in various degrees, in the light of the new project.[4] This is particularly conspicuous in the case of the "Aeolus" episode. While it was originally perfectly representative of the initial style, it now bears the visible traces of a drastic overhaul: Joyce did not alter deeply the

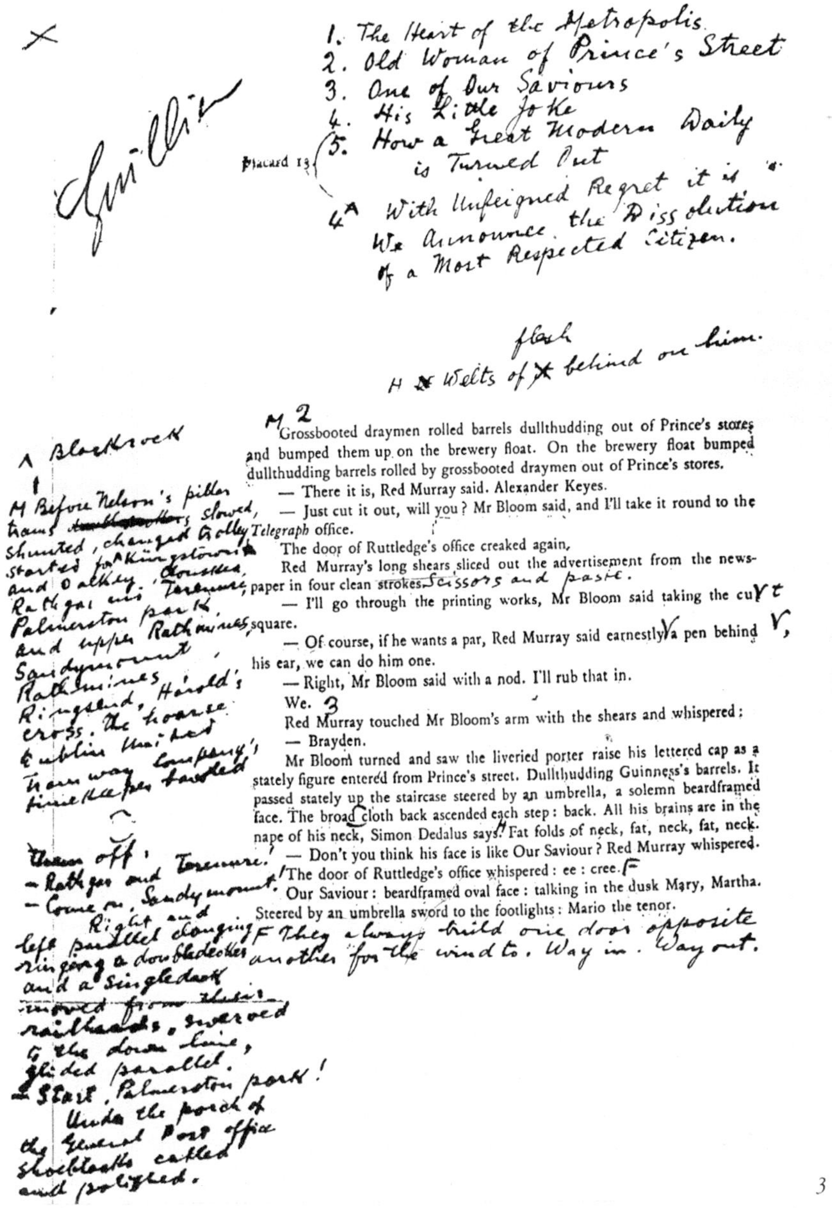

1. The Heart of the Metropolis
2. Old Woman of Prince's Street
3. One of Our Saviours
4. His Little Joke
5. How a Great Modern Daily is Turned Out

4ᴬ With Unfeigned Regret it is
We Announce the Dissolution
of a Most Respected Citizen.

Placard 13

flash
H Welts of behind on him.

M 2
Grossbooted draymen rolled barrels dullthudding out of Prince's stores and bumped them up on the brewery float. On the brewery float bumped dullthudding barrels rolled by grossbooted draymen out of Prince's stores.

— There it is, Red Murray said. Alexander Keyes.

— Just cut it out, will you? Mr Bloom said, and I'll take it round to the Telegraph office.

The door of Ruttledge's office creaked again.

Red Murray's long shears sliced out the advertisement from the newspaper in four clean strokes. Scissors and paste.

— I'll go through the printing works, Mr Bloom said taking the cut

— Of course, if he wants a par, Red Murray said earnestly, a pen behind his ear, we can do him one.

— Right, Mr Bloom said with a nod. I'll rub that in.

We.

Red Murray touched Mr Bloom's arm with the shears and whispered:

— Brayden.

Mr Bloom turned and saw the liveried porter raise his lettered cap as a stately figure entered from Prince's street. Dullthudding Guinness's barrels. It passed stately up the staircase steered by an umbrella, a solemn beardframed face. The broad cloth back ascended each step: back. All his brains are in the nape of his neck, Simon Dedalus says. Fat folds of neck, fat, neck, fat, neck.

— Don't you think his face is like Our Saviour? Red Murray whispered.

The door of Ruttledge's office whispered: ee: cree.

— Our Saviour: beardframed oval face: talking in the dusk Mary, Martha. Steered by an umbrella sword to the footlights: Mario the tenor.

3

Figure 2.3. "Aeolus" Placards 13, MS Eng 160.4, (39). Houghton Library, Harvard University (JJA 18:3).

structure of the episode but dramatically changed its external form, on its first galley proofs, by injecting the startling newspaper headlines in accordance with the radical modernist aesthetics of the later chapters (fig. 2.3). As for the later episodes, not only do they have to ensure the continuity with the early ones—the inertia of what is already written is a condition of any writing—but one of the major aspects of the late style of *Ulysses* consists in a recycling of the material of previous episodes: this is something that any reader of "Circe" will notice and that can also be detected in "Ithaca" and even in "Penelope."

Interference of the genetic context

By now it must be clear from the preceding examples that the superimposition of temporal layers in the genesis of a passage is not independent from the modifications of the genetic context. It is significant that the assembly of the portmanteau that completes the transformation of the cork/hopk passage of "Sirens" takes place on the galleys of another, more advanced, episode. Joyce was revising "Sirens" in the context of an altered project that was developing as he was rewriting new episodes.

Because of Joyce's self-imposed publication deadline, the printing schedule of *Ulysses* had been arranged in such a way that Joyce was rewriting the last episodes at the same time as he was correcting the proofs of the earlier ones. As a consequence, the (extensive) correction of the proofs for "Telemachus," "Nestor," "Proteus," "Calypso," and "Lotus Eaters" belong to the chronological context of the writing of "Ithaca" and "Penelope." This means not only that the early episodes, some of which had been drafted many years before, were actively present on Joyce's writing table as the end of the book was being written (or rewritten)[5] but also that the revisions of the first part were introduced from the perspective of the late style. We must also keep in mind that during a single week of October 1921, Joyce marked proof for "Lotus Eaters," "Hades," "Aeolus," "Lestrygonians," "Scylla and Charybdis," "Wandering Rocks" and "Sirens": all the modifications entered at this moment in this wide array of episodes should be studied in the context of each other.

During the sixteen years of the writing of *Finnegans Wake,* major inflections modified the original project, but the more drastic changes were structural reorganizations. The stylistic alterations were much more gradual, so that we cannot assign major "styles" as convincingly as in *Ulysses.* Since the book was not written linearly from beginning to end and given the nature of the final text, it is not so easy to detect in it the traces of the process of evolution. However, if we take a bird's-eye view of the genesis of two of the more accessible passages in the book, the "Anna Livia Plurabelle" chapter (I.8) and the soliloquy of Anna Livia at the end of the book, we can make a few useful general remarks about genetic contextuality.

"Anna Livia Plurabelle" was drafted in 1924 and then revised at least seventeen times in the next fourteen years.[6] The main characteristics of the very first draft are still visible in the final text: the oral quality of the exchange between the two washerwomen, the fluidity of the rhythm, the humor. But many other features were added by the successive revisions, reflecting different visions of the work as it took shape between 1924 and 1928. The multilingual aspect, absent in the first layer, was introduced at different stages, beginning with Scandinavian elements and northern dialects. Joyce then increased the number of colloquialisms and made the sound patterns more complex. But the most conspicuous feature is the addition of river names: for instance "Go on, go on," the injunction to continue the story, from one of the washerwomen to the other, is replaced by "Garonne, garonne" (*JJA* 48:125; BL 47474–175). Later on, Joyce added "I amstel wainting" (*I am still waiting,* combined with the *Amstel—JJA* 48:354; 47475–83), so that in the final text ("I amstel wainting. Garonne, garonne!," *FW* 205.25), the impatient prompting alludes to a Dutch and a French river. This process began with a few scattered fluvial references but became a major preoccupation of Joyce, who, for years, harvested hundreds of river names in his notebooks in order to weave them into the sentences of this episode. Most of these names are unknown to the majority of readers, so that the allusions cannot be detected without the help of a comprehensive encyclopedia or, even better, of Joyce's notebooks. It has often been pointed out that these elusive allusions obscure the original meaning of the sentences. Obviously, by the time Joyce finished writing *Finnegans Wake,* direct accessibility had ceased to be a concern.

As a partial counter example, one can mention the final soliloquy (*FW* 619–28), which was drafted, copied, typed five times and further revised on galley proofs within a few months at the end of 1938. In the process, the passage was considerably expanded—the last two short sentences ("I only hope the heavens sees us. Abit beside the bush and then a walk along the") were expanded to eighty-seven lines in the printed book (*FW* 625.36–628.16)—but no spectacular change of direction is taken in this last and concentrated bout of writing, only a development and a progressive intensification. By this time, the stylistic evolution of *Finnegans Wake* had run its full course. We can even detect a certain "regression" toward a greater transparency, due perhaps to the fact that the final monologue of Anna Livia was a paradigmatic equivalent of Molly Bloom's soliloquy, so that the finishing of one book brought memories of the completion of another and the end of *Ulysses* formed another kind of context for the ending of the *Wake*.

Paradoxes of overdetermination

Because we usually read literary works linearly, from beginning to end, we have the impression that they were written in the same way, or even that they are the product of a single, instantaneous perspective. This can never be true, but the falsity of such an impression is particularly in evidence in the manuscripts of Joyce, because of his constant wish to renew his writing and because his working method implied multiple revisions, so that these revisions were made in the light of a profoundly altered project.

The layering of successive levels of intentionality can be observed in any work that is produced in time (that is to say, everywhere except perhaps in very short extemporizations), but it is particularly accessible to a genetic approach within the framework of Joyce's aesthetics of saturation (as opposed, for instance, to an aesthetic model based on deprivation, like Beckett's). We have seen that Joycean meanings pile up without canceling one another on the model of the portmanteau word (the "ray of hope" does not obliterate the underlying "cork"; "go on" is still narratively and rhythmically perceptible beneath the surface of "Garonne"). Using the manuscripts to follow successive stages of writing produces an effect of ex-plication, a gradual unfolding of the packed riches. And yet it poses specific difficulties, linked with the paradoxes of the notion of overdetermination. The multiplication of levels in a work like *Ulysses* implies that each element is heavily overdetermined: it is determined by its narrative import, by its various meanings, literal and symbolic, by its thematic and intertextual references, and by the tight web of symmetries and echoes that binds it to other parts of the book. It was impossible, however, logically and empirically, for Joyce to conceive and adjust these multiple levels at the same time. We hardly need the confirmation of the manuscripts to know that the infinitely complex structures of *Ulysses* and *Finnegans Wake* cannot have sprung like Athena fully armed from Joyce's brain (although Joyce sought to persuade some of his admirers that this had been the case). This implies that the majority of the determinations were discovered retrospectively by the writer rather than projected, so that they paradoxically reflect a basic indeterminacy. An open attitude toward the potentialities of writing is required on the part of the critic (reflecting Joyce's own disposition) to interpret genetically the mechanics of meaning.

The unforeseen consequences of the ink accidentally sinking through the proofs of the Black Mass scene provide a strong illustration of this phenomenon. We have seen how it prompted the Satanic inversion of the Alleluia and the Gooooooooooood/Dooooooooooog mirror effect, establishing a whole network of unforeseen connections with preexisting thematic networks.

This connective propensity is the best ally of writers in general and in particular of an author like Joyce who was keen to take advantage of it. He seems to have been aware very early of the role played by contingent relationships in the dynamics of invention. In the "Esthetic" section of what is known as the "Alphabetical Notebook" (1910), the young Joyce notes:

> The instant of inspiration is a spark so brief as to be invisible. The reflection of it on many sides at once from a multitude of cloudy circumstances with no one of which it is united save by the bond of merest possibility veils its afterglow in an instant in a first confusion of form. This is the instant in which the word is made flesh. (*JJA* 7:121–22)

We can hear a distinct note of regret: the bright flame of inspiration is dimmed by the multitude of cloudy circumstances that reflect it, related only by mere possibility, that is to say devoid of the character of necessity that is ideally manifested in the completed work of art. But the fire shines so briefly as to be a mere spark: it cannot live if it is not incarnated ("made flesh") in a contingent form. The necessity of the work of art is an effect, a posteriori, of its completion.

Even if we do not share this youthful romantic nostalgia,[7] we must acknowledge that this faculty of generating unexpected echoes or reflections, which contributes so much to the enrichment of the work, can also cause, from the point of view of the reader of the final text, a blurring, or even a blunting, of the edge of the inventive moment.

We can find an example of this in a passage from "Circe" that is probably the most radical undermining of the extraordinary illusion of life created by the characters of *Ulysses* but that remains rather inconspicuous and is rarely quoted. This is the passage in the final text:

> (*A panel of fog rolls back rapidly, revealing rapidly in the jurybox the faces of Martin Cunningham, foreman, silkhatted, Jack Power, Simon Dedalus, Tom Kernan, Ned Lambert, John Henry Menton, Myles Crawford, Lenehan, Paddy Leonard, Nosey Flynn, M'Coy and the featureless face of a Nameless One.*)
> THE NAMELESS ONE
> Bareback riding. Weight for age. Gob, he organised her.
> THE JURORS
> (*all their heads turned to his voice*) Really?
> THE NAMELESS ONE
> (*snarls*) Arse over tip. Hundred shillings to five.
> THE JURORS
> (*All their heads lowered in assent*) Most of us thought as much. (*U* 15.1139–51)

What is this "Nameless One"? We recognize the voice, the language and the attitude of the anonymous narrator of half of "Cyclops," the "debt-collector." But why this absence of features and of a name? Up to that point, the debt-collector has never appeared outside his own discourse. The "shot-reverse shot" technique, which is so important for the rounding out of the characters of Bloom, Stephen or Molly, for their naturalization both as subject and represented object, has not been applied in this case. He has not been presented from the outside; therefore, narratively speaking, he has no face! He has not been called by his name; therefore, he has no name! Much is at stake here: the face—the stamp of individuality, the primordial sign from which the infant takes his bearings toward the breast—is reduced to a blank page; the name—the mainstay of symbolic and social identity—is annihilated. This character—and a very lively one it was—is abruptly reduced to a ghostly presence by this sudden refusal to go on playing the usual game of inference: a discourse implies a voice, a subject, a human being. . . . We are brutally reminded that characters are nothing but literary artifacts, temporary clusters of linguistic elements. The apparently solid figures that the earlier episodes had presented are threatened with a contagion of decomposition.

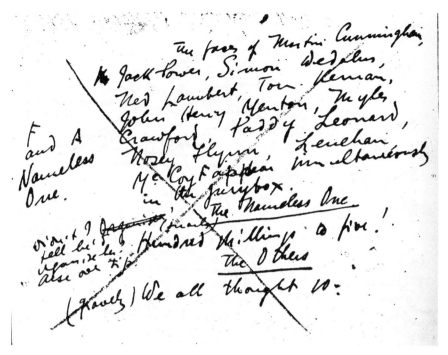

Figure 2.4. Draft for "Circe." Buffalo V.A.19–8 (*JJA* 14: 210).

Now if we look at the genesis of this passage, we can see that it was elabo-rated in the earliest extant draft for "Circe" (Buffalo V.A.19), on a verso, as part of a scene of indictment of Bloom for various misdemeanors (fig. 2.4).

To pass judgment on Bloom, a jury is summoned, consisting of various Dubliners that he has encountered during the day. We can notice that it was only as an afterthought that the "Cyclops" narrator was included, in a mar-ginal addition, but it must have occurred to Joyce immediately after he drafted the first paragraph, since "The Nameless One" is present in the main text that follows. Presumably, it is at this moment that Joyce realized that this lively character, as an anonymous but intradiegetic narrator, was the only one of its kind and could be called literally "The Nameless One," offering the occasion for an allusion to one of his favorite poems by James Clarence Mangan but transgressing the implicit convention that fictional characters must have a name even if the reader is not informed of it.

It was at a relatively late stage (the manuscript is missing, but it was later than the third extant version, the NLI Quinn draft, and earlier than the Rosenbach fair copy) that Joyce carried his initial gesture to its logical conclusion and added the even more disturbing "featureless face," transgressing another implicit convention that fictional characters have a physiognomy, even if it is not described. But in the same way as the *Nameless* appellation immediately found its place in *Ulysses's* dense network of intertextual references, the *featureless* characteristic perfectly agreed with the mutilated aspect of many apparitions in "Circe," from the "visage unknown injected with dark mercury" (*U* 15.213) to Paddy Dignam ("Half of one ear, all the nose and both thumbs are ghouleaten." *U* 15.1208) and the Mother ("her face worn and noseless, green with gravemould." *U* 15.4159). However, this retrospective cohesion has the disadvantage of diluting the strength of this exceptional passage, making its metaleptic transgression somewhat inconspicuous in the fantastic universe of "Circe."

It could be argued, then, that in this case, the connective propensity tends to have a somewhat weakening effect, but it generally works as a very effective ally for Joyce, who counts on it and knows how to multiply its effects. The word *serendipity* would not be adequate here, because it would suggest that things just happened, by sheer luck, obliterating Joyce's intense labor in order to detect and develop the potentialities that presented themselves and, before that, to create the conditions for their occurrence.

Dissemination

It is interesting to compare the "Esthetic" entry from the Alphabetical Notebook quoted above with a remark by Frank Budgen describing Joyce in the early days of writing *Ulysses* ("Joyce . . . was a great believer in his luck. What he needed would come to him. That which he collected would prove useful in its time and place"[8]); with a 1923 letter revealing that his apparently fragmented writings are "active elements" that "will begin to fuse of themselves";[9] and with a note inscribed in 1924: "JJ no gambler because/his style gambles/ infinitely probable."[10] By this time, Joyce is well aware that he does not need to gamble because his style does it for him, and it cannot lose because its bets cover every possibility available on the gambling table.

Finnegans Wake is written from this perspective, and the potential for the diffusion of effects is even greater there than in *Ulysses*—or probably any other book. We will study a single example, but it demonstrates an extreme power of dissemination, as it affects a pair of letters of the alphabet (p/k) and the allusive power that they progressively acquire.

It starts with a series of notes taken by Joyce in notebook VI.B.14, during the summer of 1924 while he was on holiday in Brittany (fig. 2.5). Joyce was interested in Breton as a branch of the Celtic linguistic family and more generally in Celtic studies. He discovered that he had been anticipated and perhaps surpassed in linguistic manipulation by the eighteenth-century Celtophiles or "celtomanes," such as Jacques Le Brigant in his *Eléments succints de la langue des celtes-gomérites ou Bretons: Introduction à cette langue et, par elle, à celle de tous les peuples connus* (1779), who had revived Celtic studies in France but with questionable scientific rigor. The celtomanes asserted that Breton was the origin of all tongues, proving this by all sorts of fantastic derivations, and they even believed that Breton was the language of Eden. On page 101 of the notebook, Joyce quoted the crowning elements from the demonstration. Adam and Eve received their names from Breton words: the first man asked for a bite (*A tam* in Breton) of the apple, and when he choked on it, the first woman urged him to drink (*Ev* in Breton)! On the same page, Joyce answers in kind, as it were: he writes "Keltomaniac (Le Brigant)" and adds a "- p -" on the line below. He demonstrates that, with a manipulation of consonants similar to those performed by Le Brigant himself and the addition of a *p,* it is easy to transform "keltomaniac" into "kleptomaniac," which translates Le Brigant's name (in French a *brigand* is a bandit) and describes his activity as word stealer from every language in favor of Breton.

We find out later that the addition of the *p* is particularly appropriate. On page 188 of the same notebook, Joyce notes a particular feature of Celtic historical linguistics, the *p/k* (or *p/q*) split. It divides Celtic languages in two groups: Brythonic languages (such as Breton) admit the sound *p* where Goidelic languages (such as Irish) have the sound *k*. A consequence of this is pointed out in a note on page 218 of this notebook ("pascha I. casca/purpura Kurkura"), perplexing but clear enough when its source was discovered in a book by Stefan Czarnowski:

Dans les premiers temps les Irlandais remplaçaient le son *p* par *k* (écrit *c*) dans les mots empruntés, par exemple *purpura* devint *corcur, pascha—casc* [At first the Irish replaced the sound *p* by *k* (written as *c*) in words they had borrowed, for example *purpura* became *corcur, pascha—casc*].[11]

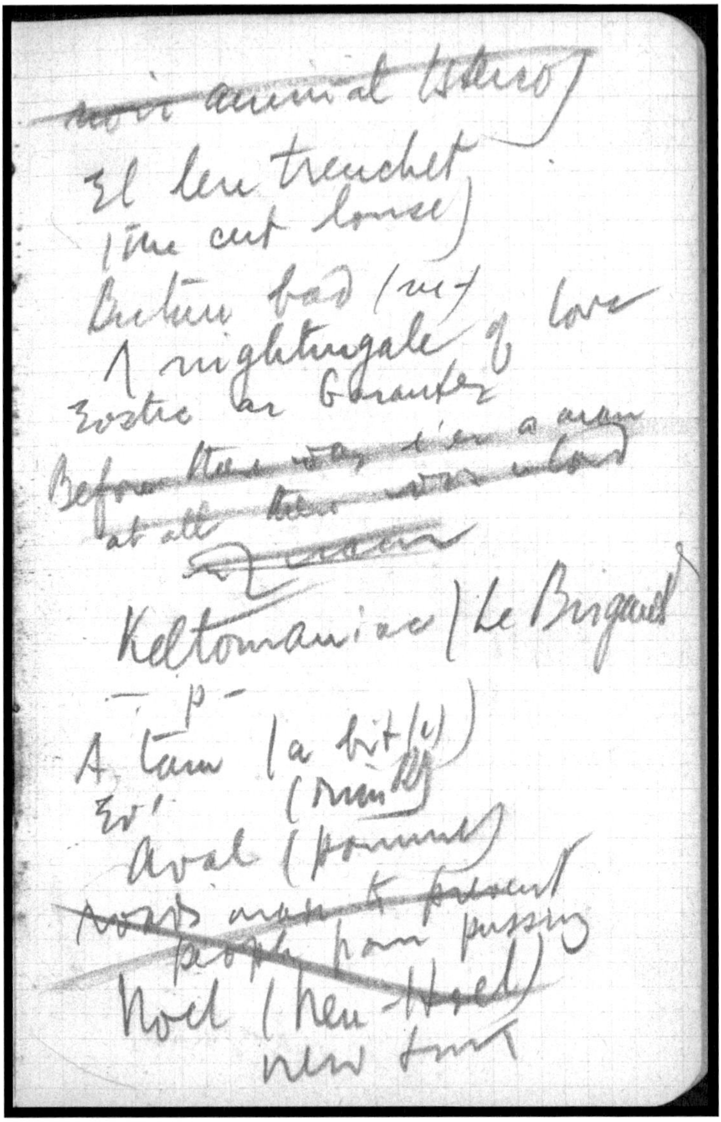

Figure 2.5. Buffalo VI.B.14–101 (*JJA* 32:172).

This national mispronunciation is a pattern of linguistic deformation that Joyce would exploit often enough in *Finnegans Wake*. But its meaning was enriched in the following year by another discovery. As Joyce was reading Freud's *Collected Papers*,[12] he took note, on page 18 of notebook VI.B.19, of an infantile phrase used by one of the young patients "do no 1" (from "Hans: 'Oh, I'll come up again in the morning to have breakfast and do number one,'" in "Analysis of a phobia in a five-year-old" *Collected Papers* 160). Number one and number two are of course nursery euphemisms for urinating and defecating. This is taken up again in the same notebook: "no 1 or no 2" (VI.B.19.168, see fig. 2.6). Then, on top of the next page, we find the letters *pp* or *kk* followed by "keykey ahah." Passing from an English to a French version of the excremental functions (in French *pipi et caca* are precisely "number one and number two," with roughly similar childish connotations), Joyce starts playing with the sounds, relishing perhaps their coincidental homophony.

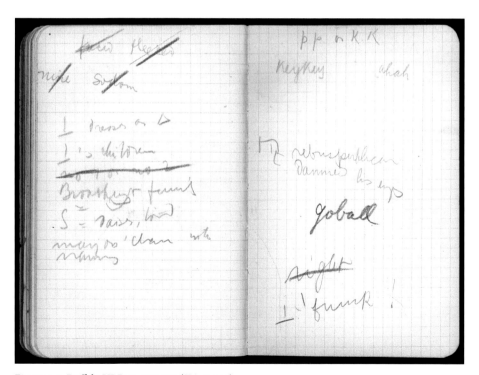

Figure 2.6. Buffalo VI.B.19–168-169 (*JJA* 33:292).

Figure 2.7. Draft for *Finnegans Wake* III.4. British Library, 47482a-23v (*JJA* 60:44).

The game is continued on a page of a draft (47482a–23v, *JJA* 60:44) that is exactly contemporary with this notebook. Apparently, Joyce had written first:

earned by Cain, outflanked by Ham, reordered by Patrick, delivered by Tristan, by Patrick's dear.

He then takes up the Irish "kurkura" from the Czarnowski note to coin the amusing "kurkle katches," which gave him the key for a transformation of the passage, prompting a series of additions, substitutions, and overwritings:
The *p*/*k* substitution is at work in the names of Irish heroes (Patrick is transformed into Kawdreg and, more surprisingly, Parnell into Karnell, with a hint of the carnality that caused his downfall), spreads to other words ("inklored," suggesting traditions penned in ink), and seems to be getting out of hand, perhaps due to its newly discovered excremental connotation, with a surplus, an overflow of *k* (of *caca*), encroaching over other letters (Kam and Kriskan!?).

Although this passage was never incorporated into *Finnegans Wake,* we do find two occurrences of "kurkle" (*FW* 95.22 and 296.13). In the first appearance in particular ("Fine feelplay we had of it mid the kissabetts frisking in the kool kurkle dusk of the lushiness"), the excremental connotation is clearly present (pissabed) and associated with the p/k substitution. But we should consider that it is also present in each of the several instances of the *p/k* inversion in *Finnegans Wake.* Taking this a step further, we become aware that no *p* or *k* in the book remains unaffected: each *k* could be a *p,* a *k* may be hiding behind each *p,* and in the shadow of each instance of these letters lurks a marginal allusion to Celtic philology and to infantile scatology.

Of course Joyce did not write every *p* and every *k* with these associations in mind, but this is not the point. Joyce knew that the signifying engine he had made up worked autonomously like the printing press gone wild that is fantasized by Bloom in "Aeolus" (*U* 7.102–4). Each word, each letter, opens up an indeterminate number of meanings or, to put it differently, produces retrospectively a multitude of determinations.

This is the reason why manuscripts do not provide us with final answers about the correct interpretation of the text. They reveal that the productivity of the text surpasses Joyce's intentions at any particular moment. Authorial intention cannot be the last word on the text: it is something that we should not neglect, something that we should pursue through its fluctuations and nuances by a rigorous analysis of extant documents, but it cannot limit our powers of interpretation. Joyce's writing illustrates—we can go as far as saying that it deliberately and thoroughly exploits—the essential "iterability" of writing, its "possibility of functioning cut off, at a certain point, from its 'original' meaning and from its belonging to a saturable and constraining context."[13]

3

From Tristan to *Finnegan*

Decontextualization and Recontextualization
in the Transition from *Ulysses* to *Finnegans Wake*

The story of the beginnings of *Finnegans Wake* can be told in many differ-ent ways: predictably, the genesis of such an unusual book is extraordinarily complex. In this chapter, we will be able to highlight only some of the factors in the creative adventure that took Joyce from the completion of *Ulysses* to the writing of his next book. I have chosen to emphasize the part played by the story of Tristan and Isolde in the transition between *Ulysses* to *Finnegans Wake*. The importance of this theme has been known to Joyce scholars for a long time,[1] but six sheets recently acquired by the National Library of Ire-land (and now available online) radically change our perspective. Studying this transitional period will give us the opportunity to observe on a larger scale the mechanisms that we have studied in the first chapter.

In October 1922, Joyce was resting in the South of France from the exertions of writing and publicizing *Ulysses,* but he could not quite let go of the book. He was reading it again and preparing a list of corrections for the next edition. By the end of the month, he had reached only the "Cyclops" episode, and on the first extant page of Buffalo notebook VI.B.10, he listed a few emendations, then stopped suddenly and wrote the following gloss: "Polyphemous is Ul's [Ulysses's] shadow." (fig. 3.1)

Joyce does not take up the errata list on this page or in this notebook, and we can consider that his work on *Ulysses* stops there, on the idea of a dark side, a nocturnal dimension of the divine Ulysses. And the work on *Finnegans Wake* somehow starts here, although Joyce did not know it. On the next line Joyce noted the words "clipper ship" from an article in the October 22, 1922,

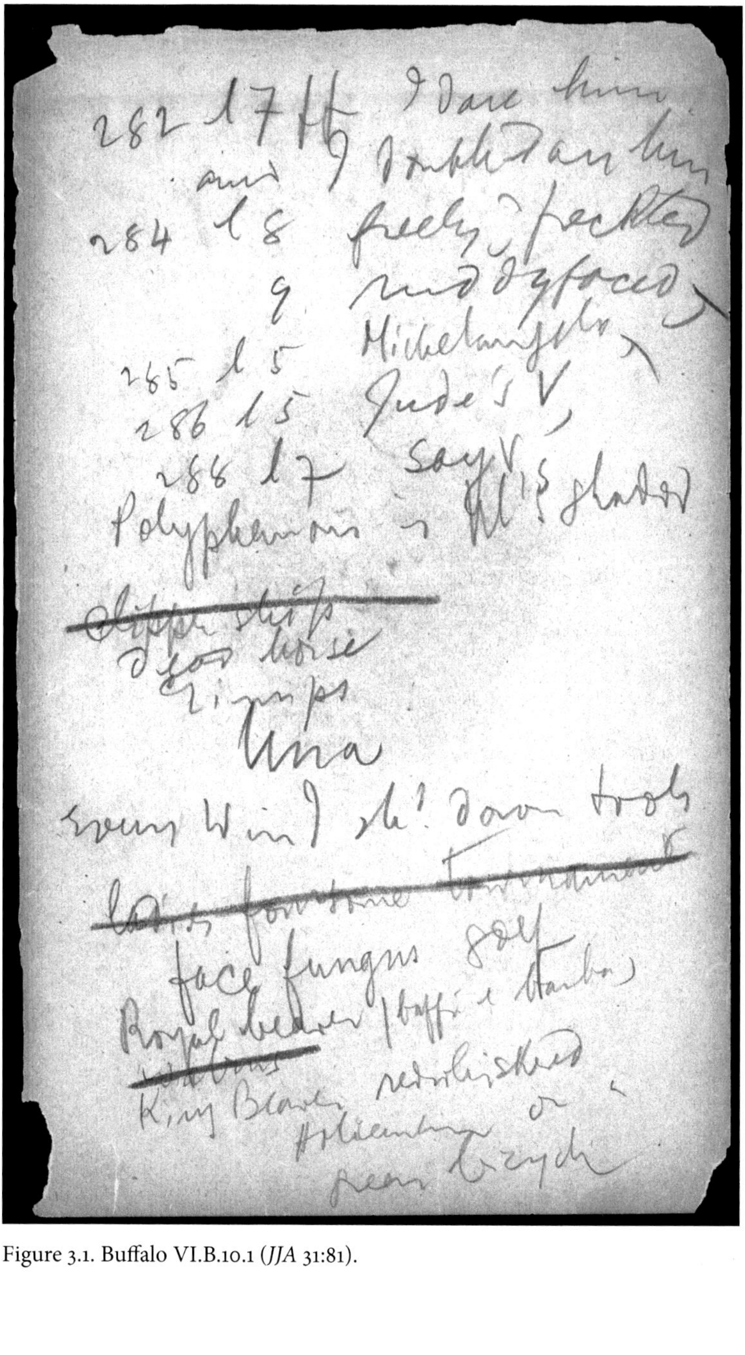

Figure 3.1. Buffalo VI.B.10.1 (*JJA* 31:81).

edition of the *Daily Mail,* which one year later he used as "the ships, [. . .] the clipperbuilt," in a draft for a sketch that would become, another twelve years later, the core of *Finnegans Wake* Book II, chapter 4. (The phrase is still present in the printed book; see *FW* 394.15–17.)

We have the feeling that we are on a ridge, a sort of dividing line between two projects. Or perhaps a trough: the tremendous energy necessary to put *Ulysses* together is now spent, and the momentum for the new venture is not yet gathered. And yet this is not a frontier: *Finnegans Wake* integrates many elements from *Ulysses,* and we have seen that *Ulysses* anticipates *Finnegans Wake* in several ways. But this is hindsight. It was impossible for anyone, and even for Joyce himself, to know which elements from *Ulysses* (or from his other works) could be transposed into the future book or how these elements would be transfigured by their integration in a new context.

From the distant perspective of literary history, the continuity between Joyce's two great books is clear. We have only to extrapolate from the more daring passages of *Ulysses* to generate *Finnegans Wake.* Or, even better, we can draw a line from *Dubliners* to *A Portrait of the Artist as a Young Man,* from *A Portrait* to the early episodes of *Ulysses,* and then follow the gradual transformation of the aesthetic project in the middle and late episodes of *Ulysses* to reach *Finnegans Wake.* While this may seem logical retrospectively, it is also quite misleading. Such a view does not take into account the dismay of most early readers of *Ulysses* when they were confronted with *Finnegans Wake.* They were shocked because this was *not* what they were expecting after *Ulysses.* Such a view is also an obstacle to understanding how the work was actually written. It does not say anything about all the possibilities that were open in the wake of *Ulysses,* and it does not say anything about all the impossibilities that had to be transgressed in order to go further. And it does not say anything about the way *Ulysses* itself could be an obstacle.

It is difficult to imagine what it must have been like for a writer who had just turned forty to be the author of *Ulysses.* The work had been famous, as well as infamous, all over the world, for several years before it was published as a book on February 2, 1922. The early episodes had been serialized in the United States in the *Little Review* (and in part in the United Kingdom by the *Egoist*) until a series of obscenity trials stopped publication altogether. An impressive number of critical articles had already been published about

Ulysses, simply based on the expectations raised by *A Portrait of the Artist as a Young Man* and the already published episodes, which were less than one half of the final text of the book. While some extolled the extraordinary innovative power of the unpublished book, others preemptively denounced its pernicious influence.

When Valery Larbaud presented Joyce to the Parisian public in December 1921, he claimed that "it is not an exaggeration to say that, among literary people, his name is as well-known and his works are as much an object of discussion, as the names and theories of Freud and Einstein are among the scientists."[2] When the book was published two months later, it produced an even greater number of reviews and a fresh crop of superlatives: "A perverted lunatic who has made a speciality of the literature of the latrine" was one of the gentlest appreciations among its detractors.[3]

On the other hand, some of the admirers declared that it was "the greatest English writing since Shakespeare,"[4] and T.S. Eliot claimed that Joyce's use of Homer was as important a scientific discovery as Einstein's theory of relativity.[5] In the same essay, he also wrote that "it is a book to which we are all indebted, and from which none of us can escape." This *all* implies that Joyce himself incurred that immense debtorship and that he could not escape from *Ulysses.*

At the same time as he was publishing his essay on *Ulysses,* Eliot was telling Virginia Woolf in private that, after such a book, Joyce was left "with nothing to write another book on."[6] Eliot's assumption seemed true enough. It is clear that the shadow of *Ulysses* inhibited a good many writers of Joyce's generation. As she was writing her own works, Woolf could not help thinking that what she was doing was "probably being better done by Mr. Joyce."[7] Djuna Barnes declared that she could not write a single line after *Ulysses* and spoke of a literary suicide.[8] But it was not easy for Joyce himself to live up to his own reputation and to write a successor to the novelistic summa that *Ulysses* claimed to be. Indeed, when the early fragments of Joyce's new work were published, the first preoccupation of someone like William Carlos Williams was: "Has he gone backwards since *Ulysses?*"[9]

Joyce's future writing was constrained by the expectations of his public but also by his own requirements. He wrote to his father that it depended "on my eyesight and my own internal approbation of what I write—two difficult matters."[10] While in this letter he gives his father some news about his eyesight, unfortunately he does not say anything about his criteria for "internal approbation"; it would have been most interesting to know what they were. But he probably could not have defined them precisely at the time: he was in the paradoxical situation of having to write something new to continue in the track of his previous works and of having to do the unexpected in order to fulfill the expectations of everyone, including himself.

When Harriet Shaw Weaver asked him, in August 1922, what he planned to write next, he answered "a history of the world."[11] Sixteen years earlier, with *Dubliners* he had intended only to write "a chapter in the moral history of my country" (*SL* 83), but in the meantime the stakes had been considerably raised. People expected no less from him (and in some ways *Finnegans Wake* is indeed a history of the world), but it was not so easy to get started on such a project.

Joyce used to say that he needed only the slightest point of departure to get started, but he had yet to find something to catch his attention during this postpartum period. His state of physical and moral exhaustion coincided with the end of a writing cycle: he had cannibalized *Stephen Hero* to write *A Portrait; Ulysses* had started as a sequel to *A Portrait*, combined with elements from *Dubliners*. This time, the new book could no longer be a narrative sequel to his former work. It would still include, however, a strong element of continuity, that is to say the transposition of former elements into a new context.

Joyce was still very much under "Ul's shadow." He asked Sylvia Beach to send him the first issue of Eliot's *Criterion* because it contained the translation of Valery Larbaud's article on *Ulysses*. The issue also includes "The Waste Land," but Joyce does not say anything about it in the moment. What drew his attention was a rather insignificant article by Thomas Sturge Moore, "The Story of Tristram and Isolt in Modern Poetry."[12]

From Tristan to *Finnegan*

There are several aspects in the legend of Tristan and Isolde that were likely to interest Joyce.[13] It is a Celtic legend, with an Irish component: Isolde is an Irish princess and Chapelizod is a suburb of Dublin. Joyce believed that "in the particular is contained the universal," and it was predictable that the "universal history" that he had in mind would be anchored in an Irish context. Moore's article doesn't mention this aspect at all, but it is immediately followed, in the *Criterion*, by "The Waste Land," which includes a quotation from the sailor's song in the first act of Wagner's *Tristan und Isolde:*

Frisch weht der Wind
der Heimat zu:
mein irisch Kind,
wo weilest du?[14]

[Fresh the wind blows
towards home:
my Irish child,
where are you now?]

So Joyce would have been reminded, if he needed to be, that Isolde was an *irisch Kind.*

The story has other characteristics that relate it to Joyce's own work. It is about adultery as betrayal, a theme that was central to *Exiles* and essential to the story of *Ulysses.*[15] But it is another point that seems to have caught Joyce's attention. Sturge Moore begins by praising the writers who have dared to take up a theme that has already been illustrated by other great writers. Joyce, who had just finished his own version of the *Odyssey,* could not disagree. Then, Sturge Moore remarks that among the subjects with a universal appeal, the story of Tristan and Isolde has produced many modern versions. In his notebook, Joyce makes up a list based on the first page of the article:

Tristan—Binyon
    Tennyson
    Wagner
    Michael Field
    Swinburne
    Arnold
    Debussy
    Gordon Bottomley.[16]

On the first page, we can find all the names in Joyce's list, except Debussy (Joyce is probably referring to his *Pelléas et Melisande,* which can be considered as a version of Tristan and Isolde), but if we look more closely, we are surprised to find that Moore mentions Gordon Bottomley only because he has written on Shakespearean themes. As so often, Joyce seems to have been reading very quickly and taking notes superficially.

The idea of vying with these writers was rather appealing to Joyce. When he arrived in Paris in 1920, he had written to his brother:

> *Odyssey* very much in the air here. Anatole France is writing *Le Cyclope*, G. Fauré the musician an opera *Pénélope*. Giraudoux has written *Elpenor* (Paddy Dignam). Guillaume Apollinaire *Les Mamelles de Tirésias*. (*Letters* III 10)

It is remarkable that Joyce, who was then in the process of writing *Ulysses*, seemed to be rather more pleased than distressed by this proliferating competition.

The other thing that Joyce noted from Sturge Moore's article is the reference to the two Isoldes: Isolde of Brittany (or Isolde of the White Hands), Tristan's spouse, and Isolde of Ireland (or Isolde of the Golden Hair), Tristan's lover. He immediately referred this duality to the Homeric framework of his own *Ulysses* and the duality between "Penelope" and "Calypso" (which he had noted very early in the conception of *Ulysses*, in what is known as the "Subject Notebook"):[17]

Isolde of Britt—Pen
——white hands Calyp[18]

These structural and thematic similarities with his own previous work were apparently sufficient to start on a "new" track. Since several pages are missing from the end of that first notebook (Buffalo notebook VI.B10) as well as from the beginning of the subsequent notebook (VI.B.3),[19] we cannot know precisely how and when Joyce took up the Tristan and Isolde story. Nonetheless, at the end of February or the beginning of March 1923, they had grown into well-established characters as he started to take notes for several fragmentary scenes involving them.[20]

More or less at the same time, on March 11, 1923, Joyce announced that he had written the first two pages since "the final yes of *Ulysses*" (*Letters* I 202). This was a short comical sketch devoted to Roderick O'Connor,[21] the last high king of Ireland. In the next few weeks, Joyce wrote four short texts: one described the kiss of Tristan and Isolde, one described Saint Kevin's strange rituals of purification, and two of them were devoted to the childhood of Isolde and Saint Kevin, respectively.[22] Of these, two were abandoned, one was incorporated, at a very late stage, in the last chapter of *Finnegans Wake,* and one ("the kiss") would become the starting point of the genesis of chapter 4 of Book II and a crucial element in the shaping of *Finnegans Wake.*

Until recently, the only trace of the early Tristan draft was one enigmatic page among the British Library holdings (BL 47480–267v) that could be dated spring 1923 because it was written on the verso of a draft of the Roderick O'Connor sketch that Joyce had sent to Harriet Shaw Weaver. It was clear that it was somehow connected with another almost contemporaneous "Tristan and Isolde" sketch also in the British Library (BL 47481–94), but it was impossible to define the logical and chronological relationship.

Moreover, this page contained a puzzling element: in the middle of a grotesque duet between a vulgar pair of lovers, there was a version of "Nightpiece," one of Joyce's own poems that he later published in *Pomes Pennyeach*[23] and that had already appeared five years earlier in *Poetry* magazine.[24] The status of the poem on this draft, its presence in such a context, is so surprising that it was the basis of a controversy between the two most experienced specialists of the *Finnegans Wake* archive, David Hayman and Danis Rose.[25] Hayman noted the thematic relevance of the poem to Tristan and Isolde and believed that it played an important role in the early development of *Finnegans Wake,* while Rose argued that there was no relation between the poem and the surrounding text and that Joyce had just happened to use a piece of paper on which the poem was previously written and then wrote the sketch around it.[26]

One of the folios acquired by the National Library of Ireland in 2006 is the complement of this mysterious page. A foolscap of the same size, folded in a similar manner, it ends with a sentence ("Her mournful embracer pointed to the sidereal host. By them he bade her swear, them that were and are and shall be, the silently") that is continued on the British Library manuscript: "strewing, the strikingly shining, the twittingly twinkling, our true home and (as he uranographically remarked), the lamplights of lovers in the Beyond."

Thus, we now have a complete first draft of the kiss of Tristan and Isolde

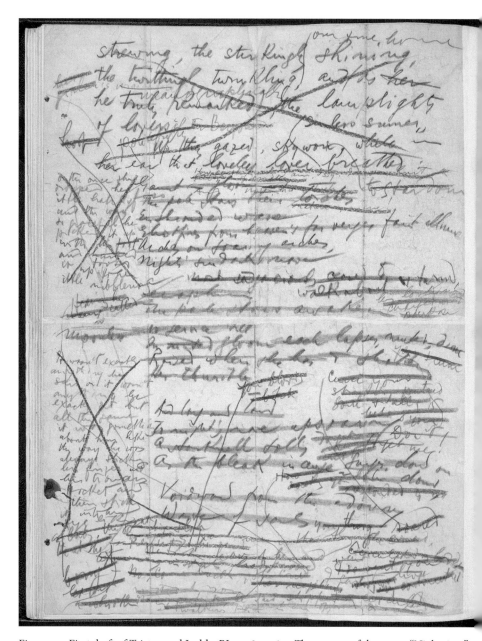

Figure 3.2. First draft of Tristan and Isolde. BL 47480–267v. The stanzas of the poem "Nightpiece" are clearly visible in the centre. (*JJA* 56:6–7).

comprising two pages in the National Library of Ireland and one page in the British Library. This earliest version can be seen as a transposition of the "Nausicaa" episode of *Ulysses*. In "Nausicaa," the meeting of Bloom and Gerty Mac-Dowell is told from the girl's point of view, in the manner of the sentimental novels that she enjoys reading, but jarring notes, petty thoughts, and vulgar subjects constantly disturb the otherwise pseudo-genteel style. Obviously, Joyce is making fun of Gerty and literature for young women. He deflates the illusions conveyed by that cheap version of romanticism by contrasting them with the point of view of a Leopold Bloom, all the more sober and disillusioned because he has just masturbated. However, speaking of parody and ironic distance is quite insufficient. Joyce enjoys the identification with this silly perspective and immerses himself with a great pleasure in the deplorable style (and so do his readers). We are quite far from the fin de siècle aesthetics of Stephen Dedalus and of some of Joyce's own poetry. In the Tristan and Isolde sketch, both attitudes are summoned and equally ridiculed.

In this sketch, it looks as if the second half of "Nausicaa," told from Bloom's skeptical, detumescent, point of view, has been mixed up with the first romantic half. This prudent masculine perspective, which, in *Ulysses,* may seem to have the upper hand because it comes after the girlish first half, collides abruptly with the cheap romanticism: neither remains unscathed. We will find this process of reshuffling and intermingling heterogeneous material at various stages of the genesis of this chapter.

Here is the first paragraph, in a simplified transcription:

> He, the gentleman, was sodavisaged. First he was a martyr to indigestion, rather liable to piles procured by sitting on stone walls while revelling in the beauty of nature and over and above that by medical advice of Dr Codd he had been lowering daily potions of extract of willow bark to keep off the Hibernian flu when he contracted a stubborn cough. With feverish pallor, indicating the action of the high seas on a teetotal stomach, he beheld the holy ghosts of his undergradual loves [. . .] Ghastlily, he pastloveyed her with a blackedged expression.[27]

Bloom, who was dressed in black because he had attended a funeral, appeared to Gerty as a dark mysterious Byronic hero—"the gentleman in black who was sitting there by himself" (*U* 13.349–50), "the quiet gravefaced gentleman" (*U* 13.542). Likewise, Isolde's "gentleman" is interestingly pale and melancholy, with a mournful ("blackedged") expression, but we are immediately told, with Bloomian matter-of-factness, that this romantic aspect is due to such things as indigestion, piles, and seasickness. (Cf. Bloom's remark in "Nausicaa": "Bad for you, dear, to sit on that stone. [. . .] Might get piles myself." *U* 13.1081–83)

This young girl covers the same territory as her *Ulysses* counterpart but in a much more frankly down-to-earth manner. Whereas Gerty "wondered why you couldn't eat something poetical like violets or roses" (*U* 13.230), Isolde is:

> waiting patiently all through the damned old dinner of burnt loinchops and ignoble potatoes with everybody talking from soup to nuts all about loinchops and mash murphies and the pig's arse and cabbage of the day before and they saying it wasn't a patch on the silverside boiled cowbeef of the stewsday day before that again & the potroast with purpletop swedes and equally ignoble colicflower without a morsel of appetite when a plain bottle of porter & a gooseberry tart would have done her.

When she addresses Tristan, she expresses herself *gynelexically:* ("Smiling Johnny, pleaded she gynelexically, do you keer for meemeee just a weeny mossel?"), in a baby talk reminiscent of the young women's way of speaking to children in "Nausicaa."[28] In sharp contrast, her beau answers with absurd grandiloquence: "Why this strangulation, this yearning for a *bonum arduum* as distinguished from a *bonum simpliciter?*" This time, Joyce's own alter ego is the target, in a parodic transposition of Stephen Daedalus's pedantic invocation in *Stephen Hero* of the Thomistic distinction between two different kinds of good.[29]

This is interrupted by a sharp request to stop the moaning and become more active: "O, can that sobstuff let you. My own loveman must not talk like that, the bold puss answered impatiently." Tristan is all too happy to oblige, switching to salacious innuendo. But before proceeding, he interrogates her bluntly on the state of her virginity. She answers in an archaic and poetic language (and with a German *Nein* alluding to Wagner's Isolde) that she is "innocent as the undriven snow." Tristan asks her to swear on the stars, and this leads both of them to gaze heavenward, triggering the incongruous poetic sequence. "Up they gazed, skywon to stardom, while in his girleen's ear that loveless lover sinless sinner, breathed:

Gaunt in gloom
The pale stars their torches
Enshrouded wave
Ghostfires from heaven's far verges faint illume . . . etc.

Joyce's entire poem is recited by this grotesque Tristan, but it is immediately deflated by Isolde's confession that what she finds seductive in him is

the way he was always sticking his finger into his trousers pocket and then sticking it into his eye like a borny baby, the great big slob or the once she dropped her ittle hankyfuss and the way so graceful he picked it up with his hoof and footed it up politefully to her ittle nibblenose.

Second version and *Scribbledehobble*

The next version of the scene,[30] still very much in a "Nausicaa" vein, describes the meeting of a girly-girl and a football and rugby player, mostly told from the point of view of the young woman, in a rather adolescent style, borrowing phrases from sentimental novels and metaphors from the sports pages of newspapers. It is not quite as heterogeneous as the first version: for instance, Joyce's "Nightpiece" is missing. It is replaced by Isolde's request "for some but not too much of the best poetry quotations reflecting on the situation" and Tristan's Byronic recital of "a favourite lyrical bloom in decasyllabic iambic hexameter: /—Roll on, thou deep and darkblue ocean, roll!"

The lexical creations that were introduced in the margins and between the lines of the early version (neologisms such as "gynelexically" and puns like "stewsday" and "colicflower"), similar to those that he had produced in *Ulysses* (see first chapter), have become more numerous in the second version ("milkymouthily," "rightjingbangshot," "dazedcrazedgazed"), and we also find experiments in syntax and rhythm that are reminiscent of the "Sirens" episode, mimicking passion ("his deepsea peepers gazed O gazed O dazed-crazedgazed into her darkblue rolling ocean orbs"), desire ("they both went all of a shiveryshaky quiveryquaky mixumgatherum yumyumyum"), or esoteric metaphysical jargon:

when theeuponthus I oculise my most inmost Ego most vaguely senses the deprofundity of multimathematical immaterialities whereby in the pancosmic urge the Allimanence of That Which Is Itself exteriorates on this here our plane of disunited solid liquid and gaseous bodies in pearlwhite passionpanting intuitions of reunited Selfhood in the higher dimensional Selflessness.

Obviously, Joyce is using this trifling scene between two vulgar protagonists (encumbered, however, with a heavy mythical and artistic background)[31] as a pretext to review the resources that he had previously deployed and try them out in different combinations. But another phenomenon was going on at the same time that suggests that this process of decontextualization and recontextualization had deeper and more complex motivations.

We are going to see in chapter 6 of this volume that Joyce had acquired the habit of noting words and phrases in workbooks and then to reorganize these elements in second-order containers before inserting them in his drafts at various stages of the writing process. At about the same time as he was starting to write the Tristan and Isolde sketches, he introduced a different note-taking procedure. He acquired a very large copybook (over a thousand pages) and pre-divided it in sections according to the index reproduced here. The vast majority of the divisions in this copybook (known as the *Scribbledehobble*)[32] refer to Joyce's own published works: his collection of poetry, the stories in *Dubliners,* the parts of *Portrait of the Artist as a Young Man,* the three acts of *Exiles* and the episodes of *Ulysses.* Once he had established this grid, Joyce poured into it material that he had previously compiled. It seems that he felt the necessity to acclimatize external elements before admitting them into his text: notes must be situated in the context of Joyce's previous work before they can be used in his current work.[33]

Once the external elements had been irradiated, reenergized by this routine of joycification, their energy level was sufficient for them to be inserted in the text of the new work. Such a preliminary organization of the writing in progress in terms of the already published is, to my knowledge, unique among writers.

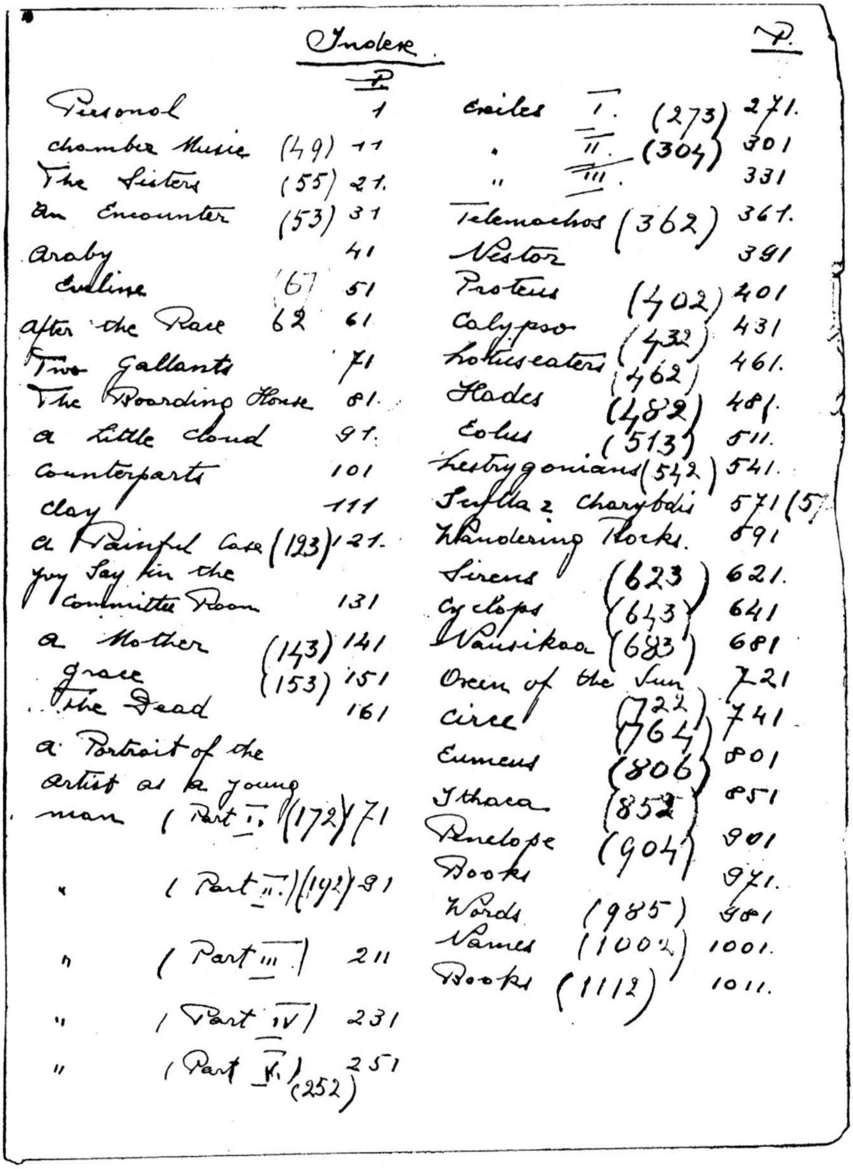

Figure 3.3. Buffalo VI.A (*Scribbledehobble*). Contents table (*JJA* 28:1).

The Four Old Men and the Kiss

The next step in the process of recontextualization is less drastically original. It involves changing the narrative perspective from one that more or less coincided with the protagonists' to an external viewpoint. In the recently discovered next version,[34] the emphasis is not on the kiss in itself but as an object of voyeurism. First, there is public opinion, represented by a flock of seabirds who have *heard of* the kiss of Tristan and Isolde and make fun of the poor husband, old King Mark. And then there are four strange old men, identified with the prophetic Waves of Erin.

The four old men have lived through all of Irish history, but their memories are all confused; they mix up dates and events, their own lives as henpecked husbands, as well as the main events of Irish history. Their senility does not make them less curious: they cling to the boats to spy on the cabins of newlywed couples and ladies' toilets through portholes that are as opaque as their own "cataractic" eyes. But again it is a noise, the "cataclysmic" sound of Tristan and Isolde kissing, that completely drives them out of themselves and leads them to sing a polyphonic song around the shores of Ireland.

This song comes as another surprise and as a confirmation that David Hayman was right in the controversy mentioned above: Joyce was willing to use his best lyrical poetry in a grotesque context. It is indeed one of Joyce's poems, which he had published seven years earlier under the title "Tutto è sciolto"[35] and which would also later be included in *Pomes Pennyeach*. We could never have expected to see it reappear here, sung by four senile old men.

After the poem, the two lovers continue their dialogue: it is as silly as ever and as grotesque. Isolde "murmured googooeyes":

> My precious since last we parted it seems to me that I have been continually in your company, even when I close my eyes at night, I am continually seeing you hearing you, meeting you in different places so that I am beginning to wonder whether my soul does not take leave of my body in sleep and go to seek you and what is more find you, or perchance this is only a phantasy.

This is not a simple parody of a stilted style. After his most lyrical poetry, Joyce is recontextualizing here something that is related to his personal history. Isolde uses sentences that come from the first letter that Nora wrote to him,[36] which Joyce thought she had lifted from a manual of correspondence. It must be noted that Joyce, who was suffering from acute conjunctivitis and was almost blind at the time, had to dictate this piece to Nora. In the manuscript, we recognize her handwriting and her idiosyncratic spelling. It means that Joyce was forcing Nora to copy once again these empty sentences that she had plagiarized many years before. This may be considered a rather perverse game, but the important point is that it proves that Joyce knew the letter practically by heart and it shows how important this episode had been for him in 1904. We can suppose that it was a source of inspiration for one of the main features of Joyce's mature style: a repetition of stereotyped discourse that is both parodic and serious.

Mamalujo

At this point, something very strange happened. At first, the four old men were only witnesses of the kiss. Their function was to provide us with a quadruple point of view on the scene, but they proved to be such absorbing characters that Joyce decided to make them autonomous figures and detach them from the Tristan and Isolde narrative. The four old men were to be developed separately and they eventually become identified with the Four Evangelists: Joyce's "Mamalujo." They are key elements in the elaboration of *Finnegans Wake,* and their perspective will become the most important in the book.

In the next version of their narrative, the same phrases return again and again, in a kind of senile loop.[37] This time, Joyce could take as a starting point another episode of *Ulysses.* In "Eumaeus," Bloom's exhaustion was expressed by means of a terribly clumsy style, piling up syntactically incompatible stereotypical expressions one on top of the other. It was the implementation of a very effective aesthetics of ugliness. But in this new sketch, it is not only the style but also the whole narrative that runs in circles like a repetitive music in which chronology is destroyed, with the compulsive return of a few obsessional dates.

"Mamalujo" is the first piece that Joyce decided was publishable. After many revisions, it appeared in the *Transatlantic Review* in April 1925.[38] At this point, we may consider that the transition between *Ulysses* and *Finnegans Wake* is complete. It remains only for us to see what became, in the later history of the book, of the elements that allowed Joyce to bridge the gap and to get started. It is remarkable that systematic procedures of decontextualization and recontextualization continued to be applied to them until the very last stages of the genetic process.

Aftermath (the genesis of *Finnegans Wake* II, 4)

The tryst of Tristan and Isolde was not discarded but left aside for a long time. It was only in 1938, when Joyce was finishing his book, that he reinstated the scene at the center of what became the last chapter of Book II. After fifteen years, Joyce reunited the scene of the two lovers' kiss with the four old Peeping Toms (Mamalujo) who are spying on them. This time, we could speak of deferral and *re*-placement. But it does not mean that the early vignette was reconstructed. The re-placement was not a return to the original context because, during the long deferral, Joyce's style and aesthetics had evolved considerably. While the early vignettes were clear, simple, and relatively easy to read, we now have a text that is as opaque as the "cataractic portholes" through which the Old Men were spying on Tristan and Isolde. In accordance with his new literary project, Joyce radicalized his technique of recontextualization: he sliced up the scene of the kiss into short fragments (from a single word to a paragraph) and injected them here and there in the "Mamalujo" text.[39]

In the illustration below (fig. 3.4), one can see the typescript on the right, representing the last version of "Mamalujo" before the reunification, marked with handwritten figures indicating the points of insertion of the numbered additions listed on the left-hand page. These additions are (revised) fragments of the scene between the two lovers. They are listed and numbered in a sequence that does not coincide with the original text of Tristan and Isolde, and they are inserted into the Mamalujo typescript in yet another different order: 2, 4, 1, 6, 14, 8, 7, 10, 11, 16 (5 and 15 being additions to 2, 9 to 7, 12 and 17 to 9 . . .).

Predictably, this technique completely disrupts the narrative logic of both pieces, adding a layer of obscurity to the senile ramblings of the Four Old Men.

Joyce will continue in the same direction until the last moment. To take a single example, we can see that, as late as October 1938, he notes, on a verso of

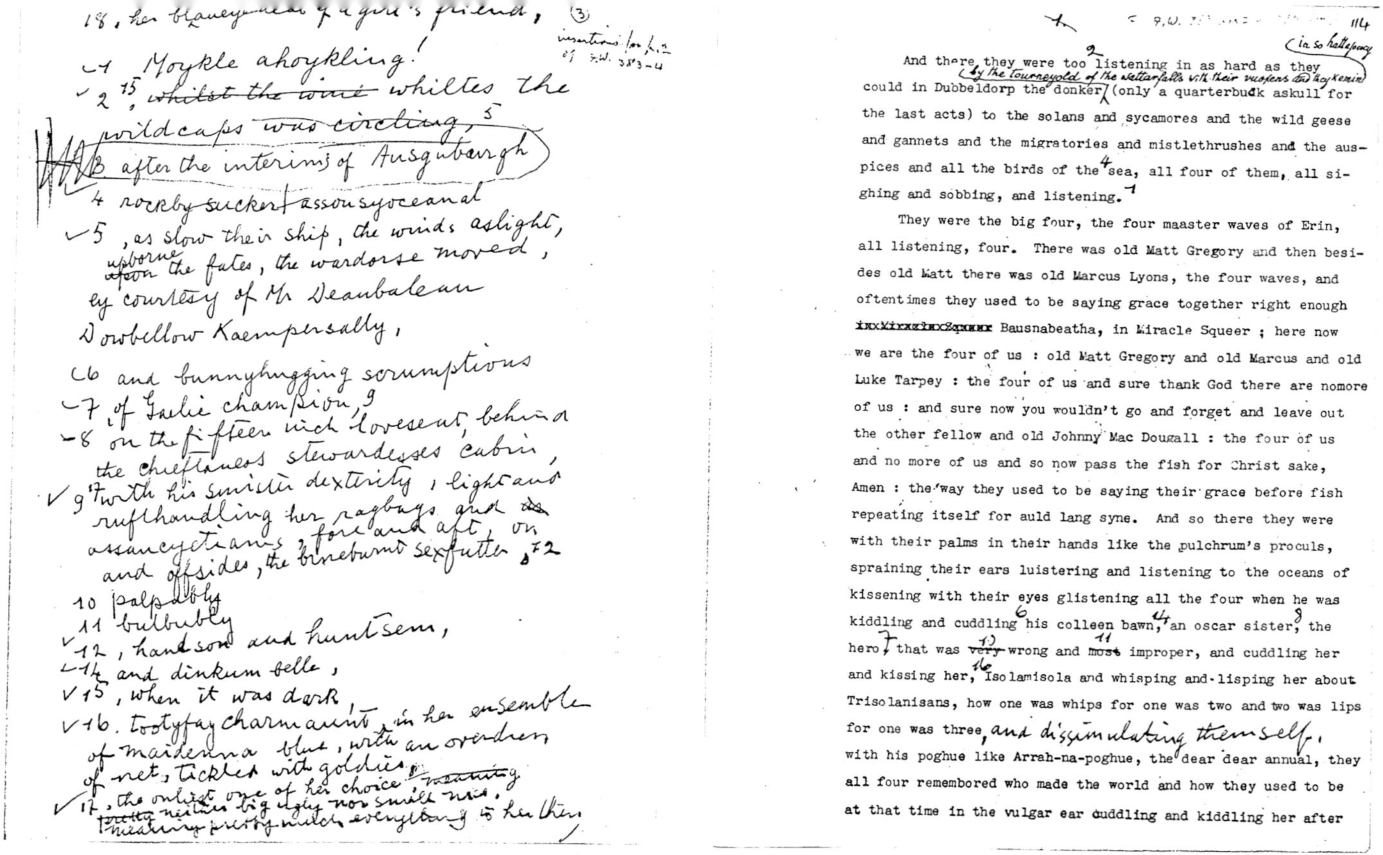

And there, they were too listening in as hard as they could in Dubbeldorp the 'donker'(only a quarterbuck askull for the last acts) to the solans and sycamores and the wild geese and gannets and the migratories and mistlethrushes and the auspices and all the birds of the sea, all four of them, all sighing and sobbing, and listening.

They were the big four, the four maaster waves of Erin, all listening, four. There was old Matt Gregory and then besides old Matt there was old Marcus Lyons, the four waves, and oftentimes they used to be saying grace together right enough Bausnabeatha, in Miracle Squeer ; here now we are the four of us : old Matt Gregory and old Marcus and old Luke Tarpey : the four of us and sure thank God there are nomore of us : and sure now you wouldn't go and forget and leave out the other fellow and old Johnny Mac Dougall : the four of us and no more of us and so now pass the fish for Christ sake, Amen : the'way they used to be saying their grace before fish repeating itself for auld lang syne. And so there they were with their palms in their hands like the pulchrum's proculis, spraining their ears luistening and listening to the oceans of kissening with their eyes glistening all the four when he was kiddling and cuddling his colleen bawn, an oscar sister; the hero that was very wrong and most improper, and cuddling her and kissing her, Isolamisola and whisping and-lisping her about Trisolanisans, how one was three and dissimulating itself, for one was two and two was lips for one was three and dissimulating itself, with his poghue like Arrah-na-poghue, the dear dear annual, they all four remembored who made the world and how they used to be at that time in the vulgar ear cuddling and kiddling her after

Figure 3.4. BL 47481-113v-BL 47481-114 (JJA 56:170-171).

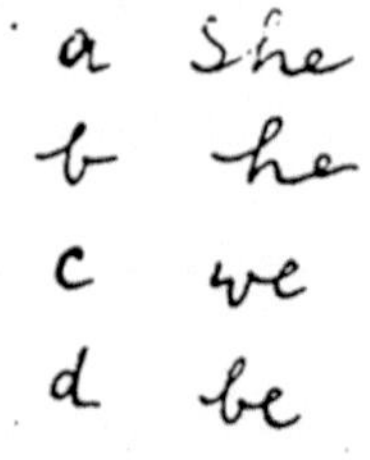

Figure 3.5. BL 47481–158v (*JJA* 56:252).

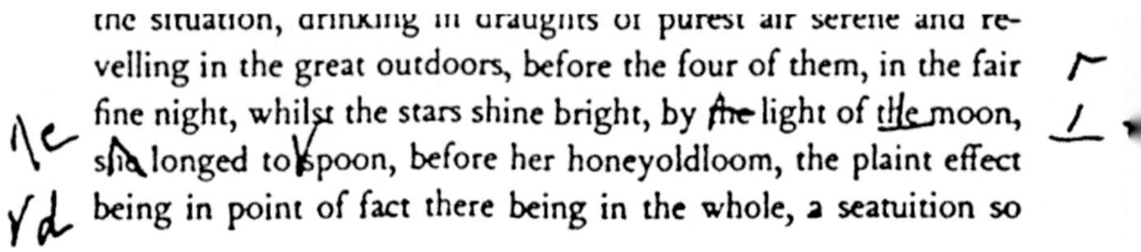

the situation, drinking in draughts of purest air serene and re-
velling in the great outdoors, before the four of them, in the fair
fine night, whilst the stars shine bright, by the light of the moon,
she longed to spoon, before her honeyoldloom, the plaint effect
being in point of fact there being in the whole, a seatuition so

Figure 3.6. BL 47481–159 (*JJA* 56:253).

the galley proofs for *Finnegans Wake,* a paradigm of four words of one syllable in which the letter *e* is pronounced [i:]: she/he/we/be.

Joyce then inserts the elements of this paradigm into a short phrase that had remained intact since the second version of the encounter of Tristan and Isolde: "by the light of the moon she longed to spoon," injecting the elements of the paradigm in such a way that the simple original phrase remains faintly perceptible but the meaning becomes entirely obscure: "by she light of he moon, we longed to be spoon."

In the same way, the published version of chapter II.4 completely differs from the original vignettes: we are in a quite different literary universe. And yet, if we have followed the genetic process, we feel that we are somehow in familiar territory: we recognize the fragments and we recapture at least some of the logic of their use.

Now, if we take one step back, we will find that Joyce's extraordinary procedures are a radicalization of the usual practice of writers: every redrafting is, to some extent, a recontextualization of the material, implying a creative oblivion of the original context (the previous version). The final version some-how retains the memory of all the different contexts it has left behind, but the traces are normally too faint to be recovered from the printed text.[40] The purpose of genetic investigation is to revive this memory. The next chapters should make this easier to understand.

4

The Spatial Dynamics of Invention
(*Nebeneinander* and *Nacheinander*)

The space that was most familiar to Joyce and that had the most influence on his writing was not the landscape around him or the rooms of his often relocated residence, nor even the urban space of Dublin that features so prominently in his books. He spent the greatest part of his days gazing at "paperspace" (*FW* 115.07): this phrase, which has often been used metaphorically, must be taken quite literally. The space that Joyce had before his eyes most of the day, the space he spent most time exploring, as long as he could see and sometimes even when he could not see and had to grope,[1] was the space of a rectangular sheet of white paper, written or in the process of being written on. The majority of his waking life was spent in front of books or manuscripts, reading or writing, most often reading *and* writing.

Let us begin with a survey of this field, which remains invisible in usual circumstances. The reader of Joyce's books does not normally have access to this space: he does not see the volumes that Joyce read, he does not see his manuscripts. And yet we have reasons to think that the published text, and therefore our reading experience, is somehow influenced by this hidden space, in the same way as, according to psychoanalysis, our waking life is influenced by the "Other Scene" of the Unconscious.

The relation is not homological: the printed pages of Joyce's works do not reflect the spatial disposition of the manuscript pages in the way the printed text reflects, more or less faithfully, the manuscript text. It is true that the typographical peculiarities of some printed chapters, for instance "Circe" in *Ulysses* or "The Night Lessons" (II.2) in *Finnegans Wake*, can be traced to specific genetic documents: we are usually able to determine the point at which the idea for the layout first occurred or the decision to adopt it was made. In the case of "Circe," this came very early: in the first extant draft, we see the narrative being transformed, after two and a half pages, into stage directions. Correspondingly, the characters' speeches immediately assume a theatrical disposition, with the name of the speaker appearing before them underlined and centered on the page. In the case of "The Lessons," on the contrary, the marginal annotations that give it its visual identity appear late in the history of the chapter, much like the headlines in "Aeolus," which appeared only at the first galley proofs stage, as discussed above.

However, each page of Joyce's printed books has many antecedent manuscript pages, from the first draft to the fair copy, as well as a number of typescripts and corrected proofs, each with its own characteristic spatial disposition. There is no way that the book page can resemble all of these. Some of these documents are as neat and regular as printed matter—their layout could be compared to the elegant symmetry of Georgian Dublin—but others are more like the organic chaos of a Brazilian *favela,* or perhaps like the labyrinthine medieval plan that underlies and secretly conditions the apparently rational urbanism of the Irish capital.

Expansion

A few of Joyce's manuscripts, such as the *Ulysses* "notesheets," are arranged in multiple columns; others bear only a few stray lines, with no particular orientation, but most of them include a more or less rectangular[2] block of text, a column of writing, usually parallel to the longer side of the sheet of paper. This is something they have in common with the printed pages of most books, but the difference is that the rectangle of printed text is a static presence on the page (we know that it was printed as a block), while the textual column did not come on the manuscript page as an instantaneous unit. It had to be inscribed word by word, letter by letter, stroke by stroke, and the dynamics of progress, usually from top to bottom,[3] is perceptible in the layout. In the words of Stephen in "Proteus," the *nebeneinander* implies a *nacheinander,* proximity can be translated in terms of succession, space in terms of time. The shape of the paragraphs and the parallelism of the lines even suggest the rhythm of the progression, irregular and halting in the case of a first draft, smooth and easy in the case of a fair copy—indeed, it is often the spatial disposition of the words, lines and paragraphs on the page that reveals, with a fair degree of certainty, that a particular manuscript is a first draft or a fair copy.

However this onward movement of writing, the progression of the textual column, is not the only dynamics that can be observed on the manuscript page. It is combined, in variable proportions, with a process of revision that applies itself, perpendicularly as it were, to the forward motion of the growing text and induces an entirely different occupation of space.

Whereas the space surrounding a printed textual block is a frame setting it off, a delimitation of the textual column, the marginal space of a manuscript is a field for actual or potential expansion. This is particularly true for such an expansive writer as Joyce. Writers often use the top and bottom margins and even, when it exists, the right-hand margin, but conventionally, the left-hand margin of the page is the reservoir for the overflow of the central textual column. Many authors, Joyce among them, set aside a copious supplementary marginal space by writing only on the recto of folios (on the right-hand pages of copybooks), reserving the versos for additions and corrections, turning them in effect into a vast extension of the left margins.

In some cases these two dynamics, the forward movement of the developing text and the lateral accretive expansion, collide and have to compete for the same space. For instance, in the Buffalo "Sirens" draft,[4] the versos were meant for revisions, but Joyce came to the end of the copybook before the chapter was quite finished, so that, instead of starting a new copybook for a single page, he reversed his course and used the blank verso of the penultimate page (V.A.5–22)[5] to complete the basic version (fig. 4.1). As a result, this single surface accommodates successive waves of textual expansion of a different nature and that work in different directions: first the continuation (and conclusion) of the draft, then an addition to the text on the facing verso, additions to this addition, and finally a revision of the continuation.

The relation between the basic text and the marginal material can be seen as centrifugal or centripetal. The marginal additions are like shoots growing from the stem, or tentacles reaching out. Indeed, they are often linked to their point of insertion by connecting lines that look like warped sunbeams: the text irradiates its margins (fig. 4.2).

On the other hand, insofar as the marginal additions are often composed of external material intruding into the work, the text can also be seen as a

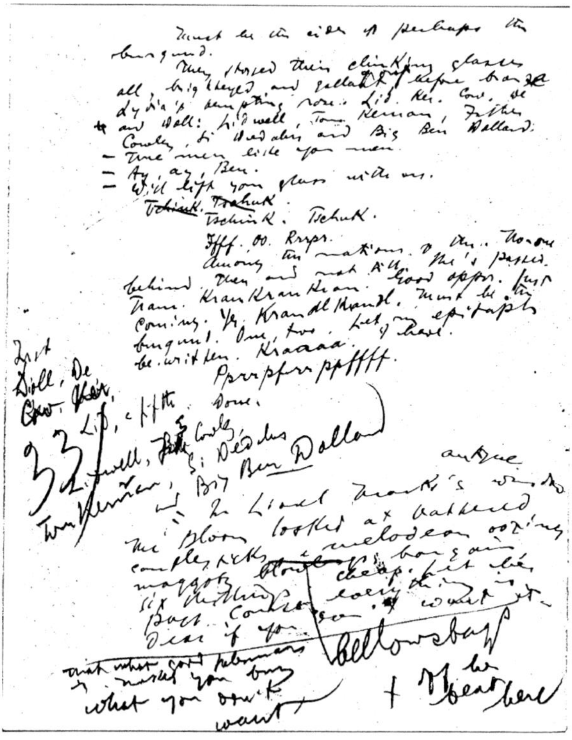

Figure 4.1. Buffalo V.A.5–22 (JJA 13: 54). The two expansive flows competing for the same space.

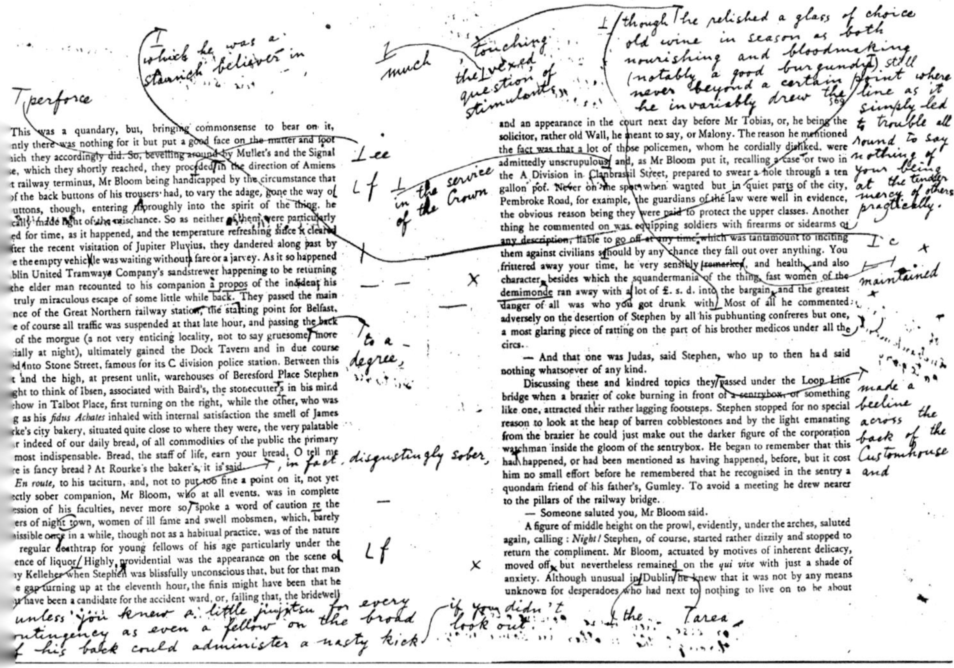

4.2. Proofs for "Eumaeus." Buffalo V.C.1–36a (JJA 27:10).

pin cushion, or rather a Saint Sebastian, ecstatically transfixed by a volley of arrows. But the arrows never fall at random; clearly, there is a gravitational pull from the text that guides and even initiates the supplementary material. The image seems particularly appropriate in the case of the "Eumaeus" episode: from the earliest extant draft to the last proofs, the text absorbs, like a black hole, an enormous quantity of extraneous matter that comes to clutter its syntax and increase its density beyond all proportions.

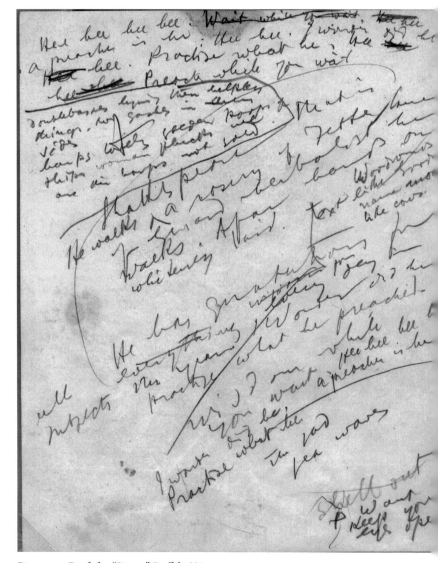

Figure 4.3. Draft for "Sirens," Buffalo V.A.5.14–15.

Let us have a closer look at another double page from the "Sirens" copybook mentioned above (fig. 4.3).

This definitely does not look like an open printed book. Perhaps a closer visual analogy would be a double page in a newspaper. Arbitrarily, I have chosen for comparison an opening of the June 16, 1904, Dublin *Evening Telegraph* (pink edition), which was used as a source by Joyce for *Ulysses* and even for this particular passage[6] (fig. 4.4).

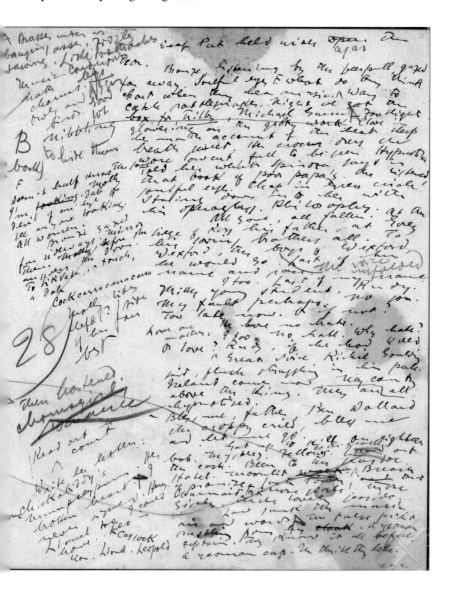

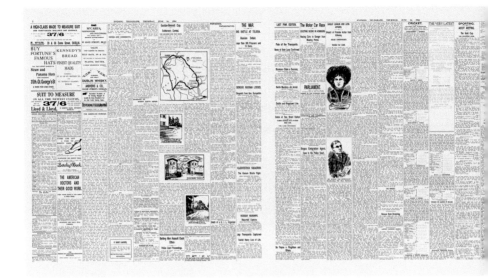

Figure 4.4. *Dublin Evening Telegraph* for June 16, 1904 (pink edition).

In spite of obvious differences, there are some common points. Both make use of the surface of the double page, and both occupy it in a not entirely sequential way: they are not meant to be read from the top of the left-hand page to the bottom of the right-hand page. Both openly acknowledge the de facto tabularity of writing (as opposed to the linearity of spoken discourse). Moreover, they are composed of discontinuous but not unrelated fragments of writing (news of the same day in one case, material for the same passage in the other).

We have said that printed matter is transferred instantaneously to the paper as a block, so that the layout does not reflect the progression of the composition—but this is not entirely true in the case of this newspaper. We do find a vestigial trace of the sedimentation of time. The stop-press column on the right ("The very latest"), printed with a different system in a blank left available for this purpose, is visibly paler, so that the practiced reader does not even have to read the heading: he is able to catch an instant glimpse of the fainter column indicative of the most recent news (or to be more precise, indicative of the most recent printing and indirectly of the most recent news).[7] In the same manner, the student of the "Sirens" draft will use indexical clues, like the change of writing instrument (pen then pencil then crayon) and the different shades of ink, as well as the position of the writing blocks, to try to establish the chronology of the different marginal additions.

There is however another important difference: the newspaper is addressed to its readers and strives to be as clear as possible, while the draft is meant exclusively for the writer himself, so that our deciphering is parasitic. We have to rely on involuntary clues or on signals that the writer left for his own perusal at a later stage and that are under no obligation to conform to an established or consistent code. The geneticist is a decipherer of indices,[8] like the hunter following a track in the forest or like the physician examining a patient's symptoms. We do not expect the prey to make things easy for the hunter or the disease to assist the physician. Indices are ambiguous, sometimes misleading, but here (see fig. 4.3) they are clear enough for us to see that additions accumulate in the left margin, until no vacant space is left. They infiltrate the main column, squeezing themselves into the residual blanks between the paragraphs. Then they start overflowing on the facing verso, at first sprawling across the page, as if enjoying the luxury of that wide open area, and then soon becoming crowded again, occupying the remaining surfaces. Ultimately the next verso (V.A.5.16) is also used for a continuation of the additions (cued by the indication "B (back)").

Without going into great detail, we can distinguish in the margin of the right-hand page, a first layer of additions to the main text, which comprises the following insertions, in ink, from top to bottom: "Music hath charms owls and birds," "nibbling," "Doesn't half know [. . .] Cockcarracarracarra," "Molly likes left (?) side of her face best," "Read out in court," "Write her letters [. . .] Lionel. Leopold." It is difficult to ascertain a chronology for these, although it seems clear that the long insertion, "Doesn't half know [. . .] Cockcarracarracarra," came after "Music hath charms owls and birds," for it is situated much lower in the margin than its point of insertion (the "F" on the fourth line), which suggests that its natural space was already occupied. Then came a second round of additions, in pencil: the "A" insertion, "Basses under us [. . .] to hide them," starting on top of the page and working round the preexisting "Music hath charms owls and birds," and lower down "then hastened" and "chorusgirl's romance."

The left page was used as an overflow when the margin was full, to inscribe additions such as "Woodwinds like Goodwin's name mooing like cows," "doublebasses lying there [. . .] their harps not said," "shell out," "want to keep your eyes open." But the whole cluster organized around Shakespeare and "a rosery of Fetter lane . . ." predates those additions. The way it is written—across the page, in a large hand—proves that the page was empty, while the long passage, "doublebasses lying there [. . .] their harps not said," is boxed in between preexisting inscriptions, squeezed in an exiguous space.

Taking all this into consideration, we can tentatively suggest that the writing of the additions followed approximately this chronological sequence,[9] which will serve us as a basis for an interpretation of the genesis of the passage in the next chapter:

Figure 4.5. A chronological hypothesis.

The fact that manuscripts are written solely for the writer's eyes does not mean that there is a perfect identity between the writing and reading agencies. The draft page is the site of a dialogue between the writer and his later self or selves. This dialogue can be more or less intense, and the lag or deferral, inherent in the notion of writing, can be more or less important. The writer can read his own signs almost at the same time as he writes them, or months, or even years later: we have seen in chapter 3 that Joyce left aside the Tristan and Isolde sketch for more than fourteen years before he started to work on it again for *Finnegans Wake.* In some cases, the writer knows that what he writes is going to undergo an almost immediate revision and rewriting and that his reading will be supplemented by fresh memory, so that the indications need not be very precise. This is clearly the case in our "Sirens" draft: the connecting lines are very loosely positioned, the relation between some fragments is not made explicit at all. It is one of the paradoxes of the semiotics of the draft page. The lack of indications is itself indicative: it tells us something about the circumstances of composition. On this draft, we can see immediately that there have been at least two distinct phases of revision: one using a pen and ink, probably contemporaneous with the writing of the main column, and a later one that used a pencil.

If we accept, then, that the writer who inscribes the first layer is not quite the same as the one(s) who make(s) the changes (see introduction), we can consider that the position of the student of manuscripts is not entirely divorced from the author's, who, in the process of revision, must become a decipherer of his own writing on the page and sees in it more (and sometimes less) than he has put, in an act of creative interpretation.

"From space to space, time after time,
in various phases of scripture" *FW* 254.26–27

The hydraulic vocabulary (reservoir, overflow, infiltration, wave . . .) that I have used and that comes naturally when one tries to describe this irresistible tide of textual expansion flooding over every available space points us to the "Proteus" episode of *Ulysses.* The episode is ostensibly about a walk on the strand, a journey on the seaside, but we know that the "art" assigned to it in the various schemas is philology, that it deals with language and its transformations, stylistic or historic, rhetorical or etymological.[10] Sandymount strand is a *limen,* a threshold between the land and the sea, occupied by "the lacefringe of the tide," a transition between the solid and the liquid elements, made of shifting sands and strewn with jetsam and flotsam; in other words, it is a marginal space. It is tempting to read its mobile, iridescent surface as a representation of another site of protean transformations, the frontier between the text and its other, the margin of the manuscript.

The margin is a transitional space where the text in progress deals with different forms of alterity: the outside world, other books, other parts of the same text, and other versions of itself. This last form of confrontation is particularly important. It is in the margin that the text faces its own future. Whereas the main column is usually a witness of the textual past (it is often copied out from a previous version), the marginal changes represent the text in a state of becoming; they are directed toward the next state.

Take a page from the first extant complete draft of "Proteus" (fig. 4.6). On the ninth line of the main column, we find this passage: "Behold the handmaid of the moon. The wet sign rules her courses, visits her. Rise up, according to the word." Everything after "wet sign" is deleted and replaced, between the lines and in the margin, by a new version: "calls on her and bids her rise. Bridebed childbed bed of death, ghostcandled." We can verify that the words inscribed in the base text come from the recently discovered early draft, now at the NLI, probably through a lost intermediate version: they are a record of the early history of the passage. We can also verify that the substituted words inscribed in the margin are integrated in the next available state, the Rosenbach fair copy (Rosenbach 15, see also the final version at U 3: 395–96): they represent the future of the passage.

The marginal transactions between past and future are sometimes much more complex. On the same page of the Buffalo "Proteus" draft, we find a particularly spectacular example.[11] The words "Mouth to her mouth's kiss" originate in the earlier version: on page 8 of the draft now in the National Library of Ireland, Joyce had first written "a man's lips to her kiss" and then revised it to "mouth to her mouth's kiss." On the Buffalo draft (and in the final text) the hesitation is dramatized. The phrase comes fully formed to Stephen's mind. He then considers modifying it, but he deliberately restores the symmetry "Mouth to her kiss. No. You must have two of em. Glue em well together. Mouth to her mouth's kiss." This rejection helps us to understand what is at stake here, what Stephen's aesthetic criteria are (they appear to be rather traditional: he is looking for symmetry, for a particular rhythm, he wants to insist on the carnality of the kiss . . .). After that, however, Stephen attempts a much more daring variation ("His lips lipped and mouthed fleshless lips of air: mouth to her moongmbh."), incorporating into the second term a range of echoes (moon, womb, tomb) suggested by the adjacent marginal substitution ("handmaid of the moon . . . Bridebed childbed bed of death").[12] But at

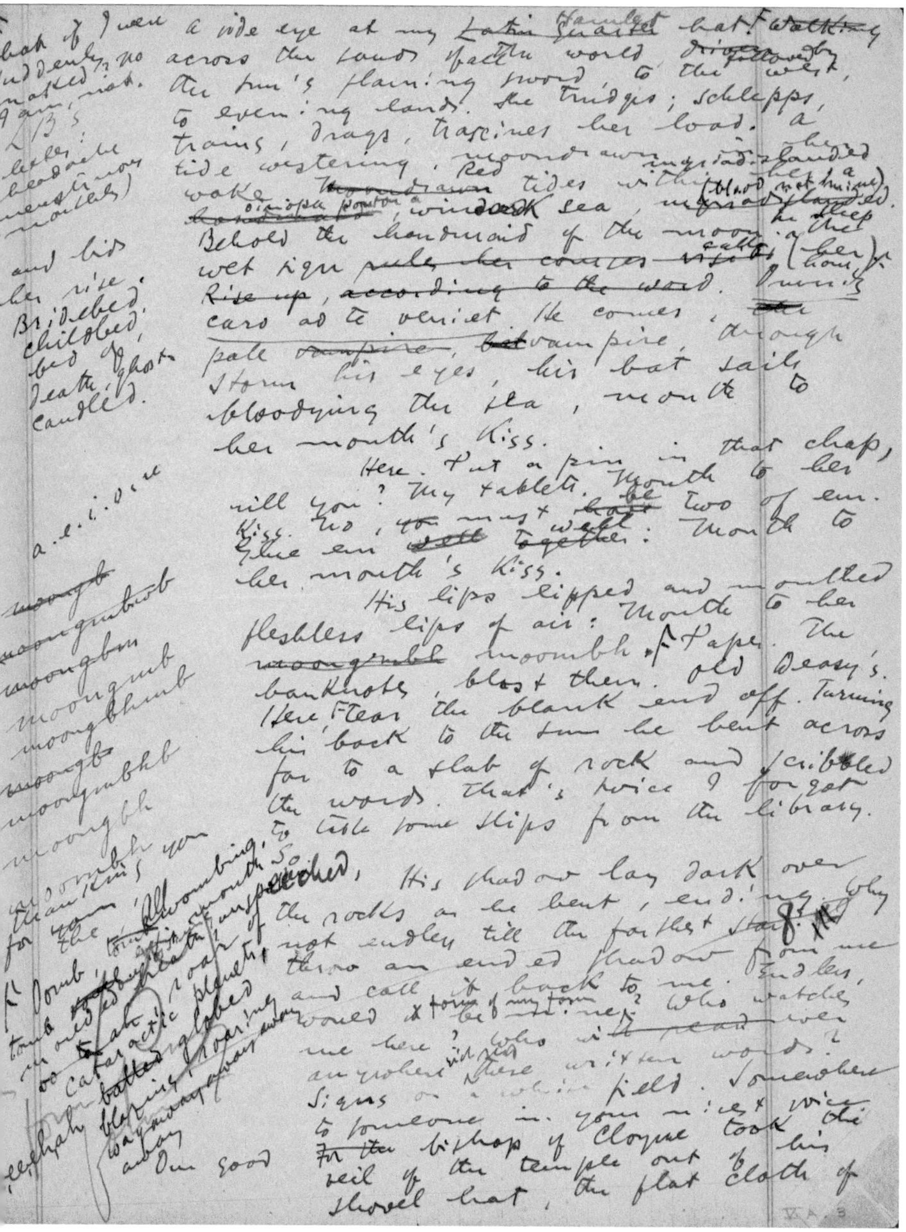

ıre 4.6. Draft for “Proteus.” Buffalo V.A.3.15 (*JJA* 12:253).

this point, it was Joyce himself who hesitated. He crossed out "moongmbh" and used the margin to try out, in the form of a list, a long series of permutations of the components, some of them immediately crossed out, some of them simply displayed in juxtaposition: "~~Moongb~~ /~~Moongmbwb~~ / ~~moongbm~~ / moongmb / moongbhmb / ~~moongb~~ / moongmbhb / moongbh / moombh." He finally chose the last element of the marginal array and reimported it into the text, just after the crossed out "moongmbh," to continue the main paragraph. It is as if a wave had deposited an object on the beach and the next one had taken it back into the sea, or rather, to reverse the image, as if an object had been thrown into the ocean, there to suffer a sea change into something rich and strange, and then was spewed back on the shore and returned to terrestrial usage.

In the Rosenbach manuscript, this element will be modified again, simplified into "moomb." In the final version, it will be replaced (perhaps by mistake) by a mere "womb." In spite of this superficial disappearance, we can consider that the history of this transmutation remains present and active, its traces can be found disseminated in the final text and we can say that this *womb* is big with all the marginal variations that led up to it, that it incorporates the fertile space of the margin that was its matrix.

The discarded portmanteau words will resurface, a few years later, in the revisions of *Ulysses*[13] and then extensively in "Work in Progress," richer and more complex than ever. But a different process of dissemination is already at work in the margin of the "Proteus" manuscript. After having inserted "moomb," the carefully selected compound, Joyce drafted in the margin another insertion that literally unpacks the portmanteau: "Oomb, ~~tombwombing~~ ^+allwombing+^ tomb ~~vowel~~. His mouth moulded ^+issuing+^ breath, unspeeched [. . .]." This is a good illustration of Roman Jakobson's analysis of the poetic function of language as a projection of the axis of selection (or virtuality) upon the axis of combination (or actuality). The elements of the paradigm that has been piling up in a list are linearized, rearranged and projected on the syntagmatic chain of a sentence. The marginal space proves to be simultaneously a field of virtualities (the trying ground for potential variants) and a locus of actualization in the elaboration of new sequences.

Marginal connections

One of the concerns of any writer is the coherence of his or her work. In a simple, linear text, this is hardly a problem: the natural memory of the writer and the momentum of writing are enough to ensure a reasonable degree of consistency. But within the frame of Joyce's post-Symbolist aesthetics, the tightness of structure that he is striving to achieve, unprecedented on such a scale, is combined with a systematic interlinking of the different parts and a strong overdetermination of each element.

Joseph Frank, in his famous study of spatial form, has emphasized the burden that is placed on the reader of *Ulysses:*

> the reader is forced to read *Ulysses* [. . .] by continually fitting fragments together and keeping allusions in mind until, by reflexive reference, he can link them to their complements. [. . .] The reader is intended to acquire this sense as he progresses through the novel, connecting allusions and references spatially and gradually becoming aware of the pattern of relationships. [. . .] A knowledge of the whole is essential to an understanding of any part; but [. . .] such knowledge can be obtained only after the book has been read, when all the references are fitted into their proper places and grasped as a unity.[14]

Frank mentions Joyce's "unbelievably laborious fragmentation of narrative structure," but he is not interested in investigating the kind of labor that was required to generate it. Obviously, when Joyce was writing the parts of *Ulysses,* he did not have that essential "knowledge of the whole," since the whole did not exist and could never have been anticipated in the form it finally took. To palliate this inevitable deficiency and generate the hypermnesia that characterizes his work,[15] Joyce could not rely exclusively on the "connective propensity" that we studied in chapter 2 or on his natural memory. The most elementary form of "artificial memory" is simply to note ideas as they come, on the readiest available surface. In the course of writing, it is evidently the margin that is nearest.

One of the functions of the no-man's-land of the margin is indeed to weave connections between different parts of the text. On the same "Proteus" manuscript page that has been occupying us, in between the marginal additions and substitutions, we find the words "LB's / letter: / headache / menstruous /

(monthly)." This is suggested by Stephen's poetical rambling about women's periodical bleeding.

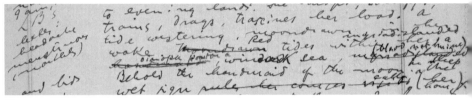

Figure 4.7.

At this point in the writing of *Ulysses,* a series of correspondences, parallelisms and antitheses between the three early Stephen episodes and the subsequent Bloom episodes are being established. Joyce notes that the romantic letter from "Martha" should contain a reference to a headache that Bloom will interpret prosaically as a menstrual migraine. Readers of "Lotus Eaters" know that the note has been effective and that the link has been created (*U* 5.285— see also chapter 6, this volume).

On the "Sirens" draft pages mentioned earlier (V.A.5.14–15), the connection works in the opposite direction: a note in the center of the left-hand page attempts to link Bloom's monologue to an earlier passage, Stephen's Shakespearian musings about Gerard's rosery of Fetter lane in "Scylla and Charybdis." As we will see in the next chapter, however, the transaction is more difficult to complete: the passage resists integration, and the graft will not be completed at this point. It will eventually migrate to a different part of the episode.

Marginal assimilation

So far, we have seen how the text uses its margin to face up to different versions of itself or to reach toward different passages in the same work. We must now consider more radical forms of otherness.

The marginal inscription of the writer's personal life on the manuscript requires only a brief mention. Some writers (Stendhal, for instance) practice this extensively: they keep a kind of diary in their margins, noting down the external circumstances of writing and personal as well as historical events.

Not so for Joyce. Michael Groden has shown that Joyce and Nora used a "Cyclops" draft for playful or angry exchanges and that this private dialogue probably interfered in some measure with the writing and revision of the episode,[16] but this is quite exceptional. It is only in his notebooks that remarks about Joyce's personal life and material circumstances alternate freely with his literary work, to the point that it is sometimes difficult to distinguish the one from the other.

The inscription of a new text in the margins of the writer's previous work is an intermediary problem. We have seen in chapter 3 that some of the early sketches for *Finnegans Wake* were written (literally in one case) in the margin of Joyce's own lyrical poems. We have also described his strange storage procedure in *Scribbledehobble* (notebook VI.A): by dividing it into sections corresponding to his previously published books, Joyce turns it into a schematic model of his opera omnia, so as to be able to lodge newly gathered material under its auspices and to write his future work as a marginal expansion of the old one.

The significance of the marginal inscription is dramatized in *Ulysses*. We know that the "mouth to her mouth" fragment, composed in "Proteus," is transcribed on the lower margin of Deasy's letter. Stephen takes care to detach it, to sever the marginal from the central (master) text, but in vain: Stephen's complete stanza is called up into "Aeolus" (its only consecutive appearance in the book) through its surface of inscription, the bottom of Deasy's letter, or rather through the absence of that surface, missing in its place:

Stephen handed over the typed sheets, pointing to the title and signature.
—Who? the editor asked.
Bit torn off.
—Mr Garret Deasy, Stephen said.
—That old pelters, the editor said. Who tore it? Was he short taken?
> *On swift sail flaming*
> *From storm and south*
> *He comes, pale vampire*
> *Mouth to my mouth.*
Good day, Stephen, the professor said, coming to peer over their shoulders. Foot and mouth? Are you turned . . . ?

Bullockbefriending bard. [. . .]
—Good day, sir, Stephen answered blushing. The letter is not mine. Mr
Garrett Deasy asked me to . . . (*U* 7.521–25)

We discover, together with Stephen, that writing in the margin of his em-
ployer's epistle is not a neutral gesture. A close relationship is established between the poem and the letter. The detached slip retains the negative shape
of the other piece: it is literally an *indenture,* the written contract binding an
apprentice to his master, which (like the *symbolon*) used to be divided in two
so that each of the parties could prove the authenticity of the contract by a
comparison of the torn edges. It asserts a relation of subordination to "Domi-
nie Deasy." The binding is so strong that it leads to a relation of identification.
The poem has been written on the bottom of the sheet, just after the formal
ending (which happens to be dealing with the obligations entailed by *insertion*[17]), that is to say in the place reserved for the signature: the poem becomes
a virtual cosignature of the letter and, by writing it, the poet not only signs
himself as an apprentice to the schoolmaster, but he becomes, in spite of his
repeated disavowals, the "bullockbefriending bard."[18]

Consequently, Joyce was careful not to place his writing in that subordinate
position. He would try to turn the tables and situate other texts (potentially
the whole of world literature) in the margin of his own text. He could not
physically achieve this by leaving even the widest possible marginal space
around his drafts, so he made it possible by annexing to his margins a whole
array of notesheets and notebooks that created an infinitely extensible space
for his enterprise of subjugation. We will study the workings of that extended
marginal zone and the way it metabolizes the intertext in chapter 6.

5

"Sirens"

Hesitations and Tipping Points

We will now have a closer look at the double page described in the previous chapter: page "27)"[1] verso and "28)" recto from the second extant "Sirens" draft (Buffalo mss. V.A.5–14–5, *JJA* 13:46–47. See above fig. 4.3). For convenience sake, we will call it the "Shakespeare double page" because of the prominent place of the phrase "Shakespeare that is" on the left-hand page. Trying to apprehend what happens in this manuscript and what is at stake there will allow us to understand better not only how Joyce worked but also how the genetic investigator must proceed in order to overcome, by inferences and hypotheses, the inevitable lacks in his documentation. Since what takes place in this manuscript is necessarily conditioned by the previous history of the passage and can only be completely understood in relation to its future developments, we will have to recapitulate what we know—and what we can guess—of the complex, and to some extent still mysterious, genesis of "Sirens." Both the general survey of the writing of this episode and the close study of the passage in question will give us the occasion of seeing Joyce hesitating at major or minor turning points. This is a rare opportunity, since most of the manuscripts in the Joyce archive tend to show him forging ahead with great deliberation, in a direction that is not always clear to us but that seems to be perfectly clear to him, so that we may often have the impression that we are missing the major creative moments.

The first extant draft

If we leave aside a few notes scattered in early notebooks, the oldest available document related to "Sirens" is a partial draft that was discovered a few years ago and is now kept at the NLI.[2] It is evidently a very early draft, but it seems to be too continuous and regularly copied to be a first draft. This means that there must have existed one or more previous documents from which this one is derived, although we cannot know what they were like or when they were drafted. For brevity's sake, we will call it the "first draft," although it is only the first *extant* draft.[3]

Getting acquainted with this "first draft," we automatically compare it with the final version of the episode and find it to be surprisingly similar, narratively and verbally, to the printed edition. The beginning looks indeed like the beginning of "Sirens" as we know it—except, of course, that there is no *overture,* but we could not have expected to find this in an early incomplete draft, since this opening piece is a motival compendium of the episode and could only have been compiled a posteriori. "Bronze" and "gold," the two barmaids, Miss Douce and Miss Kennedy, are already present in the very first lines (except that Miss Douce is called Miss Dou*se*).[4] We recognize such familiar elements as the "viceregal cavalcade" and the "tall silk" and such expressions as "Mind till I see"(*U* 11.73). The memorable phrases "Bronze by gold" and "ringing steel" appear as interlinear corrections but must have been inserted in the first flow of writing.[5] The manipulation of language is much less obtrusive than it is in the final version: we will see that Joyce increased this aspect at each stage of the development of the episode, from draft to fair copy, from fair copy to typescript and at each of the proof stages. On the other hand, the stylistic autonomy of body parts, so characteristic of "Sirens,"[6] is already present in the very first line inscribed on the page ("Miss Douse's and Miss Kennedy's heads [. . .] saw the viceregal cavalcade go by") and becomes more and more noticeable in the rest of the draft, especially on page "8)."

In the next pages of the draft, the episode proceeds along familiar lines with dialogues almost identical to those in the final version: the rude boots and Miss Douse's haughty answer, Miss Douse's dermatological problems, the giggling conversation about the awful old wretch in Boyd's, Simon Dedalus and his flirtatious cordiality, Lenehan's pathetic efforts, the tuning fork, Simon's half-hearted singing at the piano, Boylan's entry, the *Sonnez la cloche* performance, Ben Dollard and Father Cowley's conversation, Dollard's attempt at *Love and War* . . . But by the time we get to page "10)" of the draft, we cannot fail to notice that something capital is missing from the episode as we know it: Bloom is entirely absent! No trace of his approach to the Ormond or his entering the dining room. He is not mentioned by the other characters or the narrator and, more importantly, he is absent as a point of view. Up to that point in the draft, the episode is entirely confined to the dialogue in the bar, with connecting narrative passages in the third person. There is no monologue at all (or any other form of representation of stream of consciousness and very little representation of the characters' subjectivity), and we find only faint forebodings of the counterpoint that we have come to associate with "Sirens" (snatches of song come from Simon in the music room during Lenehan's interview with Boylan, the solitary twinkling of a diner's bell in the restaurant accompanies Miss Kennedy's compassion for the blind piano tuner). We are much closer to the style of *Dubliners* than to the "initial style" of *Ulysses,* let alone the style(s) of the middle stage. This apparent regression is puzzling. Is it significant that this draft is copied in a notebook immediately following an early draft of "Proteus"? After the dense and claustrophobic subjectivity of the Telemachiad, did Joyce want to move to a more impersonal, dialogue-oriented presentation? After the lyric, the dramatic mode? Or was he simply copying from an old draft, anterior to his adoption of the "initial style" of *Ulysses?* This is perhaps more likely.[7]

In the present state of our documentation, it is impossible to recover precisely Joyce's project at the time he wrote the beginning of this draft, but what is particularly fascinating is that we can follow some of the details of the process that led him to change his mind as he was writing and to move to the contrapuntal style of "Sirens" and more generally to the style of the middle stage of *Ulysses.*

The turning point seems to be on page "10)" of the draft, but it can probably be situated even more precisely. On the occasion of Simon, Dollard and Cowley's nostalgic evocation of the famous concert at which Dollard gave "Love and War" with Goodwin at the piano, there is no mention of Bloom's saving the situation and Molly's used-clothes business. Cowley inquires about another singer present at this concert, called Marie Fallon, with the name "Fallon" immediately struck out and replaced currente calamo with "Powell." Simon answers that she is alive and married, but an ellipsis indicates that his sentence is interrupted by Dollard's singing, and the reader is never told *whom* she married. This kind of thinly disguised aposiopesis becomes significant if we remember that Major Powell was, according to Joyce himself, the original of Major Tweedy.[8] This would be enough to suggest that Marie Powell is an early name for Marion Tweedy-Bloom, or a figure that shares some of her characteristics, and this is further corroborated by a later modification that strikes out the end of Simon's sentence and replaces it with the phrase we know from the final text, "My Irish Molly O" (*U* 11.512), and a still later marginal addition indicating that Marie/Molly actually comes from the Rock of Gibraltar (see *U* 11.514).

After a few lines, the dialogue stops abruptly in the middle of the page. Obviously, an interruption, of indeterminate duration, occurred. After a blank of several lines (later occupied by additions), writing resumes, in a darker ink and a slightly more cramped hand, with the name of Mr. Bloom. The paragraph is a mixture of third-person narration, interior monologue and free indirect style conveying Bloom's point of view on the barmaid.[9]

What has happened? It seems possible that the irruption of Marie/Molly-Fanlon/Powell/Tweedy/Bloom in the dialogue brought with her not only the idea of her husband but also the necessity of varying the point of view and the technique used so far. If Molly is born of a rumor (Joyce's original plan to write a story about Hunter, who was reputed to be a cuckold), she is too sensitive of a material to be abandoned to malicious gossip alone. Introducing her husband's voice seems like a good way to counterbalance the vox populi. Hence perhaps the idea of a new departure in the development of *Ulysses:* the introduction of more than one point of view in the episode, in the form of counterpointed voices (in a loose sense of the phrase).

It is possible that at first Joyce had in mind something like the present structure of "Nausicaa": a simple cinematographic shot-reverse shot, with the second part of the episode given entirely to Bloom. But such a structure, not being combined with the elaborate parody of the first part of "Nausicaa," would have been too simple for Joyce's purpose here, so it was deferred for later use. (The thematic resemblance is striking enough to suggest that this paragraph may well be the origin of the "Nausicaa" episode: Bloom exchanges indirect but significant glances with the young woman,[10] wonders about her virginity, is fascinated by the quasi-masturbatory gesture on the beerpull[11] culminating in an orgasm of gushing beer.[12])

Almost immediately, we see Joyce preparing for the orchestration of something much more complex. On the rest of the available pages of the notebook and on at least two supplementary loose leaves,[13] a multitude of short segments follow one another feverishly. They are passages to be used like bricks to build the second, as yet unwritten part of the episode and also to be inserted in the first, already written part. Most of these segments are crossed out with red or blue crayons.

Alternating with snatches of Bloom's monologue there is more nasty gossip (some of it is not crossed out and never made it to the next draft). This time we have the impression that we have the seed of "Cyclops." We even find a triple repetition of "begod," an approximation of *begob,* the characteristic interjection of the nameless debt collector who reflects half of that episode (see above, chapter 2, 34). But without the contrasting mock-epic passages, such an exercise in meanness would also have been too simple, a kind of regression toward *Dubliners.* Something else was needed.[14]

At this stage, there is still no trace of the early passages introducing Bloom in the episode, his walk along the Quay to the Ormond, or his visit to the stationery shop. Joyce is clearly embarking on a polyphonic organization, but the details of the arrangement are far from settled.

To clarify, we can say that this draft encapsulates three different moments of the development of the episode (and of *Ulysses*). The basic layer of the text, up to page "10)," probably reflects (give or take a few changes that could have been made in the process of copying) a missing earlier draft that it recopies. It seems likely that this lost draft belonged to an early stage of *Ulysses,* perhaps anterior to the writing of the first Bloom chapters. Then there is the moment of the copying and first development (early or mid-1918?). To this moment belong the changes made currente calamo, some of the deletions and marginal additions, the reorientation that happens on page "10)," and some of the fragments that follow. And finally there is a different layer of additions (i.e., the one that contains the form "Miss Douce" and the one that comes from notebook 36,639/5/A) and some of the final fragments that were probably added just before a new drafting of the episode (in the first months of 1919?). We are not able to distinguish with great precision what belongs to these three moments, but we know that they are present in this document.

The second extant draft

The second *extant* draft (we will call it "the second draft") is written in two notebooks. The first is now in the NLI and the other one, which includes the Shakespeare double page, is in the Buffalo collection. This version already has the narrative structure of the published episode: impersonal descriptions of the events and dialogues in the bar alternate with passages of Bloom's interior monologue, introduced by an impersonal narrator who is much more intrusive than in the episodes written in the "initial style." The overture is still absent, but on the top left corner of the first page, we find the words "repeat / phrases / episodes" written in bold pencil. This can be interpreted as a self-prescription: Joyce is reminding himself that he should write an opening made of repeated phrases, which he apparently assimilates to fugal episodes.[15]

A remarkable feature of this draft is that a list of musical terms, in Italian, arranged in eight paragraphs and titled "*Fuga per Canonem*" is written in pencil on the inside of the front cover of the first notebook. This is not entirely surprising, since Joyce claimed that the episode had the structure of a fugue and that it contained "all the eight regular parts of a *fuga per canonem*."[16] That such a list would appear at this stage proves that the fugal idea is not consubstantial to the episode but a second thought, something induced by the need to integrate the different voices and perspectives that Joyce, halfway through the first draft, had decided to include. But there is another problem. From a musicological point of view, it seems very difficult to understand the logic of the arrangement of the (very heterogeneous) items of the list. After much searching, the source for this list was discovered.[17] Joyce had taken notes in a dictionary of music, but the nature of those notes reveals that his reading had been very superficial: it is clear that Joyce had made no effort to understand the structure of a fugue and that he had been content to note a few terms as they occurred in the dictionary entry, selecting the most conspicuous ones from a typographical point of view. This is typical of Joyce's attitude toward some of his sources: he was often more interested in a kind of token reference to the text than in a deep understanding of the contents.[18] In the case of "Sirens," Joyce intended a kind of magical reference to the intricate structure of the most demanding form of polyphony.

The consequences are nevertheless very important. The reference to the *Fuga per canonem* inaugurates the radical congruence between style and subject matter that is so much in evidence in the published schemata. This episode devoted to the seductions of music assumes (or rather pretends to assume) a musical form with a vengeance: not a vague Paterian allusive nostalgia, but the intricate structure of one of the most forbidding musical forms. Applied to barroom singing of facile operatic music, humming of music-hall tunes, not to mention smacking garters, twanging elastics and resounding farts, this imposing model cannot but acquire a parodic dimension. We can see this as (one of) the starting point(s) of the parodic strain that characterizes the central episodes of *Ulysses*.

The combination of the first and the second drafts gives us the impression of observing at close range a crucial turning point in the history of *Ulysses* (and, we might go as far as to suggest, in the history of twentieth-century literature). We see how the change of the name "Marie Fallon" into "Marie Powell" seems to trigger a chain of consequences that, after planting the seeds for "Nausicaa" and "Cyclops," completely changed the face of the episode and of the novel.

Missing documents

The available archive for this episode is rich but incomplete. We mentioned that the first extant draft was most probably not the first, although we know nothing of what came before. We must also wonder whether Joyce could have gone directly from this draft to the "second draft" without an intermediary stage. This seems possible for the first nine pages of the early draft and their transposition into the first fourteen pages of the second extant draft: there is not that much of a difference, and it would not have been too difficult to insert the new passages, sketched at the end of the notebook and on loose leaves, into the main body of the already drafted text. After that, however, there is no real first draft in the NLI notebook, only a multitude of hastily sketched short passages. A glance at the last part of the second extant draft, the Buffalo manuscript, is enough to be certain that it is not a first drafting: it is clearly copied from a previous source before being enriched with numerous additions. That source is lacking, so we must imagine either a lost intermediary draft, a partial draft covering the last two-thirds of the episode, or at least a series of partial drafts on loose leaves integrating the most difficult passages.

As it happens, we do not have the fair copy that Joyce made from the second extant draft, but we have two documents derived from it that allow us to have a fairly precise idea of what it was like: the Rosenbach manuscript of the episode (a copy that Joyce made from the lost fair copy in order to send it to John Quinn), and the typescript that was derived from the fair copy and that was later used as a basis both for the *Little Review* publication of the episode

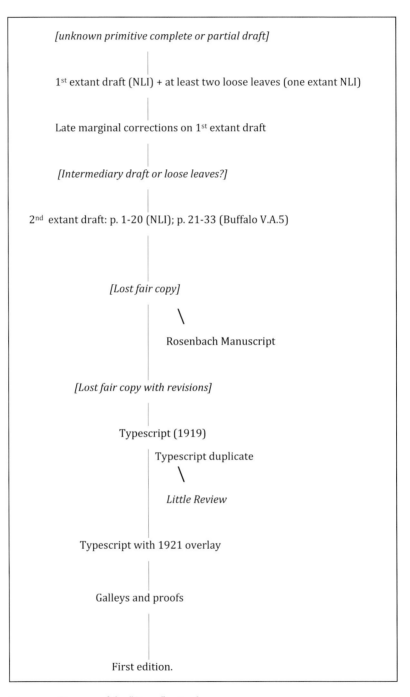

[unknown primitive complete or partial draft]

1st extant draft (NLI) + at least two loose leaves (one extant NLI)

Late marginal corrections on 1st extant draft

[Intermediary draft or loose leaves?]

2nd extant draft: p. 1-20 (NLI); p. 21-33 (Buffalo V.A.5)

[Lost fair copy]

Rosenbach Manuscript

[Lost fair copy with revisions]

Typescript (1919)
Typescript duplicate

Little Review

Typescript with 1921 overlay

Galleys and proofs

First edition.

Figure 5.1. Stemma of the "Sirens" episode.

and for the printing of the 1922 book.[19] We can observe that Joyce revised the fair copy after he made the Rosenbach copy and before it was typed.

After that, the remainder of the episode's genesis is well documented. We can distinguish at least two levels of corrections on the typescript, then we can follow the abundant additions and modifications on the galleys and proofs. We saw an example of them in the first chapter ("ray of hopk"). They all tend to go in the same direction: an increasingly radical manipulation of both syntax and morphology (supposed to represent a musicalization of language, but describable in terms of rhetorical tropes)[20] and a progressive saturation of the text with allusions to music or noise. Figure 5.1 shows a simplified stemma presenting the development of the episode.

Unbridled expansion

We can now return to the "Shakespeare double page" that was described in the last chapter as an example of the gradual occupation of available space by the irrepressible growth of textual matter (see fig. 4.3 and fig. 4.5), being aware that we cannot have recourse to the usual method for understanding what is going on in a draft: confronting it with the previous and the next version. We cannot do that in the usual way because we have seen that we do not have access to either the passage's immediate descendant (the lost fair copy) or to its immediate ascendant (the missing level between the first and second extant drafts).

We will concentrate on the first few lines of the main column. Here is the base text, before emendation:

Deaf Pat held wider open the door.

Bronze, listening by the beerpull, gazed far away. Soulful eyes. What do they think about when they hear music. Way to catch rattlesnakes. Night we got the box for *Trilby,* Michael Gunn. Footlights glowering on the gilty work. Clove in her mouth account of the heat. Keep breath sweet. Her crocus dress she wore lowcut, full to be seen. Hypnotism. Told her what Spinoza says in that book of poor papa's. She listened, soulful eyes. Chap in dress circle staring down into her with his opera-glass. Philosophy.

In several respects, this is a transitional passage in a transitional episode. The location is a transitional space: Bloom has chosen a table conveniently situated near the door that separates the dining room from the bar (in order to be able to spy on Boylan). He has asked Pat, the waiter, to leave the door ajar, and Pat is now opening it wider. Bloom can hear the music that is going on in the saloon, but he cannot see what happens there. He has a side view of the barmaids behind the bar. The words "door" and "doorway" recur fifteen times in this draft (twenty times in the final text of the episode). They designate the threshold between the dining room and the bar and occasionally the passage between the bar and the saloon, but they also come to signify the door of Bloom's house, which is about to open in order to admit Boylan into Molly's intimacy.

Narratively speaking, nothing much takes place. "Sirens" is a kind of lull in the action of *Ulysses*. Bloom is having a late (second) lunch while waiting for the encounter between Molly and Boylan to happen off-stage. He is desperately trying to think of something else ("Wish they'd sing more. Keep my mind off" *U* 11.914 and also *JJA* 13:35), and yet every trend of thought tends to bring him back to Molly and the impending adultery. In keeping with the episode's constant intertwining of the visual and the aural, Bloom is here looking at the barmaid's eye as she is listening to the music. This reminds him of an evening at the theater with Molly and her similar fascinated look as he was speaking to her,[21] but it also reminds him of the stare of a voyeur peering through an opera glass at her décolleté from the dress circle.

In the book as it is published, "Sirens" can be considered as a stylistic transition: it still resembles the "initial style," as Bloom's monologue plays an important part in it, alternating with impersonal narration, but the emphasis is no longer on verisimilitude and psychological realism but on verbal pyrotechnics, thematic saturation and parody. This is not yet perceptible, at this stage, in the fragment we are studying. Bloom's interior monologue is prevalent, but by then it has acquired a considerable plasticity in Joyce's hands, allowing indefinite textual expansion, since each element of the stream of consciousness can trigger a number of associative processes that will in turn generate new elements and new possibilities for associations. There is potentially no limit to this expansive process,[22] and we can see here how a short fragment is ready to accommodate a heavy burden of additions.

Although the immediate antecedent of the second extant draft is missing, we can find, among the fragments of text that follow the continuous part of the first draft, on pages "16)" and "17)," an early version (probably the first drafting) of our passage, fairly complete, consisting entirely of Bloom's monologue:

> Soulful eyes. What do they think about? Night we were in ^+Michael Gunn gave me+^ the box ^+stalls+^^+box+^ at the *Gaiety* for Tree in *Trilby* (?). I spoke to her about the // soul what Spinoza says in that book of papa's. She listened. Her crocus dress low cut. ^+Full to be seen ^+Footlights glowering on the gilt pillars of the stage.+^ ^+Clove in her mouth ^+nibling, breath. To keep it sweet.+^ She listened Listened+^. Quietly meditative eyes. Chap in evening suit ^+in dress circle+^ staring at ^+down into+^ her through his operaglasses, from Of course philosophy.

Already, at this early stage, we can recognize most of the features of our passage. Bloom's reminiscences of the evening with Molly are anchored in the present of the bar scene: it is the barmaid's eyes that remind Bloom of a scene with his wife in the theater. There is an effort to render the stream of consciousness as naturally as possible. Definite and indefinite articles are elided. Some pronouns are deleted: the second "She listened" is replaced by "Listened." There is, however, a remarkable difference. Music and sounds are not explicitly present at all in this fragment. The marginal additions are devoted to visual (the footlights and gilt pillars of the stage) or olfactory (the clove on Molly's breath) impressions.

This means that the musical and aural dimension of the passage ("Bronze *listening* by the beerpull gazed far away. *What do they think about when they hear music.* Way to catch *rattle*snakes.") has been added in the lost intermediary draft that was used to integrate the fragments of the later part of the first draft. The gaze that is the starting point of the whole reminiscence has now been explicitly linked with music.

Our draft goes in the same direction. The first (if we are to believe the graphic clues noted in the previous chapter) addition on the Shakespeare double page, indicated by a caret (^) between "hear music" and "Way to catch rattlesnakes," is "music hath charms owls and birds," Bloom's reminiscence of Congreve's famous quotation: "Music hath charms to soothe a savage breast," often misquoted as "Music hath charms to soothe a savage beast."

Later, a series of successive additions in the margin, on the left-hand page and on the preceding verso, bring music (or noise) to the center of the evening in the box at the Gaiety with Molly:

Tuning up.—Tootling, psa, psa, psi : psipsa—Shah of Persia liked that best of all. Also wipes his nose in curtain. Custom of his country.—Brasses under us braying asses. Fiddles sawing. Like toothaches. Conductors legs jigging good job to hide them—doublebasses lying there helpless things, two gashes in their sides—harps lovely golden poops of ships woman plucks we are their harps not saw—Woodwinds like Goodwins name mooing like cows

(This simplified transcription doesn't reproduce the chronology of the inscriptions, but it retains the resulting narrative logic, as far as we can understand it)

Alternating with these additions, however, another trend reinforces the visual dimension. The point of insertion is marked by an **F**, just after "gazed far away. Soulful eyes."[23]

Doesn't half know I'm looking. Molly devil of an eye—dab—to see anyone looking. All women.—Bronze gazed far sideways. Mirror there.—Molly likes left (?) side of her face best—before she answers the door. To titivate, a touch, a dab—Cockcarracarracarra

(Simplified transcription)

Associated with narcissism and seduction, this visual trend leads inevitably to the adulterous meeting (expressed by a reverberating phallic onomatopoeia) that is about to take place and that Bloom is so desperately trying to forget.

The concurrence of the visual and aural themes (the respective additions are literally interlaced on the page) is very much in keeping with the rest of the episode. But there is another group of (tentative) additions that is quite unexpected. We will call it the "Shakespeare trend." We have seen in the previous chapter that the core of this trend ("Shakespeare that is—a rosery of Fetter Lane of Gerard herbalist he walks. Afar hands on whiteness laid.") was introduced rather early: not among the first additions that were inscribed in ink in the margin, but at a time when the left-hand page was still mostly empty. At this stage, the sentences seem to be floating on the page, apparently unrelated to the rest.

These words are indeed unexpected, for they come directly from Stephen's Shakespearian musings in "Scylla and Charybdis":

Do and do. Thing done. In a rosery of Fetter lane of Gerard, herbalist, he walks, greyedauburn. An azured harebell like her veins. Lids of Juno's eyes, violets. He walks. One life is all. One body. Do. But do. Afar, in a reek of lust and squalor, hands are laid on whiteness. (*U* 9.651–54)

The reason that this is so surprising is not that there is no thematic relevance. On the contrary, the "hands on whiteness laid" chime in with Bloom's obsession with the adulterous encounter that is about to take place.[24] But these words have never been spoken aloud. They belong to Stephen's inner discourse. There is no way that Bloom can have any knowledge of them. In all the preceding episodes, we have been trained to separate what belonged to the character's thoughts from external or narratorial voices. We have become extraordinarily intimate with Stephen and especially with Bloom because we (have the illusion that we) have direct access to their innermost thoughts and sensations. That the separate consciousnesses should suddenly encroach on one another, against all verisimilitude, threatens to shatter our belief in these characters as realistic entities. The intrusion of these words is so shocking, both in the "Sirens" draft and in the final text, that we are tempted to think that it is an aberration, an oversight on Joyce's part, but we will see later that we have proof that Joyce performed this transgression very deliberately.

At this level, we can follow Joyce's effort to integrate these extraneous sentences into Bloom's monologue. Shakespeare is introduced through the misattribution of Congreve's quotation "music hath charms owls and birds—Shakespeare that is." *On ne prête qu'aux riches,* as the French saying goes. Then the idea of Shakespeare as a purveyor of gnomic utterances is developed at length in a long insertion between "Shakespeare that is" and "a rosery of Fetter Lane...":

He has quotations for everything,—all subjects—wisdom—text—for everything, every day in the year. Wonder did he practise what he preached—wisdom while you wait. Hee hee hee hee. a preacher is he.— I wonder did he. Practise what he—*Hee hee hee hee. Wait while you wait. Hee hee a preacher is he. Hee hee I wonder did he. Hee hee. Practise what he, hee hee hee hee Preach while you wait*[25]

We can see that Joyce is trying to anchor this trend into the barroom situation and in Bloom's psyche: it starts with a Bloomism, the misidentification of the quotation (and perhaps a double Bloomism if "savage breast" is implicitly replaced by "savage beast" as the context seems to suggest), and it ends with Bloom mindlessly repeating phrases in order to keep his thoughts away from the impending encounter between Molly and Boylan. In this context, however, Stephen's poetic diction is all the more jarring.[26]

Contraction and reorganization

At this stage, it is not clear how Joyce intended to combine these different trends. The drafting seems to remain fluid, the connecting lines tentative. To understand Joyce's final take on this, we would normally refer to the next stage, but we have seen that it (the fair copy) is not available. If we refer to the typescript issued from this lost fair copy, the corresponding passage reads like this:

> Bronze, listening by the beerpull, gazed far away. Soulfully. Doesn't half know I'm. Molly great dab at seeing anyone looking.
>   Bronze gazed far sideways. Mirror there. Is that best side of her face? They always know. Knock at the door. Last tip to titivate.
>   Cockcarracarra.
>   What do they think when they hear music. Way to catch rattlesnakes. Night Michael Gunn gave us the box. Tuning up. Shah of Persia liked that best. Wiped his nose in curtain too. Custom his country perhaps. That's music too. Tootling. Brasses braying. Doublebasses helpless, gashes in their sides. Woodwinds mooing cows. Woodwind like Goodwin's name.
>   She looked fine. Her crocus dress she wore, lowcut, belongings on show. Clove her breath was always in theatre when she bent to ask a question. Told her what Spinoza says in that book of poor papa's. Hypnotised, listening. Eyes like that. She bent. Chap in dresscircle staring down into her with his operaglass for all he was worth. Met him pike hoses. Philosophy. O rocks![27]

We find that a good part of the additions inscribed on the second draft is missing. The musical trend has been shortened: the fiddles, the harp, the conductor are no longer there. And the whole of the "Shakespeare trend" is missing. What may have happened?

One possible motivation for removing these elements could be aesthetic. We have seen that the form of the interior monologue offers the possibility of an indefinite expansion, but Joyce may have judged (at this stage of the writing of *Ulysses,* that is to say early in 1919) that cramming all these additions into just a few lines would distend the thread too much and lead the reader astray. This is probably the reason for the shortening of the musical trend. It must have happened relatively early, since what was removed here was reinserted as a late marginal addition to the first part of the second draft:

> Tiresome shapers scraping fiddles, sawing the cello. Remind you of toothache. Night we were in the box,[28] the orchestra under, puffing, blowing, screwing, emptying out spittle. Conductor's legs, bags trousers jigging. The rill the rill the rillledy rill. Do right to hide them. But the harp was lovely, glowering gold light. Girl touching it. Poop of a lovely golden ship. Erin. The harp that once. Cool hands. We are harps. (NLI MS 36,639/9, page "14)," corresponding to *U* 11.576–83)

The removal of the "Shakespeare trend" seems to have occurred later and for a different reason. Joyce probably noticed that the quotation that served as an anchor for this trend had already been used a few pages before: "Too poetical that about the sad. Music did that. **Music hath charms.** Done anyhow. Postal order and stamp. Postoffice lower down. Walk, walk." (2nd draft, Ms. Buffalo V.A.5.—7; *JJA* 13:39)

It is not surprising that at first Joyce should have overlooked this repetition, as the earlier occurrence was part of the main text, while the second one is a marginal addition to our passage.[29] It seems that Joyce did not notice it either when he faircopied the draft and that it was only later that he crossed out the second occurrence and the whole "Shakespeare trend" that depended on it, probably when he copied it again for the Rosenbach manuscript. How can we know this, since the earlier fair copy is lost? I believe that we can find indirect evidence in the Rosenbach manuscript.

First of all, the "Shakespeare trend" is entirely absent from the Rosenbach, while it reappears (at a different place) on the typescript. And in the Rosenbach overture we find the words "Preacher is he," which are entirely absent from the body of the episode in this version and in all later ones. Based on these elements, we can make the following hypothesis. Taking his cue from his own instruction at the beginning of the second draft ("repeat phrases episodes"), Joyce composed the overture with selected phrases from the episode as he was fair copying it. This means that the "Shakespeare trend," of which "Preacher is he" is a part, was still in place. When the trend was crossed out (probably during the establishment of the Rosenbach manuscript), Joyce forgot to go back to eliminate the motif from the overture. It is a peculiar form of what I have called "memory of the context" (we will soon see an even more striking manifestation of this phenomenon). Later (after the Rosenbach was copied but before the typescript was made) he noticed the oversight and eliminated the superfluous element from the overture on the fair copy.

Although Joyce was always loath to waste any material, in the Rosenbach he did not reuse anything from the "Shakespeare trend" that he had eliminated. When he revised the fair copy before having it typed, however, he saw that it could be salvaged, at least in part, simply by linking it to the remaining occurrence of "Music hath charms," and this is what happened as can be seen from the typescript:

> Too poetical that about the sad. Music did that. Music hath charms. Shakespeare said. Quotations every day in the year. To be or not to be. Wisdom while you wait.
>
> In Gerard's rosery of Fetter lane he walks, greyedauburn. One life is all. One body. Do. But do.
>
> Done anyhow. Postal order, stamp. Post office lower down. Walk now. Enough. Barney Kiernan's I promised to meet them. Dislike that job. House of mourning. Walk.

The pretext remains the same (the misattribution of the quotation). The profuse trend from the second draft is compressed here to a minimum: "Shakespeare said. Quotations every day in the year. To be or not to be. Wisdom while you wait." But the shocking intrusion of Stephen's words is still there.

In fact, these words are not quite the same as they were on the draft. In the second draft, we had "a rosery of Fetter Lane of Gerard herbalist he walks. Afar hands on whiteness laid," while in the typescript we have "In Gerard's rosery of Fetter lane he walks, greyedauburn. One life is all. One body. Do. But do." The change was certainly contrived in order to adjust the insertion to the preexisting text, in which "Music hath charms" was immediately followed by the words "Done anyhow," referring to the letter to Martha that

Bloom had just finished. To the reader of the final text, "Done anyhow." seems to be generated by "Do. But do." and the twice repeated "Walk." in the following paragraph echo Shakespeare's walking in Fetter Lane. We can see, however, that it was a kind of retrospective arrangement that suggested this continuity. Also, at this particular moment of the episode, Bloom, writing to his clandestine pen pal, is less preoccupied with the adulterous encounter, so the traumatic image of the "Afar hands on whiteness laid" is less appropriate in the situation.

Memory of the context(s)

The inserted passage is thus determined by the preexisting local context, with the presence of the Congreve quotation and the word "Done," but its current shape is the result of a series of deferrals and displacements. It is overdetermined by a number of factors that are exterior to its present context: Stephen's monologue in "Scylla and Charybdis," whence the verbal material originated; the double draft page that we have been studying, since it is there that Stephen's monologue first intrudes in the genesis of "Sirens" and becomes associated with the Congreve quotation, with Shakespeare as a provider of daily wisdom and with Pat the waiter; and last but not least, a portentous aesthetic choice, that must have happened early in 1919, implying a major turning point in the novel.

For it must now be absolutely clear that the stunning inclusion of a portion of Stephen's monologue in the midst of Bloom's thoughts is not a blunder or an oversight and that it is not tied to a local context. We have seen the extraneous material appear, boldly written across a blank page. We have seen Joyce's effort to weave it into the narrative in one place and, when this failed, his efforts to rescue it and integrate it into another context. It is clearly a deliberate attempt to undermine the well-oiled narrative machinery that he had mounted in the first episodes and to call into question the interior monologue as the last refuge of psychological realism.

The Shakespeare fragment, such as it appears in the final version, has thus been affected by each of its genetic contexts. We can say that it retains the memory of its past environments, but the previous contexts reciprocally retain the memory of its former presence. This is usually a faint, practically imperceptible trace, but we can find a very conspicuous case if we consider the further development of the paragraph in which the "Shakespeare trend" had first tried to anchor itself. This is the version that was typed in 1919:

What do they think when they hear music. Way to catch rattlesnakes. Night Michael Gunn gave us the box. Tuning up. Shah of Persia liked that best. Wiped his nose in curtain too. Custom his country perhaps. That's music too. Tootling. Brasses braying. Doublebasses helpless, gashes in their sides. Woodwinds mooing cows. Woodwind like Goodwin's name.

Before sending the typescript to the printer in 1921, Joyce used two notes from the "Sirens" section of notebook NLI MS 36,639/5/A ("grand piano open crocodile" and "not as bad as it sounds") to manufacture additions to this paragraph. "Not as bad as it sounds" went unchanged after "That's music too." The note comparing an open grand piano to a crocodile's mouth joined the other comparisons between instruments and various animals, but it took this unexpected form: "Grand open crocodile music hath jaws."

The Congreve/Shakespeare quotation in embryonic form ("music hath") returns to haunt the paragraph two years after it had been eradicated from it. There is no textual continuity, no direct line of descent. Somehow, the quotation has remained associated with this passage. But when it returns, instead of being an inadvertent repetition of a quotation used a few pages before, it becomes a deliberate variation of the previous occurrence. This variation is spectacular by its condensation. Between the time it was re- moved from the passage and its reappearance in 1921 in the margin of the typescript—that is to say at a time when the last episodes of *Ulysses* were completed or on the way to being completed—Joyce's style has changed. The condensations made possible, in the first episodes, by the elliptical character of the interior monologue are becoming more radical and more arbitrary. As in the case of the "Circe" proofs discussed in chapter 1, the deferral gives us the opportunity to observe Joyce's style moving forward, in the direction of *Finnegans Wake*.

Recycling the remainder: from *Ulysses* to *Finnegans Wake?*

We have just seen an example of Joyce's recycling of an unused element from his drafts. In this case, the element was reinjected in the same environment from which it came.[30] This is far from being the most frequent case. Usually such elements are grafted in a very different location: elsewhere in the same episode, in other episodes of *Ulysses,* or even in another project altogether.[31]

Let us return, for the last time, to the array of additions that are displayed on the Shakespeare double page. Most of them have finally been inserted either in the text on the right or in two other places in the episode. But since the "Shakespeare trend" in its final form is finally reduced to a very concise form, some of its components were abandoned. This is the remainder:

> Wonder did he practise what he preached—[. . .] Hee hee hee hee. a preacher is he.—I wonder did he. Practise what he—Hee hee hee hee. [. . .]. Hee hee a preacher is he. Hee hee I wonder did he. Hee hee. Practise what he, hee hee hee hee Preach

The "Hee hee" cannot be said to be lost, since it was already disseminated throughout the episode (there are a dozen of occurrences) before it appeared on this page. But the idea of *practising what you preach* disappears completely from the episode and from *Ulysses* in general.

Had it been forgotten by Joyce? Perhaps not: in 1925, in a notebook for *Finnegans Wake* (VI.B.19, p. 60) Joyce inscribed the words "Practise preaching." The injunction to "practise" what you preach has been grotesquely changed into something that sounds like an advice to beginning curates (to Shaun who delivers a sermon in III.2?), but the underlying phrase and the biblical reference (to Matthew 23:3) are clearly perceptible. In the present state of our information, it is impossible to tell if the idea resurfaced in Joyce's mind six years later or if the unused phrase from the draft had been stored in some intermediary repository.

Shortly after it was inscribed in the notebook, the phrase was crossed out and used in a draft for chapter 4 of Book III of *Finnegans Wake.* Here is a reproduction of the manuscript in which the phrase was inserted and a partial transcription:

> They are coming back, down the scale, the way they went up, sweetheartedly, hot and cold and electrickery with air ^+autumn+^ and lounge and porter free ^+In spate of all that science could boot or art could skill. Close ^+Bolt+^ the gate. Cave the canem ^+and cane em+^. Beggars outside^+outdoor+^. Scrape your soles. My time is for sale. ^+Help yourself+^ Credit tomorrow. By faith alone. +^**Practise preaching.**+^ Lovely weather. Gomorrn. Godeven. ^+Solong+^ +^

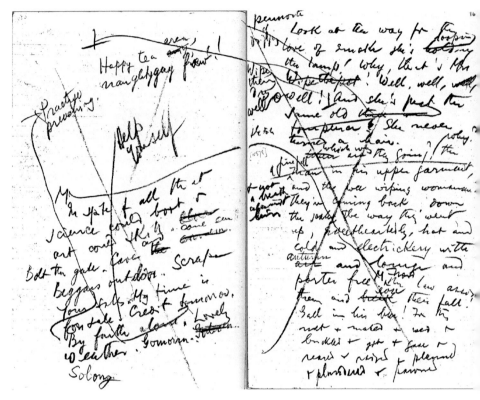

Figure 5.2. Draft for *FW* III.4. BL 47482a–15v–16 (*JJA* 60:28–29).

We can see that the manuscript is quite similar to the Shakespeare double page. The main text, on the right, is augmented by interlinear and marginal additions that soon overflow onto the left-hand page. The phrase "Practise preaching." appears as an addition to a massive addition. However, there is nothing tentative here. The limitations that stopped and reversed the expansive flow of Bloom's monologue no longer exist. The psychological pretext (mental associations between similar events in Bloom's mind, mindless repetitions meant to keep the thought away from an obsessive preoccupation) is no longer required. The fear of distending excessively the narrative thread is completely forgotten.

The additions consist of a series of grotesque injunctions and deformed phrases accompanying the parental couple to their matrimonial bed. The list, started in this manuscript, continues to grow as Joyce rewrites the passage in successive drafts, fair copies, typescripts, partial publications and proofs. Here is the ultimate version in the published book:

Hot and cold and electrickery with attendance and lounge and promenade free. In spite of all that science could boot or art could eke. Bolt the grinden. Cave and can em. Single wrecks for the weak, double axe for the mail, and quick queck quack for the radiose. Renove that bible. You will never have post in your pocket unless you have brasse on your plate. Beggards outdoor. Goat to the Endth, thou slowguard! Mind the Monks and their Grasps. Scrape your souls. Commit no miracles. Postpone no bills. Respect the uniform. Hold the raabers for the kunning his plethoron. Let leash the dooves to the cooin her coynth. Hatenot havenots. Share the wealth and spoil the weal. Peg the pound to tom the devil. My time is on draught. Bottle your own. Love my label like myself. Earn before eating. Drudge after drink. Credit tomorrow. Follow my dealing. Fetch my price. Buy not from dives. Sell not to freund. Herenow chuck english and learn to pray plain. Lean on your lunch. No cods before Me. Practise preaching. Think in your stomach. Import through the nose. By faith alone. Season's weather. Gomorrha. Salong. Lots feed from my tidetable. Oil's wells in our lands. Let earwigger's wivable teach you the dance! (*FW* 579.06–24)

We can see that the enumeration of distorted clichés and injunctions has grown beyond all measure. The only limitation seems to be the exhaustion of the writer (and of the reader). Such an absolute plasticity of texture seems to be the *telos* of one side of Joyce's efforts in "Sirens." It will be reached in *Finnegans Wake* after several intermediary stages, with the mock-epic enumerations of "Cyclops," the hyper-density of syntax in "Eumaeus," and the hyperrealist descriptions of actualities and potentialities in "Ithaca." The other side of his effort goes in the direction of condensation, observable everywhere in *Finnegans Wake* with the generalized use of portmanteau words, but we have seen in chapter 2 that "Sirens" already went quite far in that direction, even if it is not particularly in evidence in the passage we have been studying here.

6

The Reading Notes I

Ars Excerpendi

In chapter 4, we saw that Joyce made a note in the margin of the "Proteus" draft: "LB's / letter: / headache / menstruous / (monthly)" (Buffalo V.A.3.15, see fig. 4.7). It is reasonably easy for us to understand why he made that note, what it means, why it was inscribed in that particular place and how it was later used. We need not go far to discover the source that inspired it: Joyce's own text on the same page. The note is inscribed next to Stephen's divagations about women's periodical bleeding and its relation to the lunar rhythm.[1] We can guess that when he read this passage in the process of revising it, Joyce decided to establish a thematic connection between Stephen's and Bloom's monologues, so he made a memorandum to this effect in a blank space in the margin. Like Stephen, anxious to "Put a pin in that chap" (*U* 3.399), or Bloom jotting down Molly's sayings on his cuff, Joyce availed himself of the nearest available surface. It is possible that he subsequently transferred this material to a notebook for later use, but since it is not crossed out, it is more likely that he was working on "Lotus Eaters" while he was revising this draft (see above, chapter 2 on the interference of contemporary acts of writing). The linking was effected on a lost document, anterior to the Rosenbach manuscript of "Lotus Eaters." "Martha" writes: "I have such a bad headache." (see *U* 5.255) and Bloom comments: "Such a bad headache. Has her monthlies probably." Joyce later added: "Or sitting all day typing. Eyefocus bad for stomach nerve." and finally, on proofs, changed "monthlies" to "roses," in accordance with the flowery theme of the episode (*U* 5.285). These late changes weaken the connection to the lunar rhythms, but the attentive reader can still note the contrast between Stephen's poetical imagination and Bloom's matter-of-fact attitude about the subject.

This relative transparency of note-taking and note usage is unfortunately untypical of Joyce's annotations. For one thing, we usually lack the spatial proximity of the note to the source that here makes the derivation immediately perceptible. Note-taking writers can be classified in two categories: the "marginalists" and the "extractors."[2] The marginalists (like Voltaire or Coleridge) write their notes in the margins of the volumes they read, contiguous to the text, while the extractors, such as Winkelmann or Woolf, leave the books intact and write down their notes in copybooks, notesheets, common place books and other external containers, thereby severing the material connection between the note and its source. Joyce clearly belongs to the latter category. The example of Stephen's involuntary indenture to the bullockbefriending cause (see chapter 4) indicates that, for Joyce, inscribing his text in the margin of someone else's writing was felt as a kind of marginalization. Therefore, his only marginal notes are to be found in the periphery of his own manuscripts (like the one discussed above).

Extractors and marginalists have different relationships to the works they read, but both practices express a subdued violence against them by selecting a passage at the expense of their cohesion and unity. Here again, we encounter a process of decontextualization and recontextualization. Whatever its form or its place of inscription, a reading note always involves the selection of a portion of text from its original context and its tentative projection into a (still virtual) extraneous context in which it will be incorporated.

The marginalists apparently preserve the textual integrity of the source text, but they interfere with the book, brand it with their marks, adorn it with commentaries of all kinds, embrace the work with their own writing and plant the seeds of their own creation in its interstices so as to feed from its substance. We can think of Bloom, who toys with the idea of a literary composition in close intertextual and genetic relation to Philip Beaufoy's "Matcham's Masterstroke": he tears "away half the prize story sharply" (*U* 4.537) and deposits an idiosyncratic annotation on the page, later claiming to be "producing a collection of prize stories of which I am the inventor, something that is an entirely new departure" (*U* 15.803–4). Philip Beaufoy, the author, understandably resents both the marking ("the hallmark of the beast" 15:844–45) and the appropriation. This is not so different from Stephen's attitude when he tears off the bottom of Deasy's letter, giving the impression that it too has been used as toilet paper ("Was he short taken?," Myles Crawford asks; *U* 7.521). On the other hand, the extractors leave intact the materiality of the annotated volume, but the violence against the source text is more in evidence. It is dismembered like Orpheus in the hands of the Maenads, cut up in pieces of varying dimensions and dispersed, somewhat like the "Sirens" episode, cannibalized to build the "overture," a compendium that completely destroys the narrative coherence of the original text.

Early notebooks

Joyce remained an extractor throughout his career, but his mode of extracting changed considerably. Before we come to the most mysterious and original part of the archive, the notebooks for *Finnegans Wake,* we must consider briefly some of the extant specimens documenting Joyce's earlier habits of note-taking.

The initial mode of extracting is represented mainly[3] by the "Paris-Pola Commonplace Book," catalogued by the NLI as "Notebook with accounts, quotations, book lists, etc., 1903–1904."[4] Joyce first used this copybook as a receptacle for a conventional collection of extracts, but he progressively added different elements that changed its nature and anticipate his future method of work.[5] We can say that this document started as a traditional compilation and inaugurated an evolution toward something very different.

It is perhaps interesting to remark that the first words of this inaugural document are inscribed on the cover: "Prière de rendre à James Joyce rue Corneille, 5 Paris." Literally this means "Please give back to James Joyce 5 Corneille Street [the address of his hotel] Paris," an instruction (*rendre*) implying that the copybook would have been taken away from him, as opposed to *rapporter,* which would mean "bring back" or "return" something mislaid. And it is certainly remarkable that the first two pages of the copybook should display a log of the sums received and paid during Joyce's Parisian stay, indicating a complex pattern of borrowings and reimbursements. This will be translated, further in the notebook, into two budgets for Joyce's first and second months in Paris (each certified by his signature and a mock stamp, although we may suspect that they were doctored in the same way as Bloom's budget in "Ithaca"), emphasizing his outstanding debts.[6] This context suggests two different images for Joyce's extractive practice: a traffic of stolen goods (the artist as a thief and as a receiver), and the writing of a gigantic IOU (the artist as borrower and as a collector of bad and doubtful debts[7]).

In the early part of the notebook, the process of extraction is as respectful as it is possible (keeping in mind what has been said about the violence implicit in the act of selecting a passage and severing it from its context).[8] The fragments are copied in a neat hand; they are usually substantial, and when they are short, they remain grammatically coherent. The name of the author is carefully indicated. The *Ars excerpendi* was a well-known practice among the Romans, at least since Pliny. It was also a mainstay of Jesuit education, and Joyce must have been trained in the technique of anthologizing fragments of texts, chosen as examples to be admired and to be imitated. In other words, he is reproducing here a model for a collection of models. As such, we may think that (to take the authors most frequently quoted in this notebook) Aristotle and Aquinas, on the one hand, and Ben Jonson, on the other, make strange bedfellows, but their juxtaposition on the page expresses a subjective polarity that is explained in *A Portrait of the Artist as a Young Man:*

> he would repeat the song by Ben Jonson which begins: *I was not wearier where I lay.* His mind when wearied of its search for the essence of beauty amid the spectral words of Aristotle or Aquinas turned often for its pleasure to the dainty songs of the Elizabethans.[9]

The young artist's moods appear as the organizing principle bringing together the dainty Elizabethans and the spectral philosophers. But it is not enough for Joyce to be present in this role of discretionary arranger, however expressive of his personality. Among the exemplary passages from famous writers of different kinds, he includes signed and dated (and geographically located) fragments of his own writing, obviously passages that he considers important and worthy of standing next to the others.[10] We can see that he is setting a standard for himself. In the same spirit, he also gathers, under the ironic title of *Memorabilia,* passages that he considers as counter-models, because they are absurd, ridiculous, or simply awkward or infelicitous.

Toward the end of 1904, after almost two years of use of this notebook, Joyce's practice started changing. The notes become shorter and their source is no longer identified. Most entries are not quotations in the conventional sense. We can see that Joyce, instead of recording his notations chronologically according to the fluctuations of his own interests and moods, experiments with different principles of organization. He first tried to sort his notes by *destination*, with two pages devoted to *Stephen Hero* and one page devoted to *Dubliners*. When some of the notes were integrated in the work of destination, they were crossed out in the notebook, confirming that they no longer represented a static collection of permanent models. And finally, in the last pages of the notebooks, Joyce tried gathering his notes by *themes*, with one page tagged "Byrne" (J. F. Byrne, the model for Cranly) and one page tagged "S.D."

The next available collections of notes,[11] traditionally called the "Alphabetical Notebook" and the "Subject Notebook," are also organized by themes. In fact the Alphabetical Notebook (originally prepared for *A Portrait of the Artist as a Young Man*) opens with a section on "Byrne John Francis" and has a section on "Dedalus (Stephen)."[12] The Subject Notebook, prepared late in 1917 for *Ulysses*, also has a section on "Stephen."[13] Joyce may not have had exactly the same Stephen D(a)edalus in mind in each of the three notebooks, but the continuity of the procedure is obvious. The difference of arrangement of the various topics (alphabetical in one case, haphazard in the others) is probably due to the nature of the containers: an address book divided into twenty-two alphabetical sections, on the one hand, and ordinary school copybooks, on the other.

There is however an important difference. The sections of the Alphabetical Notebook (and the Byrne section of the "Paris-Pola notebook") are source oriented. They mostly refer to people Joyce knew—family, friends, and acquaintances—who would become the foundation of characters in his autobiographical works. On the other hand, the corresponding sections in the Subject Notebook are fiction oriented: they bear the names of characters in the novel. John Stanislaus Joyce appears as "Pappie" in the Alphabetical Notebook and as "Simon" in the Subject Notebook. S.D./Dedalus (Stephen)/ Stephen is of course a special case, since he is both a fictional character in *Stephen Hero, A Portrait of the Artist as a Young Man,* and *Ulysses* and Joyce's early nom de plume.

For some reason, Joyce found a thematic organization unsatisfactory, and after the Subject Notebook he reverted to a sorting by destination. From then on, his notes for the writing of *Ulysses* were organized into sections labeled by *Ulysses* episodes under their Homeric titles. Although the sections do not strictly follow the order of the episodes of the book in any of the notebooks (they almost do in NLI MS 36,639/4), it is clear that the plan of the book was firmly established by the time Joyce adopted this mode of organization.[14]

In the light of this, it will be interesting to study in detail a document that is probably anterior to the final determination of the plan of *Ulysses* and that seems to have played a part in the evolution of this plan. Its notes are organized in relation to the source and, tentatively, to the destination.

The "Lacedemon" Homeric notes

The last page of the copybook that contains the earliest extant drafts of the "Proteus" and "Sirens" episodes (NLI MS 36,639/3/B, see chapter 6, this volume) has not attracted much attention.[15] The two drafts have been found so fascinating, because of their shockingly unexpected form, that the unrelated last page of the copybook has been neglected. And yet it is a unique and important document. It throws some light on Joyce's use of Homer in the early phase of writing *Ulysses* and more generally on his interaction with his sources and the way he assimilates them to his own universe, bends them to suit his own needs, also on the way he lets them interfere with his preconceived schemes. Figure 6.1 is a diplomatic transcription of this page.[16]

First, we should try to understand the nature and organization of the document. The title, centered and underlined, indicates that it is a series of notes on "Lacedemon," that is to say the visit of Telemachus to Menelaus, king of Lacedaemon, narrated in Book IV and Book XV of the *Odyssey*. This seems like a natural sequel for Joyce, after having written a "Telemachus" episode corresponding to Books I and II of the *Odyssey* and a "Nestor" based on Book III. The page is clearly divided into two parts. The top is occupied by a complex diagram, while the remainder contains a list arranged in two columns.

The schema at the top of the page conjoins two different diagrammatic representations. One of them is a kind of family tree. It indicates that *Megapenthes* is the son of *Menelaus* and a *slave* and that he marries the *d[aughter]* of *Alector*, while [Hermione] is the *d[aughter]* of *Menelaus* and *Helen* and marries the *son of Achilles*. Joyce is trying to make sense of the complex family relationships implied by Homer's convoluted narrative:

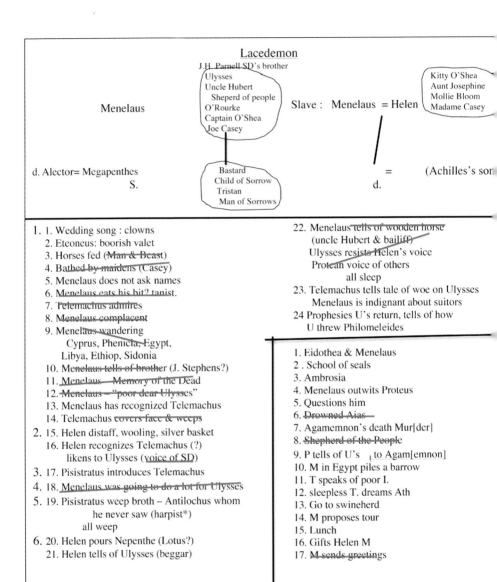

Lacedemon

J.H. Parnell SD's brother

Menelaus

Ulysses
Uncle Hubert
Sheperd of people
O'Rourke
Captain O'Shea
Joe Casey

Slave : Menelaus = Helen

Kitty O'Shea
Aunt Josephine
Mollie Bloom
Madame Casey

d. Alector= Megapenthes
S.

Bastard
Child of Sorrow
Tristan
Man of Sorrows

=
d.

(Achilles's son

1. 1. Wedding song : clowns
2. Eteoneus: boorish valet
3. Horses fed (Man & Beast)
4. Bathed by maidens (Casey)
5. Menelaus does not ask names
6. Menelaus eats his bit? tanist.
7. Telemachus admires
8. Menelaus complacent
9. Menelaus wandering
   Cyprus, Phenicia, Egypt,
   Libya, Ethiop, Sidonia
10. Menelaus tells of brother (J. Stephens?)
11. Menelaus — Memory of the Dead
12. Menelaus — "poor dear Ulysses"
13. Menelaus has recognized Telemachus
14. Telemachus covers face & weeps
2. 15. Helen distaff, wooling, silver basket
16. Helen recognizes Telemachus (?)
   likens to Ulysses (voice of SD)
3. 17. Pisistratus introduces Telemachus
4. 18. Menelaus was going to do a lot for Ulysses
5. 19. Pisistratus weep broth – Antilochus whom
   he never saw (harpist*)
   all weep
6. 20. Helen pours Nepenthe (Lotus?)
21. Helen tells of Ulysses (beggar)

22. Menelaus tells of wooden horse
   (uncle Hubert & bailiff)
   Ulysses resists Helen's voice
   Protean voice of others
   all sleep
23. Telemachus tells tale of woe on Ulysses
   Menelaus is indignant about suitors
24 Prophesies U's return, tells of how
   U threw Philomeleides

1. Eidothea & Menelaus
2. School of seals
3. Ambrosia
4. Menelaus outwits Proteus
5. Questions him
6. Drowned Aias
7. Agamemnon's death Mur[der]
8. Shepherd of the People
9. P tells of U's ₁ to Agam[emnon]
10. M in Egypt piles a barrow
11. T speaks of poor I.
12. sleepless T. dreams Ath
13. Go to swineherd
14. M proposes tour
15. Lunch
16. Gifts Helen M
17. M sends greetings

Figure 6.1. NLI MS 36,639/5/A, p. 2–3.

Menelaus [. . .] they found giving a feast in his house to many friends of his kin, a feast for the wedding of his son and daughter. His daughter he was sending to the son of Achilles, cleaver of the ranks of men [. . .]. And for his son he was bringing to his home the daughter of Alector of Sparta, for his well-beloved son, strong Megapenthes, born of a slave woman, for the gods no more showed promise of seed to Helen, from the day that she bare a lovely child, Hermione, as fair as golden Aphrodite. (Book IV: 48)[17]

We can see that Joyce's first preoccupation is to understand his source, but he does not do so passively. He combines the genealogic chart with a map of semantic counterparts. The names of Menelaus, Helen and Megapenthes are juxtaposed with circles containing the names of figures that Joyce considered comparable to them in some respects.

In the case of Menelaus, these characters are men who have been betrayed by their respective wives: the "shepherd of the people" (a Homeric designation for kings, referring here to Agamemnon, who was not only cuckolded but assassinated by his wife), O'Rourke, Prince of Breffni (See *U* 2.392–94), Captain O'Shea (the husband of Katherine O'Shea, Parnell's lover), Joe Casey (Joseph Theobald Casey,[18] the model for the Kevin Egan of *Ulysses,* who was deserted by his wife, see *U* 3.253–54), Ulysses himself (in Joyce's pessimistic interpretation of Penelope's constancy), and one "Uncle Hubert" (who has not been identified). After the first pencil circle had been filled, Joyce took into account another aspect of Menelaus and added, above the circle, the names of men who are eclipsed by their brothers: John Howard Parnell, the brother of Charles Stewart (see *U* 8.500–506), and Stephen Dedalus's brother Maurice of *Stephen Hero,* loosely based on Stanislaus Joyce.[19]

It is only logical that Helen should be associated with other adulteresses: Kitty O'Shea, "Mollie Bloom" (this spelling is used by Joyce in the early notes), and Madame Casey. "Aunt Josephine" (certainly Josephine Murray, Joyce's favorite aunt) is added to the list, but it is not clear why she is lumped in with these Messalinas.

As for Megapenthes, he is tagged "Bastard / Child of Sorrow / Tristan / Man of Sorrows." This is a confirmation of the precise source for the notes on this page. Joyce consulted various translations of the *Odyssey,*[20] but only Butcher and Lang provide an etymological footnote for Megapenthes: "*A son of sorrow: Tristram" (Book IV: 48n).

Joyce transposes the Homeric cast of characters in terms of Irish history (O'Rourke, Parnell) and personal history (Aunt Josephine, uncle Hubert[?]) but also already in terms of his projected fiction ("Mollie" Bloom), with some overlap between these categories (Joe Casey belongs both to Irish history and to the personal history of Joyce, and he is going to be transposed into the fictional world of *Ulysses*; "SD's brother" is both a fictitious character and a reference to Stanislaus). The cluster around the name of Megapenthes is less character oriented. It introduces etymological interpretation and an early occurrence of the theme of Tristan, which will play such an important part in the genesis of *Finnegans Wake* (see chapter 3 above).

Below this schematization comes a more straightforward collection of notes in the form of a list, closely following (at first) the thread of Homer's text. Spelling and phrasing confirm that Joyce was still using Butcher and Lang's translation.[21]

The notes are listed below, accompanied by the relevant passages of the source. Readers can of course skip this (austere) part, but it is an occasion to have a close look at the passages that drew Joyce's attention and to see how Joyce reformulated them and in some cases transposed them on the fly into his own universe.

1. Wedding song: clowns

Menelaus [. . .] they found giving a feast in his house to many friends of his kin, a feast for the wedding of his noble son and daughter. [. . .] a divine minstrel was singing to the lyre, and as he began the song two tumblers in the company whirled through their midst. (Book IV: 48)

2. Eteoneus: boorish valet

See next item for source.

3. Horses fed (Man & Beast)

"Menelaus, fosterling of Zeus, here are two strangers, whosoever they be, two men like to the lineage of great Zeus. Say, shall we loose their swift horses from under the yoke, or send them onward to some other host who shall receive them kindly?"

Then in sore displeasure spake to him Menelaus of the fair hair: "Eteoneus son of Boethous, truly thou wert not a fool aforetime, but now for this once, like a child thou talkest folly. Surely we ate much hospitable cheer of other men, ere we twain came hither, if even if in time to come Zeus haply give us rest from affliction. Nay go, unyoke the horses of the strangers, and as for the men, lead them forward to the house to feast with us."

So spake he, and Eteoneus hasted from the hall, and called the other ready squires to follow with him. So they loosed the sweating horses from beneath the yoke, and fastened them at the stalls of the horses, and threw beside them spelt, and therewith mixed white barley, and tilted the chariot against the shining faces of the gateway, and led the men into the hall divine. (Book IV: 49)

4. Bathed by maidens (Casey)

Now when the maidens had bathed them and anointed them with olive oil, and cast about them thick cloaks and doublets, they sat on chairs by Menelaus, son of Atreus. (Book IV: 49)

Note: In "Proteus," Stephen remembers Kevin Egan (modeled after Joe Casey) protesting: "The froeken, bonne à tout faire, who rubs male nakedness in the bath at Upsala. Moi faire, she said. Tous les messieurs. Not this Monsieur, I said. Most licentious custom. Bath a most private thing. I wouldn't let my brother, not even my own brother, most lascivious thing." *U* 3.234–38. Much later, Joyce planted an inverted echo in Bloom's thoughts "Nicer if a nice girl did it" (*U* 5.503), prepared in notebook MS 36,639/5A, p.4 and in notebook MS 36,639/4, p.5.

5. Menelaus does not ask names

So Menelaus of the fair hair greeted the twain and spake: "Taste ye food and be glad, and thereafter when ye have supped, we will ask what men ye are; for the blood of your parents is not lost in you, but ye are of the line of men that are sceptred kings, the fosterlings of Zeus; for no churls could beget sons like you." (Book IV: 50)

6. Menelaus eats his bit? tanist.

Passim

Note: The tanist was the second-in-command and heir apparent to a Celtic chief, designated among his family. This was the position of Menelaus among the Greeks, as long as his brother Agamemnon lived. Joyce suggests that he may have found this frustrating.

7. Telemachus admires

Telemachus spake to the son of Nestor, holding his head close to him, that those others might not hear: "Son of Nestor, delight of my heart, mark the flashing of bronze through the echoing halls, and the flashing of gold and of amber and of silver and of ivory. Such like, methinks, is the court of Olympian Zeus within, for the world of things that are here; wonder comes over me as I look upon it." (Book IV: 50)

8. Menelaus complacent

Menelaus [. . .] spake to them winged words:
'Children dear, of a truth no one of mortal men may contend with Zeus, for his mansions and his treasures are everlasting: but of men there may be who will vie with me in treasure, or there may be none. (Book IV: 50)

9. Menelaus wandering
    Cyprus, Phenicia, Egypt, Libya, Ethiop, Sidonia

I roamed over Cyprus and Phoenicia and Egypt, and reached the Aethiopians and Sidonians and Erembi and Libya, where lambs are horned from the birth. (Book IV: 50–51)

10. Menelaus tells of brother (J. Stephens?)

While I was yet roaming in those lands, getting together much living, meantime another slew my brother privily at unawares, by the guile of his accursed wife. (Book IV: 51)

Note: James Stephens, founder of the Irish Republican *Brotherhood,* was Joseph Casey's cousin. It is possible that Joe Casey spoke of Stephens' death that had occurred two years before Joyce's stay in Paris.

11. Menelaus—Memory of the Dead

I would that I had but a third part of those my riches, and dwelt in my halls, and that those men were yet safe, who perished of old in wide Troy Land, far from Argos, the pastureland of horses. (Book IV: 51)

12. Menelaus—"poor dear Ulysses"

Howbeit, though I bewail them all and sorrow oftentimes as I sit in our halls,—awhile indeed I satisfy my soul with lamentation, and then again I cease; for soon hath man enough of chill lamentation—yet for them all I make no such dole, despite my grief, as for one only, who causes me to loathe both sleep and meat, when I think upon him. For no one of the Achaeans toiled so greatly as Odysseus toiled and adventured himself: but to him it was to be but labour and trouble, and to me grief ever comfortless for his sake, so long he is afar, nor know we aught, whether he be alive or dead. Yea methinks they lament him, even that old Laertes and steadfast Penelope and Telemachus, whom he left a child new-born in his house. (Book IV: 51)

13. Menelaus has recognized Telemachus

See next item for source.

14. Telemachus covers face & weeps

So spake he, and in the heart of Telemachus he stirred a yearning to lament his father; and at his father's name he let a tear fall from his eyelids to the ground, holding up his purple mantle with both his hands before his eyes. And Menelaus marked him and mused in his mind and his heart whether he should leave him to make mention of his father, or first question him and prove him in every word. (Book IV: 51–52)

15. Helen distaff, wooling, silver basket

Polybus, [. . .] gave two silver baths to Menelaus, and tripods twain, and ten talents of gold. And besides all this, his wife bestowed on Helen lovely gifts;

a golden distaff did She give, and a silver basket with wheels beneath, and the rims thereof were finished with gold. This it was that the handmaid Phylo bare and set beside her, filled with dressed yarn, and across it was laid a distaff charged with wool of violet blue. (Book IV: 52)

16. Helen recognizes Telemachus (?)
   likens to Ulysses (voice of S[tephen] D[edalus])

'Menelaus, fosterling of Zeus, know we now who these men that have come under our roof avow themselves to be? [. . .] None, I say, have I ever yet seen so like another, man nor woman—wonder comes over me as I look on him—as this man is like the son of great-hearted Odysseus, Telemachus, whom he left a new-born child in his house [. . .]

And Menelaus of the fair hair answered her, saying: 'Now I too, lady, mark the likeness even as thou tracest it. For such as these were his feet, such his hands, and the glances of his eyes, and his head, and his hair withal. (Book IV: 52)

Note: In "Proteus," Stephen Dedalus calls Simon Dedalus: "the man with my voice and my eyes" (U 3.45–46). Kevin Egan insists on the resemblance: "You're your father's son. I know the voice." (U 3.229)

17. Pisistratus introduces Telemachus

And Peisistratus, son of Nestor, answered him, saying: 'Menelaus, son of Atreus fosterling of Zeus, leader of the host, verily, this is the son of that very man, even as thou sayest. (Book IV: 53)

18. Menelaus was going to do a lot for Ulysses

'Lo now! in good truth there has come unto my house the son of a friend indeed, who for my sake endured many adventures. And I thought to welcome him on his coming more nobly than all the other Argives, if but Olympian Zeus, of the far-borne voice, had vouchsafed us a return over the sea in our swift ships,—that such a thing should be. And in Argos I would have given him a city to dwell in, and stablished for him a house, and brought him forth from Ithaca with his substance and his son and all his people, making one city desolate of those that lie around, and are in mine own domain. Then oft-times would we have held converse here, and nought would have parted us in our friendship and in our joys, ere the black cloud of death overshadowed us. (Book IV: 53)

19. Pisistratus weep broth[er]—Antilochus whom
  he never saw (harpist [doubtful reading])
  all weep

Argive Helen wept, the daughter of Zeus, and Telemachus wept, and Mene-laus, the son of Atreus; nor did the son of Nestor keep tearless eyes. For he bethought him in his heart of noble Antilochus, whom the glorious son of the bright Dawn had slain, Thinking upon him he spake winged words:

[. . .] I too have a brother dead, nowise the meanest of the Argives, and thou art like to have known him, for as for me I never met nor saw him. (Book IV: 54)

20. Helen pours Nepenthe (Lotus?)

Then Helen, daughter of Zeus, turned to new thoughts. Presently she cast a drug into the wine whereof they drank, a drug to lull all pain and anger, and bring forgetfulness of every sorrow. Whoso should drink a draught thereof, when it is mingled in the bowl, on that day he would let no tear fall down his cheeks, not though his mother and his father died, not though men slew his brother or dear son with the sword before his face, and his own eyes beheld it. Medicines of such virtue and so helpful had the daughter of Zeus, which Polydamna, the wife of Thon, had given her, a woman of Egypt, where earth the grain-giver yields herbs in greatest plenty, many that are healing in the cup, and many baneful. (Book IV: 55)

Note: Joyce seems to be anticipating the "Lotus Eaters" episode.

21. Helen tells of Ulysses (beggar)

He bruised himself with unseemly stripes, and cast a sorry covering over his shoulders, and in the fashion of a servant he went down into the wide-wayed city of the foemen, and he hid himself in the guise of another, a beggar, though in no wise such an one was he at the ships of the Achaeans. (Book IV: 56)

22. Menelaus tells of wooden horse
   (uncle Hubert & bailiff)

never yet have mine eyes beheld any such man of heart as was Odysseus; even as he wrought and dared this other deed in his hardiness in the shapen horse, wherein sat all we chiefs of the Argives, bearing to the Trojans death and doom. (Book IV: 56)

> *Ulysses resists Helen's voice*
> *Protean voice of others*

Anon thou didst draw nigh, and sure some god must have bidden thee, who wished to bring glory to the Trojans. Yea and godlike Deiphobus went with thee on thy way. Thrice thou didst go round about the hollow ambush and handle it, calling aloud on the chiefs of the Argives by name, and making thy voice like the voices of the wives of all the Argives. But I and the son of Tydeus and goodly Odysseus sat in the midst and heard thy call. Now we twain had a desire to start up and come forth or presently to answer from within. But eager as we were, Odysseus stayed and held us there. (Book IV: 56–57)

all sleep

"But come, bid us to bed, that forthwith we may take our joy of rest beneath the spell of sleep."

So spake he, and Argive Helen bade her handmaids set out bedsteads beneath the corridor, and fling on them fair purple blankets and spread coverlets above, and thereon lay thick mantles to be a clothing over all. So they went from the hall with torch in hand, and spread the beds, and the henchman led forth the guests. Thus they slept there at the outer gallery of the house, the hero Telemachus and the splendid son of Nestor. But the son of Atreus slept, as his custom was, in the inmost chamber of the lofty house, and by him lay long-robed Helen, that fair lady. (Book IV: 57)

23. Telemachus tells tale of woe on Ulysses

So now am I come hither to thy knees, if haply thou art willing to tell me of his pitiful death, as one that saw it perchance with thine own eyes, or heard the story from some other wanderer; for his mother bare him to exceeding sorrow. And speak me no soft words in ruth or pity, but tell me plainly how thou didst get sight of him. (Book IV: 58)

Menelaus is indignant about suitors

Then in heavy displeasure spake to him Menelaus of the fair hair: 'Lo you now! for truly in the bed of a brave-hearted man were they minded to lie, cravens themselves as they are! (Book IV: 54) (Book IV: 58)

24. Prophesies U[lysses]'s return,

Even as when a hind hath couched her newborn fawns unweaned in a strong lion's lair, and searcheth out the knolls and grassy glades, seeking pasture, and afterward the lion cometh back to his bed, and sendeth forth unsightly death upon that pair, even so shall Odysseus send forth unsightly death upon the wooers. (Book IV: 58)

tells of how U[lysses] threw Philomeleides

Would to our father Zeus, and Athene and Apollo, would that in such might as when of old in stablished Lesbos he rose up and wrestled a match with Philomeleides and threw him mightily, and all the Achaeans rejoiced; would that in such strength Odysseus might consort with the wooers (Book IV: 58–59)

1. Eidothea & Menelaus

And now would all our corn have been spent, and likewise the strength of the men, except some goddess had taken pity on me and saved me, Eidothee, daughter of mighty Proteus, the ancient one of the sea. For most of all I moved her heart, when she met me wandering alone apart from my company (Book IV: 59)

Note: Joyce begins here a new sequence of numbers, with the beginning of the story of the encounter between Menelaus and Proteus.

2. School of seals

the seals, the brood of the fair daughter of the brine, sleep all in a flock, stolen forth from the grey sea water. (Book IV: 61)

3. Ambrosia

There would our ambush have been most terrible, for the deadly stench of the sea bred seals distressed us sore: nay, who would lay him down by a beast of the sea? But herself she wrought deliverance, and devised a great comfort. She took ambrosia of a very sweet savour, and set it beneath each man's nostril, and did away with the stench of the beast. (Book IV: 62)

4. Menelaus outwits Proteus

first among the sea-beasts he reckoned us, and guessed not that there was guile, and afterward he too laid him down. Then we rushed upon him with a cry, and cast our hands about him, nor did that ancient one forget his cunning. Now behold, at the first he turned into a bearded lion, and thereafter into a snake, and a pard, and a huge boar; then he took the shape of running water, and of a tall and flowering tree. We the while held him close with steadfast heart. But when now that ancient one of the magic arts was aweary, then at last he questioned me and spake unto me. (Book IV: 62)

5. Questions him

I am holden long time in this isle, neither can I find any issue therefrom, and my heart faileth within me. Howbeit, do thou tell me—for the gods know all things—which of the immortals it is that bindeth me here, and hath hindered me from my way; and declare as touching my returning, how I may go over the teeming deep. (Book IV: 62–63)

6. Drowned Aias

Aias in truth was smitten in the midst of his ships of the long oars. Poseidon at first brought him nigh to Gyrae, to the mighty rocks, and delivered him from the sea. And so would he have fled his doom, albeit hated by Athene, had he not let a proud word fall in the fatal darkening of his heart. He said that in the gods' despite he had escaped the great gulf of the sea; and Poseidon heard his loud boasting, and presently caught up his trident into his strong hands, and smote the rock Gyraean and cleft it in twain. And the one part abode in his place, but the other fell into the sea, the broken piece whereon Aias sat at the first, when his heart was darkened. And the rock bore him down into the vast and heaving deep; so there he perished when he had drunk of the salt sea water. (Book IV: 64)

7. Agamemnon's death Mur[der]

See source after next item.

8. Shepherd of the People / to Agam[emnon]

Then with chariot and horses he went to bid to the feast Agamemnon, shepherd of the people; but caitiff thoughts were in his heart. He brought him up to his house, all unwitting of his doom, and when he had feasted him slew him, as one slayeth an ox at the stall. (Book IV: 65)

9. P[roteus] tells of U[lysses]'s

'It is the son of Laertes, whose dwelling is in Ithaca; and I saw him in an island shedding plenteous tears in the halls of the nymph Calypso, who holds him there perforce; so he may not come to his own country, for he has by him no ships with oars, and no companions to send him on his way over the broad back of the sea. (Book IV: 65)

10. M[enelaus] in Egypt piles a barrow

So when I had appeased the anger of the everlasting gods, I piled a barrow to Agamemnon, that his fame might never be quenched. (Book IV: 66)

Note: This is another confirmation of the source. Of all the translations that Joyce might have consulted, only Butcher and Lang use the phrase "piled a barrow."

11. T[elemachus] speaks of poor I[thaca].

In Ithaca there are no wide courses, nor meadow land at all. It is a pastureland of goats, and more pleasant in my sight than one that pastureth horses; for of the isles that lie and lean upon the sea, none are fit for the driving of horses, or rich in meadow land, and least of all is Ithaca.' (Book IV: 67)

Note: Perhaps also an allusion to "poor Ireland" in "The Wearing of the Green"?

12. sleepless T. dreams Ath[ene]

The son of Nestor truly was overcome with soft sleep, but sweet sleep gat not hold of Telemachus, but, through the night divine, careful thoughts for his father kept him wakeful ever. And grey-eyed Athene stood nigh him and spake to him (Book XV: 240)

Note: Here Joyce ceases to follow the course of Homer's text. To continue the narration of the events taking place in Lacedemon, he jumps over the extended paralipsis (eleven songs of the *Odyssey*) covering the simultaneous events in Ithaca and then the further adventures of Ulysses. For Joyce, the basic unit is not the Homeric song but the narrative episode or the diegetic location.

13. Go to swineherd

for thy part seek first the swineherd who keeps thy swine, and is loyal to thee as of old. There do thou rest the night, and bid him go to the city to bear tidings of thy coming to the wise Penelope. (Book XV: 241)

14. M[enelaus] proposes tour

Menelaus, of the loud war cry, answered him: '[. . .] if thou art minded to turn toward Hellas and mid Argos, so as I too may go with thee, then will I yoke thee horses and lead thee to the towns of men, and none shall send us away empty, but will give us some one thing to take with us, either a tripod of goodly bronze or a cauldron, or two mules or a golden chalice.' (Book XV: 242)

15. Lunch

Now when Menelaus, of the loud war cry, heard this saying, straightway he bade his wife and maids to prepare the midday meal in the halls, out of the good store they had by them. (Book XV: 243)

16. Gifts Helen M[enelaus]

Menelaus, of the fair hair, spake to him saying:

'Telemachus, may Zeus the thunderer, and the lord of Here, in very truth bring about thy return according to the desire of thy heart. And of the gifts, such as are treasures stored in my house, I will give thee the goodliest and greatest of price. I will give thee a mixing bowl beautifully wrought; it is all of silver and the lips thereof are finished with gold; it is the work of Hephaestus; and the hero Phaedimus the king of the Sidonians, gave it to me when his house sheltered me, on my coming thither. This cup I would give to thee.'

Therewith the hero Atrides set the double cup in his hands. And the strong Megapenthes bare the shining silver bowl and set it before him. And Helen, of the fair cheeks, came up, with the robe in her hands, and spake and hailed him:

"Lo! I too give thee this gift, dear child, a memorial of the hands of Helen, against the day of thy desire, even of thy marriage. But meanwhile let it lie by thy mother in her chamber. And may joy go with thee to thy well-builded house, and thine own country." (Book XV: 243–44)

17. M[enelaus] sends greetings

he stood before the horses and spake and greeted them:

"Farewell, knightly youths, and salute in my name Nestor, the shepherd of the people; for truly he was gentle to me as a father, while we sons of the Achaeans warred in the land of Troy." (Book XV: 245)

The source of these notes is clear, and we have a good idea of the way Joyce interacted with it as he was reading. But it is more difficult to know what happened afterward and what use he made of the notes. When and why were the notes numbered—something that Joyce normally does not do—and then partially renumbered? Was this a system of reference for insertion in future drafts? Why are some of the notes crossed-out with a blue crayon? Joyce normally crosses out items of his notes (or passages from his drafts) when they are either transferred to another note repository or integrated in a draft. On this page, some of the crossed-out notes cannot be found in *Ulysses*,[22] while others that we identify in the text with varying degrees of certainty are not crossed out. Also, it appears that some elements from this page were integrated at a late stage of the writing of *Ulysses*. It is not likely that Joyce kept this fragile coverless notebook at his elbow during the whole time, so we can suppose that he transferred some of the elements into a notebook that is no longer extant.

The first point to be noted is that several elements of the list are present in the very early "Proteus" draft at the beginning of the same copybook, which means that the notes are *anterior* to this draft. Joyce must have used the last page of the empty copybook for his reading notes before he started to fill it, first with the "Proteus" draft and then, later, with the "Sirens" draft.[23]

For instance, the passage in the draft in which Stephen reminisces about the coy Kevin Egan (still called *Joe* Egan in the first version of the draft, after Joe Casey) in the Swedish bath ("the girls who washed and rubbed his naked body in the bath at Upsala, most licentious custom, bath a most private thing," 36,639/07/A, p. 5) must derive from the note: "4. Bathed by maidens (Casey)." It is less certain but still likely that Egan's drink, the "green fairy" (absinthe), derives from the "Nepenthe" in note 20.

The passage goes on with a description of Kevin Egan as a deserted husband (a "loveless [. . .] wifeless [. . .] castoff man") while "his madam" is coquetting with her lodgers in a separate residence ("rue Gît-le-Cœur," literally where the heart is laid to rest), directly reflecting the "Lacedemon" diagram, which identifies Casey with Menelaus and Madame Casey with Helen.

The "school of turtlehide whales stranded" (36,639/07/A, p. 7) appears to be a transposition of the note: "2. School of seals." The long passage about drowning and the drowned corpse (36,639/07/A, p. 7–8) echoes: "6. Drowned Aias." The draft also includes a passage that was later moved to the "Nestor" episode, describing the wanderings of the Jewish people and symbolically of mankind ("They sinned against the light. Old oracle. And I? And we? Wanderers to this day." 36,639/07/A, p. 7). It may derive from: "9. Menelaus wandering."

Walter Goulding, who is chided for his suspicion and for not properly welcoming his cousin Stephen (36,639/07/A, p. 4), seems to be an incarnation of Etoneous, the boorish valet of note 2. And uncle Richie, as he displays his operatic voice, may be a representation of both the minstrel and the clowns in note 1. Other possible echoes are less convincing, but we know that Joyce was fond of far-fetched correspondences. For instance, the midwife's bag with a fetus wrapped in ruddy wool (36,639/07/A, p. 6) may refer to Helen's silver basket and violet wool in note 15. The examples already given are sufficient, however, to show that the "Lacedemon" notes must precede the "Proteus" draft and therefore have been taken before the end of 1917.

The notes were used again for later drafts of this episode, and some of them were incorporated into other episodes, either directly or via some other note repository into which they had been transferred in the meantime.

For instance, the idea of the father's resemblance (from note 16) appears in the subsequent extant draft of "Proteus" (Buffalo V.A. 3), and the phrase "the man with my voice" is an addition to the passage. The word "tanist" (from note 6) also appears in this draft. Arthur Griffith, perhaps a replacement for James Stephens (from note 10), appears as a marginal pencil addition to the same passage.[24]

Note 12. "Menelaus—'poor dear Ulysses'" transited through the "Proteus" section of NLI notebook MS 36,639/5A p.29 ("poor dear Ulysses") before being used as "Poor dear Arius" on the first page proofs of "Proteus."

Other notes from this page migrated to different episodes, probably at an early stage. For instance, the constellation of betraying women, Helen of Troy/Kitty O'Shea/O'Rourke's consort, is exposed in "Nestor" (*U* 2.390–94). John Howard Parnell is presented as the shadow of his brother in "Lestrygonians" (*U* 8.500–502).

Now, if we try to look at the larger picture, these notes can give us some valuable indications about Joyce's working procedure in the early days of the writing of *Ulysses,* but also more generally about the creative process. This document shows that Joyce took detailed notes on the Homeric text at a very early stage of drafting. Is it an exceptionally preserved example of Joyce's normal writing procedure at the time?[25] Or is it an exception in Joyce's mode of writing? Did Joyce take similar, systematic and consecutive, notes on the text of Homer as the basis for drafting the other episodes of *Ulysses?* We cannot answer with certainty, but Joyce's procedures are usually very consistent, so there is a good probability that this was the way that Joyce was working, at least for the early episodes. In the case of "Telemachus," however, we know that it is based on repurposed fragments that were composed for *Portrait,*[26] so the correspondences between the episode and the Homeric text must have been found retrospectively.

We do not know why the notes were numbered, and then later renumbered, in the left margin, but this obviously indicates an attempt to arrange, and then rearrange, even if we do not know the principle of organization. The most interesting point is that Joyce starts a new sequence of numbers when he reaches the story of Proteus. The corresponding part of the source text is one of those characteristic Homeric stories within a story: Menelaus tells Telemachus of his encounter with Proteus. The new sequence of numbers shows that Joyce decided that this could be the substance for a new episode, and the decision was clearly ratified by the drawing of a box around this set of notes.[27] We can guess that the "Lacedemon" episode never went further than this initial planning and was absorbed into what should have been one of its component parts, the "Proteus" episode. This determines the realistic as well as the symbolic characteristics of the chapter: it will take place on the strand, it will be about sea change, Protean transformation, including metamorphosis of language (philology will be the art assigned to the episode in the Gorman/Gilbert schema). It will also determine the style and technique of the episode (reflecting the fluidity of stream of consciousness) in conformity with Joyce's view that "each adventure [. . .] should not only condition but even create its own technique."[28] (Joyce wrote to Édouard Dujardin on November 10, 1917, to ask him for a copy of *Les Lauriers sont coupés,* so we may suppose that it was at that time that he decided to use a form of sustained interior monologue for the third episode.)

Even if further early Homeric notes of the same kind should be discovered, this document would remain unique in that it allows us to observe at close range how the idea of one episode emerged in the process of taking notes for another one. It allows us to witness the first moment of the protean transformation of a virtual chapter into a different but actual one. And it confirms that authorial intentions are inevitably subject to a process of metamorphosis as soon as they begin to become actualized.

Ulysses notebooks and notesheets

Joyce acknowledged that he had learned from the Jesuits "how to gather, how to order and how to present a given material."[29] It would be a mistake to think that only the first part of this program is relevant to note-taking. The three verbs do not describe successive and independent actions but a single intricate process. You cannot gather without ordering in some way, and this order will largely condition the future presentation. Reciprocally, when there is an existing or contemplated order, it will influence the gathering. However, during part of Joyce's writing career, it appears that the gathering of material and the organizing of this material were performed separately, in successive phases, on distinct surfaces.

We saw that, after the Subject Notebook, all the extant notes for *Ulysses* were organized into sections labeled by *Ulysses* episodes under their Homeric titles. This is true of all the extant *organized* notes that are to be found in the "Episode notebooks," three notebooks kept at the NLI (MSS 36,639/04, 36,639/05/A and 36,639/05/B) and one notebook kept in Buffalo (V.A.2.b), and in the large notesheets in the British Library. But if we consider the way the notes are written and located on the page in these documents, we will find that they do not look like spontaneous notes taken on the spur of the moment or in the process of reading a source (fig. 6.2).

This is especially true when we compare them to another Buffalo notebook (V.A.2.a, formerly called VIII.A.5). [fig. 6.3] V.A.2.a is what Luca Crispi calls a "first-order" notebook,[30] while the others are "second-order" (at least); that is to say the materials they contain have been copied from preexisting notes.

Frank Budgen, who was very close to Joyce while he was writing *Ulysses,* speaks of his

little writing blocks specially made for the waistcoat pocket. At intervals, alone or in conversation, seated or walking, one of these tablets was produced, and a word or two scribbled on it at lightning speed as ear or memory served his turn.[31]

Budgen mentions "ear or memory" (conversations heard or ideas remembered) as sources for these spontaneous notes, but he does not mention taking notes from written sources. It makes sense, however, that notes taken in the course of reading can hardly be registered directly in a predefined grid. Indeed, this is confirmed by V.A.2.a, the only surviving first-order *Ulysses* notebook, which is almost entirely occupied by reading notes.[32]

As a repository of reading notes, largely concerned with Homeric matter,[33] it is interesting to compare this notebook with the "Lacedemon" page that we studied in the previous section. There is nothing here like the con-

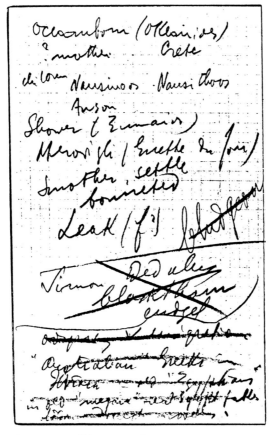

Figure 6.3. Buffalo V.A.2.a, formerly called VIII.A.5,
page 6 (*JJA* 12:136)

tinuous numbering of the notes that characterized the earlier document. Indeed, there is no sense of continuity: the notes do follow the course of the text being read, but desultorily, sometimes skipping hundreds of pages and then going back. Joyce was reading and taking notes from several books at the same time and annotations switch from one to another. The relation to the Homeric material is very different. In both cases, we can see Joyce's effort to assimilate it to his own universe, but the perspective is reversed. The source is no longer the guiding principle, just a pool of material from which elements can be arbitrarily drawn when they are liable to be adapted to the needs of a projected narrative, so as to enrich it and provide a supplement of reference.

For instance, Joyce reads in Bérard's *Les Phéniciens et l'Odyssée* that the inhabitants of Djerba, the lotus eaters, were generous with visitors and freely gave of their narcotic food to all comers. Seafarers passed the tip to each other:

Ils donnent le lotos aux marins qui les visitent; il les traite si bien que, chez eux, les équipages désertent [. . .]. Jusqu'à nos jours les navigateurs se sont transmis ce renseignement: [. . .] les habitants de Djerba sont très hospitaliers. (II, p. 107)

Joyce notes:

Get wind of it (Glasnevin)
Lotos—priest give it to any chap that
came along.
grey bootsole, petticoat (V.A.2.a, p. 3)

The Bérard passage suggests two separate ideas for two different chapters. The first is for "Hades" (Glasnevin): when someone dies, flies and rats somehow get the information that food is available:

Wonder does the news go about whenever a fresh one is let down. Underground communication. We learned that from them. Wouldn't be surprised. Regular square feed for them. Flies come before he's well dead. Got wind of Dignam. (*U* 6.990–93)

More predictably, the second idea is for the "Lotus Eaters" episode: the Holy Communion is another drug that is dispensed to anyone who wants it. This idea comes with a strong visual impression (unrelated to the source) of Bloom's rear view of the soles and laces of the priest kneeling in front of the ciborium. A whole passage derives from those three lines of note (*U* 5.344–70).

This kind of free-ranging association was Joyce's favorite mode of exploitation of his sources, the one that was most suited to his form of creativity. We know that there were many more such notebooks.[34] Joyce mentions five kilos of notes that were left in Trieste: a good proportion of these must have been first-order notes. The problem with this kind of note is that, when they are needed, it is very difficult to retrieve them among thousands of pages of scribblings randomly positioned on a neutral space. Joyce obviously felt it necessary to devise a retrieval system. The Homeric list of episodes, or rather the list of the chapters, named after Homer, of Joyce's own novel in progress, provided a grid into which the notes could be deposited and recovered when wanted.

It doesn't mean that the notes were irrevocably assigned to the corresponding episode. After some time, if they had not already been used in the process of writing and revising, they were transferred to another note repository, sometimes in a section bearing the name of the same episode but sometimes in a different section altogether, and the process could be repeated a number of times. For instance, if we take a single "Circe" notesheet, we find that it contains elements that had been stored previously in at least three different notebooks and four other notesheets. Its content was subsequently transferred to two notebooks, one notesheet and two different drafts.[35]

If we now compare the "Episode notebooks" and the notesheets to the "Lacedemon" page, we must not be misled by the superficial resemblance. Even if Joyce, when he started to take notes on the corresponding part of the *Odyssey,* had the (vague) intention of writing a "Laced(a)emon" episode, the underlined title on top of the page doesn't have the same significance as the episode titles in the various "Episode notebooks." In the first case, we see Joyce engaged in a process of mapping his own text onto the Homeric text. He is looking for points of anchor on which he will be able to establish his narrative. But in the "Episode notebooks," he is projecting various elements (including potential Homeric correspondences) onto the firmly established structure of his own book in progress. Instead of being mainly source oriented, they are destination oriented.

When Joyce completed *Ulysses,* he was forty. We could expect that his working method, in particular his method of taking and organizing his notes, would be stabilized by then and that he would simply transpose it for the preparation of his next work. We are going to see that things are not so simple.

7

The Reading Notes II

"With Some Reserve"

We have seen that Joyce tried different forms of organization for his notes as his project for *Ulysses* was developing. Before his plan for the book was completely settled, if we can extrapolate from the single example of the "Lacedemon" page, he took notes closely following the Homeric text and then tried to establish a sequence with a numbering system that unfortunately remains mysterious. At the same time, or probably a little later, in the Subject Notebook, he reverted to a solution that he had tried earlier, a classification by themes. Finally, when the plan of the book was firmly established, he used it as a grid to store the elements that he had picked in his first-order notebooks.

In the case of the writing of *Finnegans Wake,* none of these strategies could be exactly replicated and this is one of the reasons for Joyce's difficulties in the transition from one book to the other (see chapter 3).

Scribbledehobble, the second-order notebooks, and the arts of memory

In Peter Spielberg's catalogue of the Joyce manuscripts in the Poetry/Rare Books collection of the University at Buffalo, the notebooks relating to *Finnegans Wake* have been classified in four different categories: VI.A, VI.B, VI.C and VI.D. There is only one notebook in the VI.A category: the large copybook known as *Scribbledehobble* that we discussed briefly in chapter 3. It was first thought to be the "ur-workbook for *Finnegans Wake,*"[1] but we now know that it is a second-order notebook and that at least two first-order notebooks precede it.[2] In some respects, it is similar to the second-order "Episode notebooks" of *Ulysses.* Indeed, since its table of contents is modeled on the list of Joyce's previously published works, some of its sections bear the Homeric names of the *Ulysses* episodes and look very much like the corresponding sections of the "Episode notebooks." There is, however, an obvious difference: Joyce is looking backward instead of looking forward. Insofar as the "Episode notebooks" used a classification by destination, VI.A cannot work in the same way, since Joyce had no clear view of what kind of a book he was writing and there was no pilot text to lean on. (We saw that the legend of Tristan and Isolde did play an important part in the early development of the book, but it was quite incapable of playing a part comparable to the *Odyssey*.)

In chapter 3, we saw some of the specific reasons that could explain this backward turn at a crucial moment in the transition between *Ulysses* and *Finnegans Wake*. But, on the other hand, the apparent aberration of the *Scribbledehobble* helps us to keep in mind that the primary function of Joyce's second-order notebooks is not to act as convenient waiting rooms in which material could be pigeonholed in anticipation of the moment it would be poured into the marked destination: before that, these notebooks serve as a retrieval system.

As such, *Scribbledehobble* can be compared to another retrieval system, the system of memorial places (*loci memoriae*) of the Greek and Roman orators, which remained an important preoccupation for Thomas Aquinas and particularly for Giordano Bruno. It consisted in memorizing a series of rooms in a building, or a sequence of designated places in some form of organized space, and then depositing information into these, so as to be able to recover it easily by mentally visiting the building or space. Bloom makes use of a form of this technique in "Aeolus" when he uses an address in Dublin to recall the telephone number of Keyes ("Number? Yes. Same as Citron's house. Twentyeight." *U* 7.220). To make the connections he needs for his trade, he refers to the administrative geography of the city. The purpose is to anchor the evanescent flow of memories into a robust spatial structure.[3] The purpose is similar in Joyce's second-order notebooks: to be able to recover ideas that had been haphazardly scattered onto the neutral surface of thousands of undifferentiated pages. For *Scribbledehobble,* since the architecture of the work in progress was still totally undefined, the nomenclature of his previously published work offered a solid frame of reference.

The mythical origins of spatial mnemonics are suggestive. Simonides of Ceos, a Greek poet, is said to have invented it in very brutal circumstances.

He had been commissioned to sing an ode in praise of a rich man during a banquet, but he had devoted half the ode to the praise of Apollo, so the man refused to pay the full price. During the banquet Simonides was called out (presumably by a messenger of Apollo), and while he was outside, a huge rock fell from the sky and crushed the house and all the guests. All the bodies were so mangled that it was impossible to identify the guests in order to give them a burial. But Simonides found that he was able to visualize the places where each was sitting and thus to allocate the remains to the bereaved families. This discovery is supposed to have led to the invention of the method of loci.

The myth, with its unnamable substance, its bodily pulp dispersed and then reassigned to its rightful place and identity, suggests that the technique is fundamentally an instrument of discrimination and of control, imposing a stable spatial grid onto a fluid substance. At least this is the way it is theoretically supposed to operate, but it does not work as smoothly as its proponents would have it. From a Joycean point of view, the malfunctions of the system are, predictably, an important creative factor.

One of the problems with the method is that a building, or any form of spatial grid, can offer only a certain number of places before losing its usefulness and becoming a confusing labyrinth; if the rooms are not emptied (and it is not easy to empty them once the link has been made between an item and a position), they soon become crammed with a plethora of objects, competing for attention in the same location. In this respect, the worse enemy of the system is not amnesia but hypermnesia. During the writing of *Ulysses,* Joyce palliated this effect, in practice, by periodically reshuffling his notes, moving them, after a process of sifting, into new (third- fourth- and even fifth-order) notebooks or notesheets. But by doing so, he created new contexts, that is to say potential new memories that became attached to them. Uprooting and transplanting are not neutral operations: the roots inevitably retain some of their native soil. As we already had the occasion to see at different levels, a displaced element brings with it something of its place of origin, the memory of another context that interferes with the present situation. The impression of cramming, of surfeit, produced by the general structure of *Ulysses* as well as its details, down to the portmanteau words that appear there and proliferate in *Finnegans Wake,* can be related to a hypermnesiac superposition not just of one set of elements over a single spatial series but of different planes of projection competing with one another.[4]

This is compounded by another problem, which we could call "paramnesia." In a temporal sequence, each moment is contiguous with the previous and the next moment, while in a spatial arrangement, there are many possible contiguities: the atrium, for instance, is next to all the other rooms on the same floor, and then there might be a basement or an attic. . . Any element is liable to establish connections with several different neighbors. In the terms of Deleuze and Guattari, the memory systems would be described as "striated spaces,"[5] but the grooves are never deep enough to prevent frequent slippage and interference.

The trivial incidents of the daily life of Dublin are mapped onto the time-honored structure of the *Odyssey,* but also onto the Mediterranean of Bérard, but also onto Irish history, but also onto a nomenclature of the arts, of the colors, and so on, and we find that at each level there is no one-to-one correspondence: Molly Bloom is Calypso *and* Penelope *and* Helen of Troy, but she is also associated with Kitty O'Shea *and* O'Rourke's consort, and so on . . .

Beyond these complications, inherent to the system, that Joyce knows how to exploit fully, there is a deeper conflict. The techniques of *memoria artificialis* must take into account another very different, more basic, more primitive, type of memory. As Freud puts it in a letter to Fliess, "memory stinks"[6]; it brings us back to an archaic past, when we walked on all fours and our nose was very close to our neighbor's behind. Artificial (or artful) memory systems endeavor to deodorize this corporal memory, to sanitize it—after all, the point of Simonides's feat of memory was to bury properly the mangled bodies in their allotted places before they started to smell.

Joyce's work foregrounds a very carnal memory. Or rather it stages the return of the repressed, the coexistence and interference of two memorial universes: an Apollonian universe, where memory is controlled by a spatial system, a universe where marble statues of Greek goddesses, arranged between the stately memorial pillars of a library, have no anus and no smell, as Bloom finds out to his dismay; and another universe of affective and olfactive memory, where Bloom is guided home by the recollection of melonsmellonous hemispheres.

The two are inextricably associated in this passage from "Aeolus," which follows directly Bloom's use of Citron's address to recover a telephone number:

Heavy greasy smell there always is in those works. Lukewarm glue in Thom's next door when I was there.

He took out his handkerchief to dab his nose. Citron lemon? Ah, the soap I put there. Lose it out of that pocket. Putting back his handkerchief he took the soap and stowed it away, buttoned, into the hip pocket of his trousers.

What perfume does your wife use? I could go home still: tram: (*U* 7.225)

The odor of the printer's works conjures up the memory of a smell of the past: each of them is immediately pinned down to a spatial reference (*there— next door*). It is not a matter of indifference that one of the references should be to Thom's, the place of origin of the directory that maps Dublin with the greatest precision—a kind of paper reduplication of Dublin, itself reduplicated by Joyce in several respects. In the process of blocking out the offensive odor, another fragrance arises (that of the lemon soap), bringing up Citron again, this time not deliberately, as an element of an active mnemonic system, but as an involuntary recollection combining a scent and a verbal association. As soon as the smell has been assigned to its origin, the loose, fragrant soap must be confined to a buttoned pocket. But this cannot prevent a new, highly sexualized, redolent memory to arise, associating Bloom's fantasied flirtation and his wife's impending adultery. This in turn induces a temptation to reoccupy the spatial origin in order to control the drift.

After this excursus, we can return to *Scribbledehobble* and perhaps understand better its complex, composite nature. It was used by Joyce as a convenient, readily available architecture to organize some of the tentative notes that he had collected since he had completed *Ulysses,* notes that were all the more scattered since they had been taken without a really definite purpose. Concretely, it means that it was used somewhat like the Subject Notebook: the notes related to music, for instance, are regrouped in the "Sirens" section; most of the notes about Tristan and Isolde are to be found in the *Exiles* sections; the "Nausikaa" section seems to be oriented toward women and women's language, and so on. However, this thematic organization is only part of the story: many notations cannot be understood in this way. More than half of the notes in the "Sirens" section have nothing to do with music, so why did Joyce deposit them there? Very often, it is impossible to tell: it might be a simple mood, a personal reminiscence. There must be some association in Joyce's memory between the note and the published work to which it is assigned that connects it to the network of associations that had been created there. It might also be a deliberate juxtaposition. The new idea is grafted, more or less forcefully, upon the old stock of the published work so as to benefit from its roots, in the hope that it will help it to flourish.

As in the case of *Ulysses,* the fusion of the elements needed "a prolonged existence together,"[7] but there was also the hope that the process of maturation and amalgamation could be helped by putting the elements in boxes endowed with certain properties, in the same way as Bloom's handkerchief acquires a lemony scent because it is stored in a pocket contaminated by the soap or as Joyce's youthful aesthetic fragments had been dignified by being inscribed among a collection of quotations from Aristotle, Aquinas and Ben Jonson.[8]

However that may be, after only a few months Joyce abandoned this puzzling form of organization. He continued to make use of the remaining hundreds of blank pages in the large copybook, but the notes that were entered after 1923 appear completely unrelated to the titles under which they were inscribed.

The undifferentiated space of the "B" notebooks

The second kind of *Finnegans Wake* notebooks in Peter Spielberg's catalogue of the manuscripts at Buffalo is the VI.B category: it covers essentially the first-order notebooks. If there is only one extant first-order notebook for *Ulysses,* approximately fifty such notebooks are available for *Finnegans Wake.* To simplify, we can say that, taken together, these documents constitute a huge list of items, haphazardly scribbled one beneath the other, along thousands of notebook pages, without any indication of origin. Some of these are tagged, on the fly, with signs, the "sigla," that tentatively assign them to one of the protagonists of the planned book, or to a particular passage.[9] For instance, the third entry from the bottom of the left page in figure 7.1, "triliteral root," is preceded by a little drawing that looks like a capital *E* rotated 90 degrees clockwise and means that this entry is related to HCE.

Some of the listed items are conceptual notes for "Work in Progress" or details from Joyce's daily life, but the vast majority are reading notes; that is to say they are extracts from a great variety of texts, ranging from silly journalistic echoes to classical masterpieces, from advertisements and obituaries to serious works of anthropology or linguistics. The extracts tend to be brief: a single word, or a short phrase, and no reference is made to their source. Let us look for instance at the right-hand page in figure 7.1.

The source of the second and third items on the page ("redemptorist" and "quadwrangle") has not been located, but it has been possible to ascertain that the others come from Ernest Hemingway's collection of short stories *In Our Time,* which had just been published when Joyce was compiling this notebook.[10] It is not particularly surprising that he should have read this book from a young writer who was a friend. He may have been told that he appeared in the book among other avant-garde celebrities.[11] But it is interesting to see the kind of notes that result from this reading. They are so short that it would be impossible to identify the source in isolation. The cluster, however, demonstrates that they do come from *In Our Time* and allows us to follow the thread of Joyce's reading.

The first note, "in the morn," comes from the story "Indian Camp," on page 19 of the book; "canthooks" and "ojibway" both come from "The Doctor and the Doctor's Wife" on page 28; "dipper" comes from the story "The Three Day Blow," on page 54; "caboose" and "felt <u>of</u> his knee" come from the story "The Battler" on page 65. These page numbers show that Joyce was reading the book sequentially, and this confirms what the spatial disposition of the left-hand page of the notebook seems to suggest: "yeth yup / yep yis / yest yezz / yeb yedz / yeffs" and "tamarack" are additions to the list on the right. They come, respectively, from the story "The Three Day Blow" on page 49[12] and from "The Battler" on page 65 of the book and are meant to go before "dipper" and before "caboose." To this list we should add two words from "The Battler" on the top of the next page (page 17 of the notebook, see fig. 7.2): "crut," on page 65 in Hemingway's book, and "thanks a lot," on page 73.

At this point, Joyce interrupted his reading of Hemingway and took notes from other sources, including Freud's *Collected Papers.* He resumed on page 25 of the notebook with three more notes from Hemingway's book: "cuadrilla," from an interlude on page 125 of *In Our Time;* "Khuds," from the story "Cross-Country Snow," page 142; and "2 decies," from the same story on page 144. The phrase "in back," from "Out of Season" on page 131, was presumably inserted at the same time on the bottom of page 19 of the notebook.

The note-taking is sporadic and desultory: isolated words, two unusual phrases ("felt <u>of</u> his knee"—the underlining is Joyce's; "on back"), a relatively

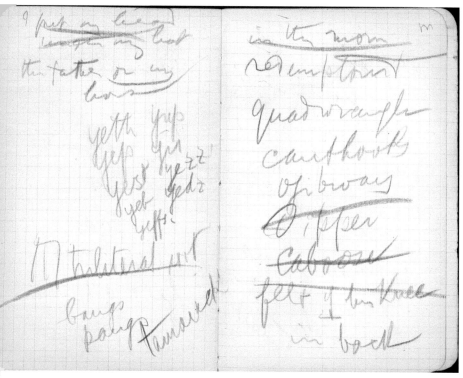

figure 7.1. Buffalo notebook VI.B.19–14–15 (*JJA* 33:215).

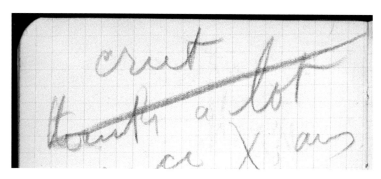

Figure 7.2. The top of page 16 of Buffalo notebook VI.B.19 (*JJA* 33:216).

recent expression ("thanks a lot"), but nothing that really gives an idea of what is in the book. What can be the point of such notes?

We have seen that Joyce had the habit of crossing out notes as he used them, so we immediately know which of these entries were incorporated in the drafts of *Finnegans Wake*.[13] Strangely, the most characteristic words ("tamarack," "canthooks," "ojibway," "crut") are not crossed out, which means that they were finally ignored. The notes crossed out in green crayon ("in the morn," "dipper," "caboose" "felt of his knee," "thanks a lot") were all used in the first draft of what will become *Finnegans Wake* Book III, chapter 4 (see 584.03, 581.14, 586.26, 565.08, and 582.03). In spite of the relative proximity (four of them appear within a span of five pages in the final text), it is absolutely impossible for the reader of *Finnegans Wake* to identify their source. Their characteristics have been erased: the dipper (in Hemingway a kind of wooden ladle) appears in the new context as a constellation; the caboose (a trainman's car at the rear of a freight train) is combined with another entry to make "caboosh," suggesting in context the French *caboche,* meaning "head"; and the oddity of the phrase "felt of his knee" is completely lost when it appears as "place my hand [. . .] upon thee knee." Even the most perceptive of readers and probably even the keenest artificial intelligence could not recognize Hemingway under the surface of Joyce's text.

The same is true of the notes that we find on the next two pages and that come from the third volume of Freud's *Collected Papers,* very recently published by "Leonard et Virginia Woolf at the Hogarth Press, 52 Tavistock Square, London, W.C. and the Institute of Psycho-Analysis."[14] It is striking that the words noted by Joyce include very few psychoanalytical terms and that most of the items that are crossed out are particularly uncharacteristic: for instance, "little girls" noted on page 17 of VI.B.19, or "Unless I am mistaken," on page 36 of the same notebook. Did Joyce really need to read Freud to think of these phrases? And when Joyce notes a phrase that is more identifiably Freudian: "father surrogate," from a sentence in the Wolfman case study ("in my patient's case the wolf was merely a first father surrogate"),[15] the pun that is introduced on the notebook page changing "father surrogate" to "vice-father" ensures that the text in *FW* 480.25–26, "a child's dread for dragon vice-father," is untraceable to its origin.

But there is another reason why the sources are lost on the reader; it is because they are often so trite that they are indistinct in the background noise

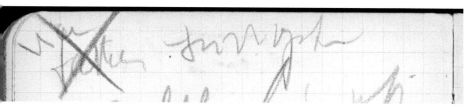

Figure 7.3. The top of page 70 of notebook VI.B.19 (*JJA* 33:243).

of culture. If a cluster of notes had not been found in notebook VI.B.6,[16] who could guess that the words "visibly unmoved" on *FW* 430.14 come from an article called "Today and Yesterday" in the *Irish Independent* of February 13, 1923? The notebooks reveal that this type of indistinguishable source is extremely common in *Finnegans Wake*.

A library of indistinction

We have seen that Joyce bragged about his usage of the eight parts of the *Fuga per canonem* to structure the "Sirens" chapter without making the effort to really understand what these terms referred to. It is significant that while he is writing *Finnegans Wake,* he, on the contrary, downplays mockingly his reference to Mesopotamian mythology in a letter to Harriet Shaw Weaver:

> The words expressing nightmares are from Greek, German, Irish, Japanese, Italian (my niece's childish pronunciation) and Assyrian (the star-group called the "gruesome hound"). I speak the latter language very fluently and have several nice volumes of it in the kitchen printed on jampots. (*Letters* I 226)

It is only by deciphering a few words in another notebook (VI.B.14) that we have been able to discover that Joyce had read Stephen Langdon's *Enuma Elish: The Babylonian Epic of Creation* (1923), whence came the reference to the "gruesome hound."[17] It would be impossible to identify the traces of the *Enuma Elish* directly in *Finnegans Wake*. For instance, who would recognize that "trying on my garden substisuit" (*FW* 487.11) comes from a note to the Mesopotamian Epic ("Theoretically the king was present at certain vital parts of every New Year festival in each city, but that was of course impossible, and as substitute he sent his royal garments.") by way of an addition to a typescript ("trying on my garment substitute," *JJA* 58:177)?

Whereas in *A Portrait* Stephen Dedalus was ready to suffer a few beatings from his peers in order to affirm his difference among them by building a secessionist library, electing Byron rather than Tennyson, Hugo rather than Louis Veuillot, in *Ulysses,* already, Stephen distances himself from his youthful hyper-selective reading of "the fading prophecies of Joachim Abbas" in the "stagnant bays of March's library" (*U* 3.107–8). The library of *Ulysses* progressively changes in character; it becomes much less exclusive and shifts toward Bloom, the common man. Alongside immortal classics, such as Homer, Dante and Shakespeare, it includes disposable literature (such as *Matcham's Masterstroke*) to read at stool, *Physical Strength and How to Obtain It,* by Eugen Sandow, as well as the *Prophetiae Abbatis Joachimi,* Aristotle's spurious *Masterpiece* as well as Aristotle's *Poetics* and *Metaphysics,* pop songs such as *The Seaside Girls,* as well as the *Fuga per Canonem* and Pope Marcellus's Mass. This becomes even more prevalent in *Finnegans Wake.* Joyce chooses precisely the type of books that Stephen disdainfully discards in the bookseller's cart: *The Irish Beekeeper, Life and Miracles of the Curé of Ars, Pocket Guide to Killarney* (*U* 10.838–39). The choice of books is much less distinguished. We can go as far as saying that they are no longer an instrument of distinction but quite the opposite. This is not to say that there are no sophisticated or rare works in the *Wake.* But they are outnumbered by leaflets, newspapers, secondhand manuals and bad books of all sorts.[18] The library of aesthetic posturing has not been replaced by the library of indistinction, but it is drowned in it.

Progressively, we come to suspect (and the notebooks go a long way to demonstrate) that every word in the *Wake,* even the most ordinary looking, is a quotation from an invisible library. In the same way, the dirt of the road is composed of the dust of our predecessors, Great Men and anonymous multitudes combined. Joyce's writing progressively becomes more and more absorbed by the rumor of the world, the indistinct babble and Babel, the continuous murmur of the printed universe.

But what is the point, one may ask, of this indistinct background? To understand what is at stake for Joyce, we will leave aside for a moment the *Finnegans Wake* notes and consider a very different kind: the preparatory notes that Joyce made for the writing of *Exiles* a decade earlier.

"A certain reserve": The *Exiles* notes

For many readers of Joyce (including myself), *Exiles* is a disappointing play, not quite worthy of his other published works. But it becomes quite interesting when we consider it together with the surviving preparatory notes (Buffalo III.A). These notes are like nothing else in the extant Joyce archive. Except for a few terse remarks, Joyce practically never comments on his work in his manuscripts. Here, on the contrary, Joyce explains his own intentions at length and reminds himself of the real nature of his characters and of their deepest motivations. Another strange feature of these notes is the methodical development of long chains of associations triggered by words or lists of words. This gives us the impression that the somewhat stilted words spoken by the characters on stage are overdetermined by an "Other Scene," a network of connections all but invisible in the play but occasionally made explicit in the notes.

Joyce confided to Frank Budgen that, in *Exiles,* characters act with "a certain reserve."[19] They also speak, like Beatrice in the following exchange, "with some reserve," that is, with reticence and "with something in reserve":

RICHARD: And you gave him your garter. Is it allowed to mention that?
BEATRICE (with some reserve): If you think it worthy of mention.
(*E* 23)

Indeed, why mention this incongruous, unwarranted detail? Why is it worthy of mention and why does it call for Beatrice's reserve? What is behind this garter? The most obvious answer would be to speak of fetishism, in the Freudian sense. The garter derives its value metonymically from the woman's thigh and the proximity to her genitals.[20] Joyce's partiality for female undergarments is well known. He even claimed that women's drawers interested him more than what was inside them. This should prevent us from saying simply that female underwear (drawers, garters) is a metonymic substitute (a "substisuit") for a woman's genitals. It would be more accurate, according to Freudian orthodoxy, to say that it stands for what is missing there. But *Exiles* openly acknowledges that women, and implicitly women's sexual organs, are just one link in a chain of association. They serve as an intermediary enabling conjunction between males.

Robert: You love this woman. I remember all you told me long ago. She is yours, your work. *(Suddenly.)* And that is why I, too, was drawn to her. You are so strong that you attract me even through her. (*E* 87)

This is made very explicit in the notes:

The bodily possession of Bertha by Robert, repeated often, would certainly bring into almost carnal contact the two men. Do they desire this? To be united, that is carnally through the person and body of Bertha as they cannot, without dissatisfaction and degradation—be united carnally man to man as man to woman? (*E* 172)

And reciprocally:

Richard, unfitted for the adulterous intercourse with the wives of his friends because it would involve a great deal of pretence on his part rather than because he is convinced of any dishonourableness in it wishes, it seems, to feel the thrill of adultery vicariously and to possess a bound woman Bertha through the organ of his friend. (*E* 174)

When Joyce analyses the play's dominant force, jealousy, he quotes Spinoza's explanation, according to which it expresses a repugnance caused by the association of the image of the beloved with the excrements and the shameful parts of someone else (*"pudendis et excrementis alterius jungere imaginem rei amatae"*), considering that this explanation is unsatisfactory. But he suggests that it would be enough to change the negative sign under which Spinoza set the *imaginem jungere* (associating the image) into a positive sign ("Separated from hatred and having its baffled lust converted into an erotic stimulus" *E* 165) to understand the force that drives Richard to push his lover into the arms of Robert.

Beatrice herself is presented as a go-between in the relation between Richard and Robert. The connection to a third party causes the attraction but also the reserve, with its double aspect of impoverished surface and underlying riches. Interpreting the nature of this vicarious sexual attraction is not our concern here. The erotic transfer is only one of the links of an associative chain that extends much further. It is primarily a verbal chain ("your names were always spoken together," says Richard to Beatrice to account for his own "reserve").

To return to the word "garter,"[21] we can see that it is the representative of a vast network of associations that is not accessible in the text but deploys itself in the notes. In a note dated November 12, 1913, we find the following string: "Garter: precious, Prezioso, Bodkin, music, palegreen, bracelet, cream sweets, lily of the valley, convent garden (Galway), sea" (*E* 167). This chain of key words is further developed in a very long note dated November 13, picking up some of these elements, glossing them ("[Bodkin's] attendant images are the trinkets and toys of girlhood (bracelet, cream sweets, palegreen lily of the valley, the convent garden)."), extending in various directions to meet some of Joyce's previously written work (*Chamber Music* XI, "The Dead," the poem "She Weeps over Rahoon").

The interesting point is that this does not represent directly Joyce's own associations. The note is prefixed with an "N. (B)," which presumably means *Nora (Bertha)*. As a matter of fact, the string beginning with Nora's recent admirer in Trieste (Prezioso) continues with her early attachment for Michael Bodkin and more generally with images from her youth in Galway. But it soon becomes clear that the words cannot really be Nora's. This is confirmed when the perspective abruptly shifts from Nora to Bertha, from Joyce's companion to the character in the play in progress. The long developments are Joyce's rambling interpretations deriving from a starting point that seems to have been provided by Nora's free verbal associations or her memories of a dream. The purpose of this strange impersonation seems to be to flesh out Bertha's character but also to accumulate a *reserve* behind his text.

Toward the end of the notes, Joyce remarks:

Perhaps it would be well to make a separate sketch of the doings of each of the four chief persons during the night, including those whose actions are not revealed to the public in the dialogue, namely Beatrice and Richard. (*E* 175)

The idea that the writer should have more in store than what is revealed to the public is what Hemingway would later call the iceberg theory:

If a writer of prose knows enough of what he is writing about he may omit things that he knows and the reader, if the writer is writing truly enough, will have a feeling of those things as strongly as though the writer had stated them. The dignity of movement of an iceberg is due to only one-eighth of it being above water.[22]

In Joyce's case, the notion should be extended beyond elements of plot or character. For him, the surface text needs to be rooted in an underlying verbal soil. As a young writer, it was enough for him to draw from Skeat's etymologies, which he read "by the hour," but he soon realized that he was not really interested in words embalmed in a dictionary. In the same way as, for Richard Rowan in *Exiles* (and, to a certain extent, for Bloom in *Ulysses*),[23] women derive their value from having been associated (*imaginem jungere*) with other men, for Joyce, words and phrases become interesting (I would go as far as to say that they acquire a libidinal charge) when they have been used by someone else: Nora, people around him, or the author of any work that he happened to read. The words stolen[24] from such sources carry with them a wealth of associations that are valuable for Joyce, even if they remain cryptic for his reader. This becomes increasingly important when his texts, from mid-*Ulysses* onward, become less and less representational and more and more associational.

Invisible intertextuality and generalized agrammaticality

This raises an interesting theoretical question: can we speak of an intertextual relationship between two texts (as opposed to a simple relation of derivation) when the relationship is imperceptible to the reader? I am not referring to the many esoteric allusions concealed in *Ulysses* or in *Finnegans Wake* that are a challenge to the sagacity of the reader, nor to the burlesque deformations that transfigure the most famous quotations to such an extent that they become difficult to recognize. For instance, when we read "trespassing on the space question where even michelangelines fool to dread" (*FW* 160.36–161.01) or "A king off duty and a jaw for ever!" (*FW* 162.35), it takes us a few moments to recognize Pope's "Fools rush in where angels fear to tread" or Keats's "A thing of beauty is a joy for ever." The effect is a delayed reaction, an uncanny shock of recognition, all the stronger because we have felt momentarily estranged from our most familiar cultural background. Similarly, after a few years, the critics have taken up Joyce's challenge and published a host of scholarly works identifying *the books at the Wake*.[25] This moment of suspension induced by Joyce's delaying tactics is part of a generalized strategy of deferment:

If I gave it up immediately, I'd lose my immortality. I've put in so many enigmas and puzzles that it will keep the professors busy for centuries arguing over what I meant, and that's the only way of ensuring one's immortality.[26]

However, in such cases as the insertions from *In Our Time* or from the *Irish Independent* of February 13, 1923, professors cannot even guess that there is an enigma to solve. There is no tantalizing clue left by Joyce to tease them. It is not that he has deliberately erased his traces, but in such cases he has not bothered to leave any trail of breadcrumbs or Ariadne's thread to follow.[27]

The problem raised by Joyce's most singular practice can be related to a more general question that Michael Riffaterre has called "intertextual erosion."[28] This refers to the fact that, with the passage of time, some of the cultural references tend to be forgotten: if we read the work of seventeenth-century poets, for example, we can no longer follow the allusions that were accessible to the contemporary reader. Can we say that the intertextual relation persists in such a case? According to Riffaterre, this is a "non-issue," because the text always implies the absent intertext in its structure (for him, this incompleteness is the defining characteristic of the literary text). The interference between the two systems causes a perturbation in the text. The important point is not that readers should be able to identify the intertextual reference but that they should feel the perturbation (which Riffaterre calls "agrammaticality" or "catachresis") introduced by the presence in the text of the "connector" (the extraneous element issuing from the intertext).[29] These *agrammaticalities* are not necessarily linguistic blunders but can be anything that is somewhat out of place or unforeseeable in the new context. The connector belongs both to the text and to the intertext: it is grammatical in the intertext, but when it is imported in the text, it stands out as agrammatical.

We recognize, applied to the relation between text and intertext, the mechanisms that we have seen at work in the inner (endogenetic) development of the text: decontextualization/recontextualization and memory of the context. It can be argued that what Joyce tries to achieve, the basis of his aesthetics, from his earliest literary endeavors, is precisely this: creating or observing interferences between different systems and the resulting perturbations. Joyce's early epiphanies, if we follow Stanislaus's analysis, were already concerned with a form of agrammaticality. They were "ironical observations of slips, and little errors and gestures—mere straws in the wind—by which people betrayed the very things they were most careful to conceal."[30] Small, apparently insignificant elements open another plane of meaning because they are somehow incongruous in the context.

By the time he had reached *Finnegans Wake,* Joyce is aiming for a generalized agrammaticality.[31] Take the example of the word "Hesitency," on *Finnegans Wake* 35.20. The incorrect spelling indicates a reference to Lester Pigott's forged letter and the error that caused his downfall, but the reference is a complex one. In the context of the historical trial, the misspelling stood out as agrammatical in the forged letters, literally as an orthographic blunder but also as something that was foreign to Parnell's imitated style. Therefore, it acted as a connector to an elusive intertextuality, an involuntary reference to a hidden context. The work of Parnell's counsels was to prove that it was "grammatical" in Pigott's idiosyncratic orthography. On the other hand, in *Finnegans Wake,* if *hesitency* did not recur several times, and if Parnell's story did not feature so prominently in Joyce's work, we would hardly notice the misspelling, among the profusion of deformed words. As a matter of fact, we encounter so many aberrant variants of the same word (*Hasatency, hasitancy, hathatansy, hesitensies, Hasitatense, hiscitendency, hissindensity, hosetanzies, HeCitEncy, heth hith ences . . .*) that, when we encounter the correct form (twice), toward the end of the book, we have the feeling that something is wrong! The allusive value of Pigott's particular mistake is automatically transferred to each of these deformations (including the ultimate deformation that returns it to normal). But the process does not stop there. Beyond that, we find that the act of misspelling in general becomes a reference to this involuntary confession of guilt. Every deformed word becomes a "connector" in this respect and, since misspelling is everywhere in *Finnegans Wake,* the potential intertextual reference spreads like a circular wave across the surface of the text.

In doing so, it meets other waves propagating in different directions. In chapter 2, we discussed the case of another agrammaticality: the inversion of the letters *P* and *K* and its multiple allusive value (Celtic historical linguistics, Le Brigant, Freud . . .). We saw that agrammaticality tends to proliferate: beyond the cases where the substitution is clear (for instance in the word "kurkle"), we come to suspect that any K can be a distorted P, and vice versa, and that each of them could be a connector toward the complex intertext revealed in the notebooks.

Besides such tidal waves, wreaking havoc all around, there are also a myriad of little splashes, causing only local disturbances, with each insertion of an element from the notebooks acting as a connector to its original context. In his pioneering edition of the "Index Notebook," Danis Rose suggested that, in *Finnegans Wake*, "the function of distortions was to permit the conjunction of otherwise irreconcilable [notebook] units."[32] It now seems more appropriate to say on the contrary that the function of the multiple insertions of extraneous units was to engender systematic distortions.

This is how it worked concretely: at each stage of the writing or revision of a portion of his drafts, Joyce would go over (some of) his notebooks and select the entries that could be introduced in the current state of the work in progress. The way language normally works is that at each point of the syntagm, there is a choice between different members of a definite paradigm, so as to find the appropriate one (le mot juste), however it is defined. But Joyce would move his paradigm (the vast and heterogeneous paradigm constituted by the list of elements entered, one after the other, in the notebooks at hand) along the syntagmatic chain in search of semantic or grammatical openings that would offer available slots to insert them, slots in which they would find their place but also where they would be somewhat out of order, misplaced because they are displaced from their original context.

Sometimes the oddity is unobtrusive, or even barely perceptible. Sometimes, on the contrary, the insertion stands out as violently incongruous, but the purpose is never to blend them silently in the preexisting text: some form of agrammaticality is generated by each insertion of a notebook element.

For example "thanks a lot," the note from Hemingway's *In Our Time* mentioned above, is used for the first draft of chapter 4 of Book III: "a vote of thanksalot to the hungriest coaxing experimenter" (*JJA* 60:037). In the final text, it will become: "a snatch vote of thanksalot to the huskiest coaxing experimenter" (*FW* 582.03). The coinage "thanksalot" unsettles the subjacent phrase *a vote of thanks*.

Or take this note from Chateaubriand in notebook VI.B.5: "snow=years" / downpour=day." It derives from a Native American phrase in *Atala*—"il y aura sept fois dix neiges, et trois neiges de plus"—and also from the footnote appended in the anthology for French schools that Joyce was using, "Neiges pour année, 73 ans." When Joyce uses it, he neglects Chateaubriand's original expression and retains only his own gloss (thus making identification of the

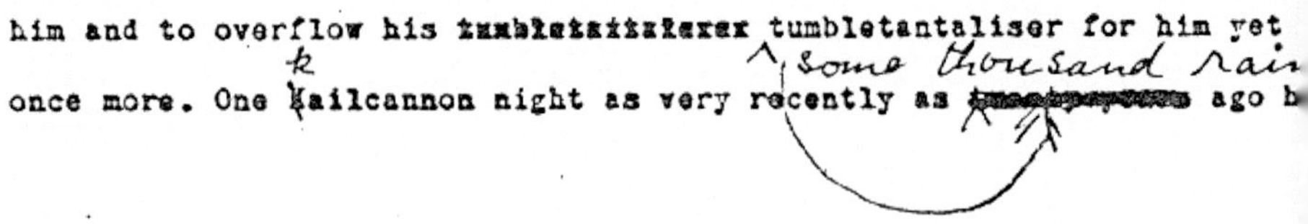

him and to overflow his ~~tumbletaitslerer~~ tumbletantaliser for him yet
once more. One ~~k~~ailcannon night as very recently as ~~twenty~~ ago b

Figure 7.4. Corrected typescript for *FW* I.7 (*JJA* 47:434).

source absolutely impossible) to suggest that in a country of frequent rains, one might count the days by counting the downpours. The insertion is made on a typescript for chapter 7 of Book I:[33]

"Some thousand rains ago" is substituted for "twenty years ago." This exotic way of measuring time clearly stands out in the distinctly Irish context. It is interesting that, shortly afterward, Joyce reinforced the rainy theme by changing "kailcannon" into "hailcannon,"[34] and then by inserting, more than twelve years later, on the galley proofs for the final publication (*JJA* 48:221), a parenthetic explanation introducing the idea of "downpour": "One hailcannon night (for his departure was attended by a heavy downpoor) as very recently as some thousand rains ago" (*FW* 174.23).

These two examples come from sources that were not explored by Joyce for a particular purpose. We have seen some of the reasons that might have led Joyce to read *In Our Time*. In the case of Chateaubriand, Joyce seems to have read him for his own pleasure, during his holidays in Brittany, because he admired his style.[35] Nevertheless, he took more than a hundred notes,[36] only a handful of which were incorporated in his drafts. Sometimes, however, Joyce's work is much more focused: he is taking notes for a particular purpose, preparing for the writing of a specific passage or for an important theme: rivers, the big cities of the world, the postal service, and so on. His work of documentation is not so different in this respect from that of other writers. The kind of notes that he takes is sometimes not unlike those of Flaubert or Zola, but the way he uses his notes is completely different. The notes prepared for a passage are entered in this passage not at one time but on several succeeding drafts, saturating the text with insertions from a particular source.[37] But once this is accomplished, the remaining notes are available for the same kind of treatment as the random notes; that is to say they are confronted to successive portions or strata of the text being written or revised until they encounter a place where they could be inserted. The same thing can be said of Joyce's tagging of some of his notes with the system of "sigla" mentioned above, assigning a note to one of the protagonists of the book or to a particular chapter. If the note doesn't prove useful in this way, it will be silently reassigned to another context.

This modus operandi probably explains why Joyce, after the early experiment of *Scribbledehobble,* did not feel the need to systematically reorganize his notes in second-order notebooks[38] as he did when writing *Ulysses:* he wished to preserve the fluidity of the direct confrontation between the syntagmatic and paradigmatic axes (the primary notes and the drafts), knowing that his method of processing material had come to such a point of sophistication that almost anything could go almost anywhere to serve the general purpose of the book (the "infinitely probable" gamble discussed in chapter 2).

The transcribed notebooks and the missing notebooks ("C" and "D")

Besides the VI.A (*Scribbledehobble*) and the VI.B (the first-order *Finnegans Wake* notebooks that we have just discussed), there are two more categories in Spielberg's catalogue of the manuscripts at Buffalo, the VI.C and the VI.D *Finnegans Wake* notebooks. Although they are not autograph manuscripts, they are worth considering, because their very peculiar nature tells us something about the status of Joyce's notes.

The "C" notebooks are transcriptions of "B" notebooks by an amanuensis, France Raphael. Between 1934 and 1938, when Joyce's problems with his eyes made it very difficult for him to read his own scribbled notes, he asked Raphael to copy the unused entries in a more legible hand. She did a relatively good job of deciphering them, but she was working against insuperable difficulties: Joyce's terrible handwriting when he was writing notes and the impossibility of anticipating what was written in the absence of any context, which is the defining characteristic of these notes.

Legrand, Poe's emblematic decipherer in the "Gold Bug," tells us that "in all cases of secret writing, the first question regards the *language* of the cipher." Raphael could not even be sure of that since Joyce would switch languages in the most unpredictable way. For instance, when he was taking notes from a French source, he would almost always use English, but sometimes he would quote a phrase in the original, and occasionally a word would come more readily to him in Italian (the language he spoke with his family). For instance, taking notes on the French text of *Les Pierres bretonnes* by Abbé Millon explaining that fairies are bribed with small quantities of fat to retrieve lost objects, Joyce would write "pay in fat to find smarriti" (using the Italian word for lost objects);[39] or, just a few lines below, when Millon reports that several Breton monoliths are thought to have been annoying pebbles shaken out of Gargantua's shoes, Joyce notes "ciotoli from boots" (approximating the Italian *ciottoli,* small stones). Not surprisingly, Madame Raphael could not make anything out of these and wrote instead the meaningless "smacrisi" and "ciotali." And we know that Joyce was liable to include words from dozens of different languages, including Swahili or Samoyed. Worse still, the notes could very well belong to several languages at once or to no language at all, in the case of Joyce's coinages. For instance "yeoroldpean" on VI.B.5, p. 30, based on Chateaubriand's use of the words "ton," "vieux," and "Europe," was understandably mistranscribed by Raphael.

The interesting point is that Joyce used these inevitably distorted notes and trusted them to a large extent. There were cases when he was able to see through the deformations and recover something of his original notes. For instance, from a passage of Dean Kinane's *Saint Patrick,* p. 127 ("'There is,' answered the Angel, 'the great sea to come over Erinn seven years before the Judgement'") he had noted, in notebook VI.B.14, p. 45: "There is the great sea to come over I[reland]—7 years before doom." In Raphael's transcription, this became "That is the great gem / to come to our J—7/ just before dawn" (VI.C.12, p. 31). Joyce was able to retrieve part of his original idea through this garbled transcription. He crossed out the first two lines and, combining this with other notes from notebook VI.B.19, wrote: "Here's the flood, the flaxen flood that's to come over fightlittle tightlittle irryland," in a draft for chapter 4 of Book III. Obviously, Joyce had remembered the great flooding sea beneath Raphael's "gem" and recognized "over I[reland]" in her "our J." An insertion on the facing page shows that he connected this flood with Saint Patrick. However, he was incapable of making anything out of "7 just before dawn," so this part of Raphael's copy was not crossed out, and the idea of the seven years before doom was abandoned (see *FW* 583.19).

In other cases, the original intention was completely lost. Joyce had written "Λc on vibrating bed."[40] Raphael, who was probably not aware that, in Joyce's shorthand, Λc meant the third chapter of the book of Shaun (chapter 3 of Book III), transcribed it as "Λ convibrating bed."[41] This resulted in an addition in chapter 4 of Book II: "convibrational bed" (*FW* 394.3–4). Joyce was completely misled—or was he? He must have been aware that such deformations would inevitably occur, but for him, as for Stephen Dedalus, errors were "portals of discovery" and "volitional" (*U* 9.229). One can understand that the "continually more and less intermisunderstanding minds of the anticollaborators" (*FW* 118.24–26) were the best collaborators in his enterprise of generalized agrammaticalization, even if it meant that his own original intention and the intention of the authors of the original sources receded further and further into inaccessibility.

The "D" notebooks are even more peculiar entities than the "C" copies: their characteristic is that they do not exist. They are notebooks that are no longer extant but were copied by France Raphael, so we know that they did exist in the 1930s. Raphael's transcriptions give us some idea of their contents, but the image she provides is severely warped by her frequent misinterpretations of Joyce's writing, for the reasons we have just seen, and necessarily incomplete, since she had been instructed to copy only those elements that had not been crossed out, while the crossed-out elements are surely the most interesting for us since they were the ones that had proved useful to Joyce.

From the remaining, distorted, shreds of evidence, Danis Rose and John O'Hanlon have undertaken to recover, as far as possible, the contents of one of these virtual notebooks (VI.D.7, based on their transcription in VI.C.16),[42] and they have succeeded remarkably in what would have seemed to be a desperate enterprise.

It so happens that this notebook had originally been prepared for *Ulysses,* almost twenty years before it was copied by Raphael. Its reconstruction sheds a very welcome light on the early days of the writing of *Ulysses,* but the interesting point for our present purpose is that it shows Joyce's resolution to make full use of everything he had written and his radical flexibility, since he believed that he could incorporate in his current work in progress material that had been collected for a completely different book (*Ulysses* as it had been envisaged in 1917).[43]

The method used by Rose and O'Hanlon to accomplish this amazing feat of philology, the partial restitution of a lost notebook, is itself revealing and tells us a great deal about the status of Joyce's notes. It is based on a confrontation between the existing transcription and the sources and destination of the original notes. The advantage we have over Raphael is that, unlike her, we know something of the context for which those notes were intended, in this case *Ulysses*, or rather the projected text that would later become the *Ulysses* we know. For instance, confronted with these two enigmatic lines:

SD Marsh library
hears again tells

Rose and O'Hanlon first of all restore a more likely original text:

S(tephen) D(edalus) in Marsh's library
heard again bells

Then they conjecture that these are not consecutive fragments but the first and last lines of a passage that Joyce had crossed out with a cross that failed to cover its first and last lines. This means that Joyce had used the passage in question but had imperfectly crossed it out, or rather that Raphael misinterpreted the large cross canceling it. This will remind the reader of *Ulysses* of a passage of "Proteus" in which Stephen Dedalus remembers his visit to Marsh's library and thinks of the anecdote of Occam hearing the elevation bell rung several times. The reconstruction implies that at this point the original notebook featured a series of notes for this passage.

It is a very particular variety of textual criticism, in which the manuscript does not serve to establish a definitive text, but the text serves to reconstitute the manuscript. This is only the first part of the process, and the most precarious, since the notes that were used were usually crossed out and would not normally have been copied by Raphael. This means that it is necessary to look in another direction: toward the source. If we discover, for example, that a number of items were collected from a particular handbook of Cockney slang,[44] we could first of all correct the approximations of Mme Raphael's transcriptions by comparing them not with their absent original but with the original of that original (the handbook consulted by Joyce); then, in noting in *Ulysses* the slang expressions that come from the handbook via the notebook (where they had been crossed out after use), they could be restored to their place in the series of notations according to their place in the handbook's series of expressions.

Thus, thanks to an intense back-and-forth between source text and destination text, the missing notes find themselves relentlessly stalked and cornered.[45] This encircling procedure illustrates the precarious status of notes in general, doubly dependent on the upstream and the downstream, a provisional repository of material that is merely in transit across it or, rather, that dwells there in a curious state of suspension, since it is partially deprived of the meaning conferred on it by its original context in the source and not yet invested with the meaning bestowed on it by its destination.

If we stop to think about it, we will see that the problems posed by the "B" notebooks are not essentially different, although the situation seems to be much simpler: the notebooks are materially present; they have not been subjected to the distorting intervention of a copyist ignorant of their context; and they were not meant for a book other than *Finnegans Wake.* But this last statement must immediately be qualified: there was no *Finnegans Wake* when these notes were first entered, only an as yet nameless "Work in Progress," a developing work that its author could discover only as he was writing, with the help of his notes. And we have seen that the text in the VI.B notebooks is a remainder: an extract subtracted from a larger whole from which it derives its value. And finally, the fact that there are no deformations introduced by a blundering copyist is amply compensated by the systematic deformations practiced by Joyce himself. Our own incapacity in this respect matches that of Mme Raphael: how do we distinguish an *o* from an *a,* a final *y* from a final *ing,* when they are graphically absolutely similar and when we cannot know in which dictionary we can find the scrawled word, if any? Our only hope of providing an adequate transcription is often to find how Joyce used the note in his drafts, usually in more legible manner, or to discover the source of the note, so as to reconstruct, following one direction or the other, something that is intrinsically indecipherable. Unfortunately, neither way affords any certainty, since Joyce would often change the words as he noted them, translating, reformulating, or playing with them; and he altered them even more as he incorporated them into his draft. It is impossible to be absolutely sure of what is written on the notebook page, and the text of the notes will always remain in a state of partial suspension, as virtual as the lost notebooks. In this respect, they are not unlike the "final" text of the *Wake,* which has been calculated to remain forever in a state of signifying and enunciative suspension.[46]

8

Virginia Woolf's Notes on *Ulysses*

A Conversational Reading

In *Finnegans Wake* I.7, the phrase "horrible awful poverty of mind" goes unnoticed among the shower of aspersions poured by a Wyndham Lewis–like Shaun on the head of a Joyce-like Shem. A very attentive student of modernism might perhaps be reminded of a passage of Virginia Woolf's famous essay "Modern Fiction," in which, speaking of the "Cemetery scene" in *Ulysses,* she wonders why a "work of such originality yet fails to compare [. . .] with *Youth* or *Jude the Obscure.* It fails, one might say simply because of the comparative poverty of the writer's mind."[1]

Notebook VI.B.6 confirms that Woolf's comment is the source of the phrase. If we look at the page reproduced here (fig. 8.1), we find a list of critical comments on *Ulysses,* starting four lines from the top.

The first two items on the list, "incoherent atoms"—derived from the often-quoted sentence "Let us record the atoms as they fall upon the mind in the order in which they fall, let us trace the pattern, however disconnected and incoherent in appearance, which each sight or incident scores upon the consciousness"—and "poverty of mind," come from Woolf's essay, or rather from a slightly different version, called "Modern Novels," that had been published anonymously in the *Times Literary Supplement* of April 10, 1919.[2]

The next item, "rancid / Joyce stuff," comes from an article in the *Sporting Times* of April 1, 1922: "The Yankee judges fined the publishers of the *Little Review* one hundred dollars for the original publication of a very rancid chapter of the Joyce stuff, which appears to have been written by a perverted lunatic who has made a speciality of the literature of the latrine." It is used in *Finnegans Wake* as "up and down the four margins of this rancid Shem stuff the evilsmeller [. . .] used to stipple endlessly inartistic portraits of himself" (*FW* 182.16–19).

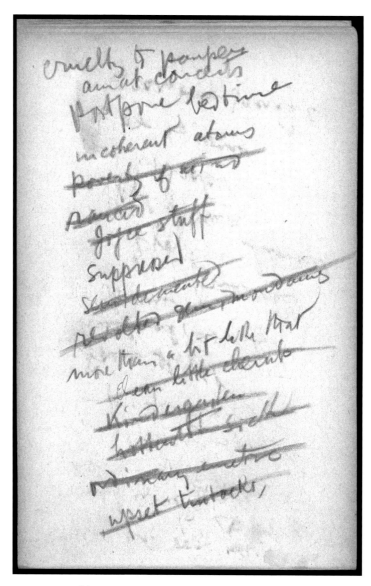

Figure 8.1. Buffalo VI.B.6.116 (*JJA* 30:130).

The list of abuse extracted from reviews and critical assessments of *Ulysses* goes on for four pages of the notebook.[3] All the items that are crossed out (like "poverty of mind") were introduced, in the first months of 1924, in the draft of what would become *Finnegans Wake* I.7 and, for the most part, remain quite indistinguishable from Joyce's own prose.

This is typical of Joyce's relation, from *Ulysses* onward, to what we might call adversative texts. He absorbs them, in the same way as he absorbs clumsy or ridiculous styles, metabolizes them, assimilates them into his own substance. This is typical of Joyce's relation to such texts—or at least of what we can perceive of it. To tell the truth, we have no direct knowledge of the way Joyce felt about these criticisms. Was he amused or shocked? It is probable that they acted as a reinforcement rather than as a deterrent, but we cannot tell if he was seriously affected or almost indifferent.

It is a special case of a characteristic of the genetic study of Joyce that must be clear by now. We have seen that Joyce's manuscripts are a blessing for the genetic critic, because so much is happening there, so much invention takes place, that it gives us a unique opportunity to catch a glimpse of the mechanics of creation. But, on the other hand, we are frighteningly left to our own devices in front of this puzzling material. With the conspicuous exception of the *Exiles* notes, Joyce practically never explains himself in his manuscripts. Of course we have the aesthetic theories expressed by Stephen D(a)edalus, but they don't seem particularly illuminating for the making of the mature works. Of course we have the various elucidations that Joyce confided to his friends or fed to critics, exegetes and biographer, but even if we could fully trust the memory of those who report them, we are not to trust completely Joyce's retrospective or biased point of view (or any other author's in such circumstances). We have seen that the multiple changes in evidence on the manuscript page or detectable by a comparison of successive versions of a passage are the result of a myriad of decisions taken at each stage and reflect a system of choices, providing us with a much richer and more reliable view of Joyce's practical aesthetics. But we have to make educated guesses about the reason(s) why each of these decisions was taken, the axiological basis for the choices. This is true for both the micro- and the macro-decisions. For instance, we do not know anything of the deliberations that led him to modify and then to abandon the "initial style" of *Ulysses*. Other writers are much more helpful in this respect. Take Zola's "Ébauches" (sketches for his novels):

they are a kind of meditation on paper, *exteriorized monologues* in which he ponders the various possibilities for the novel that he is planning to write, the motivations and the consequences of each choice.[4]

Virginia Woolf is such a writer: she likes to think on paper. In her manuscripts, in her diaries, she ruminates on her ideas, develops her plans, considers her options and explains to herself her own motivations. Even if such documents are not always to be taken at face value, even if what an author says must be confronted with what is actually being done in the drafts, it is a considerable help for the geneticist, a solid starting point that is sorely missing in the case of Joyce.

Woolf's reading notes are also relatively explicit, at least considerably more so than Joyce's. One good reason for this is that Woolf was writing these notes in preparation of newspaper reviews or critical essays. It is only natural that they should be largely discursive. Now, it is a wonderful opportunity for us that Woolf's notes on (the first episodes of) *Ulysses* should have been preserved. They practically allow us to follow Woolf's reading in real time, her engagement with Joyce's text. At the same time, these notes allow us to witness the first elaboration of the ideas, based on this reading, that formed the starting point of her celebrated essay (the essay quoted derisively in *Finnegans Wake*) and also, I would like to suggest, of important developments in her own writing of fiction.

The submerged *Finnegans Wake* quotation can be considered as the conclusion of an asymmetrical dialogue between the two most important English-speaking novelists of the time, a dialogue that had started many years earlier and that involved many different voices.

To be able to understand correctly what is going on in these notes, it is important to avoid two damaging errors of perspective. The first one gives us a comfortable feeling of superiority, because we find that we can read *Ulysses* better than Virginia Woolf: we may not be able to write *The Waves*, but at least we are better, more perceptive, or less prejudiced readers. Needless to say, such superiority is based on false premises, and not only because we benefit from the hindsight unavailable to Woolf. The first thing we must keep in mind is that the Woolf who is reading *Ulysses* (early in 1919) is not the writer of *The Waves*.[5] At the time she began writing her notes, she would not have been able to write *Jacob's Room* (published in 1922), although she was probably closer to that point when she finished writing them and the essay that is derived from them.

The second error of perspective is more general: we have a tendency to speak from a distant historical prospect that neglects or distorts the particular circumstances of the intercourse between works of art and the ambivalence of their relationships.[6] In the case of Joyce and Woolf, critics often study the influence of *Ulysses*, a book published, according to bibliographies, in February 1922, on *Mrs Dalloway*, a book published in May 1925. This bird's-eye view, which disregards the modalities of reception and diffusion of a work and the actual writing circumstances, is misleading, in the same way as the apparently smooth continuity between *Ulysses* and *Finnegans Wake* is an illusion, as we saw in chapter 3. It is important to realize that the text that Woolf is reading is *not* the *Ulysses* that we know. Because, even if we try very hard, we cannot pretend to read *Ulysses* as a new book, unencumbered by the mass of critical readings that has become an integral part of it, and also because *Ulysses*, in 1919, was not a book but a handful of episodes being published serially in the *Little Review*, and those episodes were different, sometimes extremely different (e.g., in the case of "Aeolus") from what they would be in the final version. *Ulysses* was a "work in progress" in several respects. To be more accurate, Woolf read the first seven episodes: the January 1919 issue, containing part 1 of the eighth episode, was seized and destroyed by the Post Office, and the February/March 1919 issue, containing part 2 of the same episode, presumably arrived too late for the article.[7]

What we are witnessing in these notes, then, is not the timeless intertextual relation between books that have "take[n] their place in the long procession" of literary history,[8] but a reader in progress, or more accurately a reader-writer in progress, interacting with a text in progress.

The setting

We must consider both the institutional and the physical setting of this intercourse. Woolf was reading the first installments of a novel that was being serialized in an avant-garde magazine, the *Little Review*, in preparation for an article that she was planning for the *Times Literary Supplement* (*TLS*). Each of the two contemporary periodicals has such a different status that the encounter seems improbable, but the principle of the interaction is actually preprogrammed by the vehicles themselves. One of the mottoes of *The Little Review*, usually appearing on its contents page or on the inside cover, is

Figure 8.2.

"The magazine that is read by those who write the others." This is an assertion of leadership, suggesting that the other magazines are mere followers, but it is also an assumption that its readers are actors in the same field, not just passive receptors. On the other hand, the *TLS* specializes in reviewing, which implies that it is indeed written after reading contemporary publications.

The respective positioning of the two periodicals within the institutional field suggests that the interaction will take the form of an opposition. We are not particularly surprised by the class prejudice that expresses itself openly in Woolf's notes (but not in the published article) when she deplores the fact that *Ulysses* "seems to be written for a set in a back street" (*MNJ* 643). One of the factors is certainly an opposition of *sets,* determined (symbolically?) by their socio-geographic abodes. But given Virginia Woolf's later stature as a feminist writer, we must make a particularly strong effort to recontextualize the notes and realize that, a decade before *A Room of One's Own* and two decades before *Three Guineas,* it was Joyce who was publishing in Margaret Anderson and Jane Heap's avant-garde feminist journal, constantly threatened by moral and political authorities, and Woolf who was writing for the literary stronghold of the Establishment and patriarchy.[9]

This, however, is still too abstract, or at least too distant, a perspective. If we examine the *Little Review,* we find out, for instance, that one of Woolf's main objections in the notes (that Joyce perversely positions himself outside the mainstream: "Always a mark of the second rate, indifference to public opinion—desire to shock" *MNJ* 643) is a pointed retort to the main motto of the review, appearing on the cover of each of the issues that Woolf has been consulting: *The Little Review: A magazine of the arts making no compromise with the public taste* (fig. 8.2).

The physical setting of the confrontation is an ordinary sized copybook, with a marbled cover bearing the inscription "—Modern Novels—" and a white label with the words "MODERN NOVELS (Joyce)."[10] The contents are divided into two main parts: a series of notes on James Joyce's *Ulysses* is followed by a very rough draft of an article on recent fiction based on those notes, with the heading "Sketch of article." This is the first draft of the essay that would eventually be published in the *Times Literary Supplement* on April 10, 1919, and republished in a slightly modified version under the title "Modern Fiction" in *The Common Reader* (1925).

A simple division in two parts, however, does not do justice to the diversity of the document. The *Ulysses* notes are preceded by half a page of enigmatic, apparently unconnected notes and before that, on top of the first page, before the title of the projected essay, "Modern Novels," we find a listing of the first seven episodes of *Ulysses* matched with a list of colors (fig. 8.3).

Order of Ulysses   I—Claret red.
                    II—pale blue
                    III—orange
                    IV—dark green
                    V—light green
                    VI—green
                    VII—dark blue
_____
Modern Novels

This is not an attempt to grasp Joyce's color symbolism but a description of the precise shades of the covers of the successive magazine issues in which the episodes of *Ulysses* were published. Since the covers bear no numbering or any sequential indication, Woolf obviously thought that this little exercise in material bibliography was an indispensable preliminary to her reading.

At the other end, after the draft part, the note form resumes briefly with a reference to *Pendennis* and a few related remarks.[11] More importantly, each of the two main sections is quite heterogeneous. The reading notes include sentences that seem already to be preparing a future essay, and the draft is intermingled with self-addressed questions and exhortations that are clearly not meant for the general public's eye.

The spatial disposition reflects the heterogeneity of the document. The abovementioned sections are separated by titles and blanks or dividing lines. The left-hand pages are mostly empty, with a few additions to the main text written on the right-hand pages and a series of floating notes with no defi-

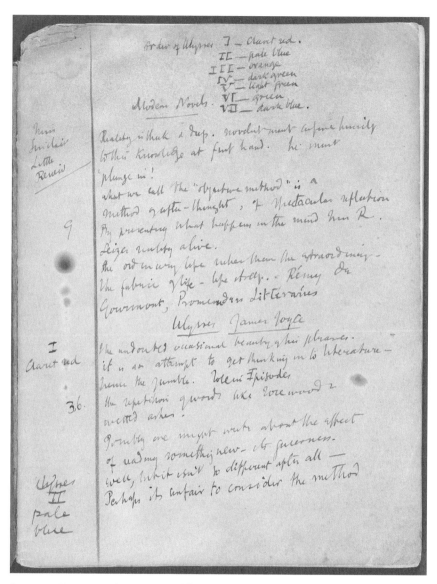

Figure 8.3. First page of Virginia Woolf's Notebook XXXI. Berg Collection.

nite point of insertion in the text. A blue crayon line is neatly drawn on the left of the right-hand pages, defining a marginal zone that is used for precise references to the text being read. This is a kind of inversion of the common marginalia system: instead of commentaries being inscribed in the margin of the text, the text, called up very concretely in its material incarnation (the page and episode numbers are invariably accompanied by a reminder of the color of the issue cover), is placed in the margin of the commentary.

We will see that one of the major stakes of this notebook is indeed a process of self-definition through opposition. But before being used ultimately as an instrument of distantiation, it serves as a transitional space (defined by Winnicott as "the space between inner and outer world, which is also the space between people[, the space where] creativity occur[s]").[12] It acts very concretely as an interface between the text of the other and the writing in progress. The thin line drawn by Virginia Woolf to create a marginal zone is less an instrument of segregation than a kind of permeable membrane through which the nutritive substance of the other text filters into Woolf's writing, where it is assimilated or rejected—or submitted to a digestive process that combines assimilation and rejection.

The time setting is not simple either. A book review is like a conversation: the protagonists share the same temporal coordinates and the same framework of reference. It is addressed to one's contemporaries, the potential readers of recently published books, but also the writers who have just written them and are eagerly expecting some feedback. For this reason, Virginia Woolf, toward the end of her life, playfully suggested that reviews could be usefully replaced by a kind of consultation, a private conversation between the author and the reviewer.[13] Now, the article Woolf has in mind when she starts taking these notes is halfway between a review and an essay: it deals with recently published books (or even, in the case of *Ulysses,* a book in the process of being written) but tries to put them in the perspective of the history of the novel and to draw universal conclusions. Woolf's strategy of revision, when she republishes the essay a few years later in *The Common Reader,* is ambiguous. Superficially, she seems to be wanting to keep the piece up-to-date, replacing, in the liminal analogy ("And yet the analogy between literature and the process, to choose an example, of making bicycles scarcely holds good beyond the first glance") the manufacture of bicycles by the more modern manufacturing of motor cars.[14] But, strangely enough, she does not actualize a much more crucial matter, her reading of *Ulysses:* some of her remarks, which could be considered acceptable in 1919, in the shock of discovery of a very incomplete text in progress, were much less so in 1925,

once the whole book had been published for three years and more perceptive judgments had been expressed in several reviews. Woolf chose not to
update the article at all in this respect: it remains a partial view in all senses
of the term. It completely ignores chapters that profoundly alter the nature
of the book, like "Sirens," "Cyclops," "Circe," "Ithaca," or the revised version
of "Aeolus." Even if Woolf had her reasons for not coming to terms with the
book as a whole, she might have tried to conceal this fact by remaining conveniently vague, but she deliberately retained a sentence like this one: "any
one who has read *The Portrait of the Artist as a Young Man* or what promises
to be a far more interesting work, *Ulysses,* now appearing in the *Little Review,* will have hazarded some theory of this nature as to Mr. Joyce's intention," in which the tense system openly refers to 1919 and is hopelessly out
of date by 1925.[15] This may indicate that Woolf was less interested in timeless
truths than in preserving a moment of conversational exchange. After all,
one of the first things that crosses her mind as she begins reading *Ulysses* is
that it would be interesting to write something about the very experience of
being confronted with contemporaneity and/or innovation ("Possibly one
might write about the effect of reading something new—its queerness."), the
process of *accommodation* that is necessary to make out what does not enter
into preexisting categories.

   On the other hand, the debate seems to transcend the moment; the reference framework seems to be larger. This is evident in the notes even more than
in the published essay. "Would my objections apply to T[ristram] S[handy]? /
Don Juan. I believe Johnson was outraged by TS." Beside innovative creative
writers (Byron and Sterne), great critical voices of the past (Dr Johnson) are
summoned to take part in the debate. In this respect, the setting of the conversation is no longer the present of 1919, no longer the literary marketplace of
Woolf's time, where she is potentially competing for a share of the public's attention, but English literature, English literary history, where she is indirectly
and preventively staking her claim.

Nested readings: Joyce through Richardson through Sinclair

Close scrutiny of the notes allows us to understand better what is going on.
Since Woolf writes sequentially in her copybook and records her impressions

along the way, we are able to reconstruct the exact sequence of the interaction by confronting these sometimes enigmatic jottings with the actual appearance of the volumes that she was perusing, and this goes a long way toward explaining some of the characteristics of Woolf's take on Joyce.

After the numbered list of episodes of *Ulysses,* or rather of issues of the periodical, and before the notes on "*Ulysses James Joyce,*" a few mysterious lines occupy the first half of the first page.

Miss	Reality is thick & deep. Novelist must confine himself
Sinclair	to this knowledge at first hand. He must
Little	'plunge in.'
Review	what we call the "objective method" is a
	method of after-thought, of spectacular reflection
9	By presenting what happens in the mind Miss R
	seizes reality alive.
	The ordinary life richer than the extraordinary—
	the fabric of life—life itself. Rémy de
	Gourmont, Promenades Littéraires

(MNJ 643)

These lines are mysterious until we notice the tags in the margin ("Miss Sinclair," "Little Review" and "9"): the "9" refers to a page number in the issue of the *Little Review* (dated April 1918) in which the second episode of *Ulysses* was published. Its first article is indeed an article by the critic (and novelist) May Sinclair ("Miss Sinclair") on "The Novels of Dorothy Richardson" ("Miss R"), and we find out that all these notes are almost verbatim quotations from Sinclair's article.

> Reality is thick and deep, too thick and too deep and at the same time too fluid to be cut with any convenient carving knife. The novelist who would be close to reality must confine himself to his knowledge at first hand. He must, as Mr. Beresford says, simply "plunge in." Mr. Beresford also says that Miss Richardson is the first novelist who has plunged in. (p. 4)

> What we used to call the "objective" is a method of after-thought, of spectacular reflection. [. . .] The first hand, intimate and intense reality

of the happening is in Myriam's mind, and by presenting it thus and not otherwise Miss Richardson seizes reality alive. (p. 9)

There are two essays of Rémy de Gourmont in *Promenades Littéraires*, one on "L'Originalité de Maeterlinck," one on "La leçon de Saint Antoine." Certain passages might have been written concerning the art of Dorothy Richardson: "[. . .] une vie où il semblerait ne rien se passer que d'élémentaire et quotidien serait mieux remplie qu'une autre vie riche en apparence d'incidents et d'aventures [. . .]. Il y a peut-être un sentiment nouveau à créer, celui de l'amour de la vie pour la vie elle-même [. . .]" (p. 11)

As Woolf was gathering the *Little Review* issues and preparing the color table of their covers prior to reading them, she was obviously diverted by Sinclair's article. Spatial as well as temporal contiguity seem to have played their part here: Woolf could hardly have failed to notice this piece, since it is the opening article and the "cover story" of the issue, "'DOROTHY RICHARDSON'S

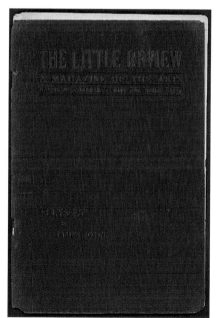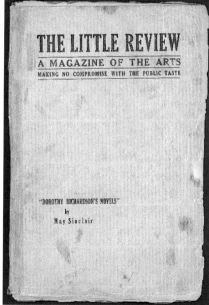

Figure 8.4. Covers of the March 1919 and April 1919 issues of the *Little Review*.

NOVELS' by May Sinclair" occupying the same place on the pale blue cover as "'ULYSSES' by James Joyce" on the claret red cover of the previous issue. She was certainly interested, if only because she herself had reviewed, just a few weeks before, Richardson's latest novel, *The Tunnel*.[16]

(Although we have no proof of it, we can be almost certain that Joyce himself must have noticed that, for this second installment, he was already being replaced, as the cover story and the opening piece, by Dorothy Richardson. It seems likely that he read May Sinclair's article, in which he is mentioned with admiration. We can speculate that it suggested to him that it was time to go in a different direction, abandon his "initial style," and do something that was *less* psychological, further away from straightforward stream of consciousness. The date of the issue—April 1918—makes this plausible, since it more or less coincides with the rewriting of "Sirens" [see chapter 7, this volume]. It is interesting to see Sinclair's article as a kind of diverging point in the respective courses of Joyce and Woolf.)

When Woolf's cryptic liminal notes are referred to their origin in Sinclair's article, they point to ideas that play an important part in the "Modern Novels" essay and that perhaps affected, directly and indirectly, the future of Woolf's writing career. But first it is clear that, together with the rest of the article, they distinctly influenced Woolf's reading of *Ulysses* that immediately followed.

Some of the details of Woolf's discussion of Joyce are conditioned by the article on Richardson: for instance, we find out that the charge of indifference to public opinion, which seemed to be a direct retort to the motto of the *Little Review,* is actually mediated by May Sinclair's first paragraph:

I HAVE been asked to write—for this magazine which makes no compromise with the public taste—a criticism of the novels of Dorothy Richardson. The editors of the *Little Review* are committed to Dorothy Richardson by their declared intentions; for her works make no sort of compromise with the public taste. If they are not announced with the same proud challenge it is because the pride of the editors of the *Little Review* is no mate for the pride of Miss Richardson which ignores the very existence of the public and its taste. (p. 3)

The impact, however, is more general. We can go so far as to say that Woolf reads Joyce through Dorothy Richardson or, more accurately, through May

Sinclair's view of Richardson. This partly explains Woolf's very psychological view of *Ulysses* (in sharp contrast to her friend T. S. Eliot's interpretation): "it is an attempt to get thinking into literature. hence the jumble" (*MNJ* 642); "It simply is the way one thinks if one holds a pen and writes on without coherence—interesting perhaps to doctors" (*MNJ* 642); "The desire to be more psychological—get more things into fiction. Everything can go in" (*MNJ* 643); "The interest is that this is psychology. Possibly like a cinema that shows you very slowly how a horse does jump" (*MNJ* 643); "here is thought made phonetic—taken to bits" (*MNJ* 643).

Woolf's perspective is actually more psychological than Sinclair's, but Sinclair introduces a very important term: stream of consciousness. It is in her article that William James's phrase first appears in a literary context. Woolf herself never uses it, but the reviewers of her subsequent novels use it liberally. "Modern Fiction" provides the most brilliant and the most famous description of the idea, including the phrase that would be singled out in *Finnegans Wake:*

> The mind [. . .] receives a myriad impressions—trivial, fantastic, evanescent, or engraved with the sharpness of steel. From all sides they come, an incessant shower of innumerable atoms; [. . .] Let us record the atoms as they fall upon the mind in the order in which they fall, let us trace the pattern, however disconnected and incoherent in appearance, which each sight or incident scores upon the consciousness.[17]

A conversation of many voices

Writing is always done with an eye on previously written texts (if not on the whole of literature). Conversely, at least for Virginia Woolf, serious reading could only be envisaged with a pen in hand. In her diary, she expresses her gratitude to the reviews she had to write for the *TLS:* because of them, she was "made to read with a pen and notebook, seriously."[18] The notes in question were precisely taken in preparation for one of those reviews, not the review of a particular book but a general overview of contemporary fiction in its relation to the tradition of the novel. The task Virginia Woolf had set for herself was very comprehensive indeed. On March 5, 1919, she wrote in her diary: "But oh, dear, what a lot I've got to read! The entire works of Mr. James Joyce, Wyndham Lewis, Ezra Pound, so as to compare them with the entire works of Dickens and Mrs. Gaskell; besides that George Eliot; and finally Hardy."[19]

It is interesting to match up this project to her actual reading as far as it is reflected in these notes and in the resulting essay. Of the writers mentioned here, only Joyce and Hardy are present, but in the case of Hardy, Woolf relies on her previous knowledge and does not engage in any new reading of his work. As she expresses it in the notes, he has become a fixed quantity, not something to be read but a point of reference, a sort of yardstick applicable to other readings: "Hardy is planted beyond reach of change; only seems desirable when we read novels not by Hardy." The entire works of Dickens, Gaskell and Eliot have been replaced by a few pages of Thackeray. But we see the traces of an intense reading effort relating to the first seven episodes of *Ulysses*. The input from this work has been so massive, so difficult to assimilate, that it absorbed Woolf's reading energies and inflected her writing project. Unpremeditated references appear, generated by the necessity to deal with Joyce: Sterne and Byron, on the one hand, as examples of eccentricity among the classics; Wells and Bennett, on the other, as foils ("It is from them we wish to start. We see how much fails to get into their books."[20]); and then Chekhov, through a single allusive word ("Gusev"). In the finished essay, some of these authors disappear and the others are manipulated like pieces in a game of chess for a particular strategic purpose; but in the notebook, particularly in the notes properly speaking, they play their part in a relatively open conversation.

We can see that the purpose of these notes is complex. At the beginning, Woolf sets out to read and evaluate a large number of novels, but the reading notes turn out to be devoted to one single overwhelming book. Then the notes are abandoned in favor of the draft of an essay. In the course of the reading and drafting, the question of norms is persistent, but it is tackled with different intentions: coming to terms with Joyce, a reflexive assessment of the norms used to assess any novelist, a reflection on modernity, on what it is to write (and read) a modern novel and, indirectly, a working-through of the definition of what a "Woolfian novel" could be.

Woolf the reader never forgets that she is also Woolf the critic, who will have to pass a judgment on what she is reading in her intended article, and she is also aware that she is Woolf the writer, striving to define a norm that will guide her own future writing. Already, in her notes from May Sinclair, she emphasized statements that are evaluative ("life is richer") and prescriptive ("the novelist must"). In the remainder of the notebook, at the same time as she tries to understand Joyce, and simply to understand what is going on in *Ulysses* ("Bloom—/ editor of a paper. / Dignam dies / Stephen Dedalus is the / son of Mr Dedalus. / Mulligan is his friend—/ What is the connection / between Bloom and Dedalus?"), she undertakes to judge him. But how is it possible to judge something that obviously supersedes existing norms? The accepted norms must be reexamined and adjusted to accommodate the new work, but how can one do that without surrendering to this work and erecting it as a more valid norm (something Woolf is absolutely not ready to do)? How can one assess the norms and the new work at the same time? The answer was already part of the original purpose: this can be achieved only through a process of comparison.[21] So Woolf deliberately compares Joyce with the traditional novelists and the *marginal* classics (Sterne and Byron), with the premoderns (Hardy, James, and Conrad), and with the Edwardians (Bennett and Wells), and then, on the basis of what she feels to be satisfactory and unsatisfactory in each, she tries to establish a new set of norms. She even goes as far as to suggest that no literary value is eternal and that norm-making is always transactional: it is because the Edwardians have been so materialistic that the modern novel must be more spiritual. Revolution ("For all I know, every great book has been an act of revolution"), in the sense of radical change in reaction to the present state of literature ("we must go on; can't stand still; move on from our immediate past"), is a perpetual necessity. The theory adumbrated here ("the big things [. . .] must be seen again, felt again; always. perpetually") is very similar to the theory of *ostranienie* (defamilarization) that was being developed by Victor Shklovsky at about the same time.[22]

This (the objective appraisal of *Ulysses,* the dialogic establishment of a new set of values and the reflection on the process of evaluation) is not the whole story. It is clear that Woolf is resisting very strongly what she is reading, or even that she is determined, before she starts, to find fault with what she is reading.[23] The norms are used as a weapon in a struggle to get the upper hand, to shift from the subjugated condition of reader, overwhelmed by the new masterpiece, to the superior stance of the discriminating critic. In her diary, Woolf explains with great lucidity what is at stake for her when she reads writers that she considers as rivals: "The truth is that when I looked at [Dorothy

Richardson], I felt myself looking for faults; hoping for them. [. . .] There must be an instinct of self-preservation at work. If she's good then I'm not."[24] Such self-preservation is even more crucial in the case of Joyce, who casts a longer shadow. Whereas, in the finished essay, Joyce appears as an ally against the previous generation of writers, in the notebook he is clearly felt to be an adversary.

This is part of a conscious or unconscious strategy of relative positioning. Analysts have noticed that, in most conversations, a great deal of time and energy is spent defining and confirming the respective status of the participants or struggling for the dominant position. Woolf obviously feels that Joyce must be put in his place, sent back to where he belongs: "in a back street" with his "set." But putting the other in his/her place is often an attempt to secure one's own place. The preoccupation of Woolf is not to establish a pecking order between authors; she is performing a kind of tug-of-war to gain territory, to clear a breathing space, a room of her own, so to speak, in which to exist and create. She feels threatened by Joyce's towering stature and she feels she must belittle him.

Like May Sinclair, Woolf mentions a number of writers in support of her argument, but their respective lists[25] do not have a single name in common, apart from Joyce. This is probably because their purpose is profoundly different: while Sinclair uses the other writers to explain Richardson and the direction in which she is going, Woolf uses them as standards or foils to create a set of distinctions and oppositions and as yardsticks to measure each other and ultimately to measure Joyce. Woolf is clearly groping for a set of values against which to judge (and condemn[26]) Joyce.

In her discussion of Joyce, Woolf uses the same kind of rhetoric as she had used in her review of Richardson: what Joyce/Richardson is doing is interesting and courageous, it goes in the right direction, but it fails in some way. Her notes on *Ulysses* begin with this very restrictive praise: "The undoubted occasional beauty of his phrases" (*MNJ* 642), which reminds us of a similar phrasing in the review of *The Tunnel:* "That Miss Richardson gets so far as to achieve a sense of reality far greater than that produced by the ordinary means is undoubted. But, then, which reality is it, the superficial or the profound?" (*E* 2, 11). In the case of Joyce even more than with Richardson, it is obvious that Woolf is looking for some (faint) praise, some ("undoubted") quality that she can concede generously before leveling her blows. Woolf's arguments against Richardson had been that she was superficial ("we still find ourselves distressingly near the surface" [*E* 2, 11]) and shapeless (she required that "Miss Richardson shall fashion this new material into something which has the shapeliness of the old accepted forms" [*E* 2, 12]) and she concluded: "The old method seems sometimes the more profound and economical of the two" (*E* 2, 12). But Sinclair produces convincing arguments against both accusations. Far from being superficial, Richardson is to be praised for "the sheer depth of her plunge" into a life that is "thick and deep," and her novels "show an art and method and form carried to punctilious perfection" (Sinclair 1918, 5).[27]

Sinclair adds that "Miss Richardson has not plunged deeper than Mr. James Joyce in his *Portrait of the Artist as a Young Man*" (1918, 5). Since the accusation of formlessness would be even more difficult to sustain against Joyce, Woolf is forced to look for other critical restrictions. And if the aesthetic norms are too fragile to serve as an effective weapon, evaluation must be transferred to other levels: Joyce is bloodless, fleshless, and brainless, he dwells too much on indecency, he is not generous enough, the temperature of his book is too low, the quality of his mind is not good enough, and so on.[28]

Then comes a series of converging remarks:

> But the worst of Joyce & c.[ompany]:[29] is their egotism. . . . perhaps this method gets less into other people & too much into one [. . .]. Funeral perhaps the best thing. But isn't it always the same mind? [. . .]
>
> Then the summing up. The necessity of magnanimity & generosity. Trying to see as much of other people as possible, & not oneself. (*MNJ* 645)

In the final text of the essay, these analytical fragments are replaced by an impressionistic image:

> [*Ulysses*] fails because of the comparative poverty of the writer's mind, we might say simply and have done with it. But it is possible to press a little further and wonder whether we may not refer our sense of being in a bright yet narrow room, confined and shut in, rather than enlarged and set free, to some limitation imposed by the method as well as by the mind. Is it the method that inhibits the creative power? Is it due to

the method that we feel neither jovial nor magnanimous, but centred in a self which, in spite of its tremor of susceptibility, never embraces or creates what is outside itself and beyond? ("Modern Fiction," 161–162)

If *superficial* and *shapeless* cannot be retained, then *narrow* and *confined* must do. This is an amplification and a reversal of Sinclair's laudatory insistence on the restrictive aspect of Richardson's technique:

By imposing very strict limitations on herself she has brought her art, her method, to a high pitch of perfection. [. . .] She would probably deny that she has written with any deliberate method at all. She would say: "I only know there are certain things I mustn't do if I was to do what I wanted." Obviously, she must not interfere; she must not analyse or comment or explain. Rather less obviously, she must not tell a story, or handle a situation or set a scene; she must avoid drama as she avoids narration. And there are some things she must not be. She must not be the wise, all-knowing author. She must be Miriam Henderson. She must not know or divine anything that Miriam does not know or divine; she must not see anything that Miriam does not see. ("The Novels of Dorothy Richardson," *Little Review* 12 [1918]: 5)

It is possible that the image of the bright room also derives from Sinclair's article,[30] more specifically from a quotation from Richardson: "Her room was a great square of happy light [. . .] Now she knew what she wanted. Bright mornings, beautiful bright rooms, a wilderness of beauty all round her all the time—at any cost" ("The Novels of Dorothy Richardson," 10).

It is much more important, however, to see how this affects Woolf's own fiction. The act of self-preservation becomes an act of self-definition. By way of rejecting Joyce, Woolf initiates a process of affirmation: the main weakness that Woolf identifies in *Ulysses* suggests, in a form of negative intertextuality, a direction for the development of her own style, a development that will find its expression, in different stages, in the novels she is going to write.

Jacob's Room will start in the opposite direction: instead of being locked up in the claustrophobic chambers of a particular mind, it will explore the space of a room, which is a locus of social, intellectual and emotional interactions between the self and its environment. In the next novel, *Mrs Dalloway,* published simultaneously with *The Common Reader* collection that includes "Modern Fiction" with its remarks on Joyce, she will develop her own characteristic technique, based on free indirect speech and the fluidity of borders between centers of subjectivity.

It may seem strange that, in spite of her importance in the genesis of "Modern Novels/Modern Fiction"—and indirectly in the genesis of Woolf's future novels—Woolf does not mention May Sinclair at all in the article. Again, if we try to reconstruct the context, we can understand that Sinclair also represented a threat and that Woolf was not eager to associate herself with a writer who was much more important than we might imagine today.

Discussing *Jacob's Room* four years later, the anonymous reviewer of the *New York Times* still presented things in this way: "It is to be suspected that Miss Woolf stems from May Sinclair, but she has carried the terse method of that excellent writer to a natural conclusion." The reviewer goes on to say: "This book again impresses upon the reader of English fiction the great quality of the women now writing in that country. Headed, of course, by May Sinclair, there is a host of names—Sheila Kaye-Smith, Mary Butts, Ethel Colburn Mayne, F. Tennyson Jesse, Elinor Mordaunt. Indeed, the list is endless. Miss Woolf is certainly one of the foremost figures in this group."[31] Woolf obviously does not want to be categorized in this manner (as part of a group of female writers, "headed of course by May Sinclair"). She knows that it is almost inevitable that she should be thus pigeonholed, and she is careful not to give any fuel to this tendency.

It is significant that Jane Austen is the only woman novelist mentioned in the published article. The single contemporary fiction writer mentioned in the notes, Gertrude Stein ("The desire to be more psychological—get more things into fiction. Everything can go in. Gertrude Stein." [*MNJ,* 643]), is absent from the final version. And Dorothy Richardson, discussed (and dismissed) elsewhere by Woolf, is conspicuously missing here.

Sinclair, Richardson, Stein, deliberately left unmentioned, Beresford and Gourmont, discarded as superseded stepping stones, William James, unconsciously smuggled in with Sinclair's ideas—the wings of "Modern Fiction" are haunted by an army of ghosts of varying importance, who play their invisible part in a multidimensional relationship that it would be much too simple to call influence. It is a great mistake to think that we can neglect the detail of the genetic context and the publishing environment and study in vitro the connection between the books of Joyce and Woolf.

Woolf's reading notes are very different from the *Finnegans Wake* notebooks. When we are able to decipher Woolf's daunting handwriting, they are much more explicit, less mysterious and easier to relate to. And yet, in the case of the "Modern Novels (Joyce)" notebook, they also reveal an invisible intertextuality that played a crucial part in the genetic process.

Conclusion

In a famous passage of *A Room of One's Own,* Virginia Woolf, or rather the female narrator that represents her, is denied access to the manuscripts of *Lycidas* and *Henry Esmond.* Her thwarted wish was to study the "alterations" made by Milton and Thackeray, in direct opposition to an essay by Charles Lamb in which he expresses a violent rejection of such a curiosity:

> Those *variae lectiones,* so tempting to the more erudite palates, do but disturb and unsettle my faith. [Footnote: [. . .] I had thought of the Lycidas as of a full grown beauty—as springing up with all its parts absolute—till, in an evil hour, I was shown the original written copy of it, together with the other minor poems of its author, in the Library of Trinity, kept like some treasure to be proud of. I wish they had thrown them in the Cam, or sent them, after the latter canto of Spencer, into the Irish Channel. How it staggered me to see the fine things in their ore! interlined, corrected! as if their words were mortal, alterable, displaceable at pleasure ! as if they might have been otherwise, and just as good ! as if inspirations were made up of parts, and those fluctuating, successive, indifferent! I will never go into the work-shop of any great artist again, nor desire the sight of his picture, till it is fairly off the easel; no, not if Raphael were to be alive again, and painting another Galatea.][1]

The final reference to Raphael's nude Galatea, supposed to have been painted on the model of a famous courtesan, points to the transgressive, voyeuristic aspect of such a revelation. It is simultaneously "tempting" and "repugnant," desirable and frightening, like a peek at the primal scene. Focusing on the "ore," the "interlined, corrected" versions, instead of the perfection of the full grown beauty delivered by the canonical text is a trans-gression equivalent to Joyce's own revolutionary decision to focus on what was considered un-representable: bowel movements and urinations, throw-aways and graffiti, and all the insignificant dross that floats on the surface of consciousness.[2]

There is something of a Charles Lamb in all of us.[3] We are shocked *and* thrilled to discover that canonical masterpieces, such as *Ulysses* and *Finnegans Wake,* "might have been otherwise"—but not necessarily "just as good," if we consider Joyce's strenuous efforts to "improve" his work by altering it until the very last moment, redefining at the same time the notion of a "good" book.

The genetic approach is perhaps a solution to the problem that Woolf found so challenging: how to assess a work like *Ulysses* that is clearly unmeasurable according to usual standards? Each of the "alterations" that can be found on Joyce's manuscripts reveals a movement from one state to another, a direction, and challenges us to understand the reasons for this movement and the evalu-ation on which it is based. When the evidence is available (genetic evidence is always deficient, but we have seen that much could be inferred from an incomplete archive), we can form a clear picture of the writer orienting and reorienting himself, altering his text to suit his standards but also readjusting his standards in the light of his creation. This gives us the opportunity to as-sess each aspect of the book according to the standards that presided over its creation.

Like Charles Lamb, we realize with some dismay that "inspirations [are] made up of parts, and those fluctuating, successive"—but certainly not "in-different," if we consider Joyce's determination and tenacity. Inspiration is in-deed revealed to be plural, time-bound, and our "faith" in the image of the godlike creator suggested by the finished work is inevitably "unsettle[d]." But do we admire Joyce the less because we have found out that neither *Ulysses* nor *Finnegans Wake* are the direct implementation of a preconceived plan? Is our respect for him diminished because the genetic documents reveal that the final form of the books result from a long and patient struggle with the potentialities of language and its perceived limitations, the laws of narration, the tradition of the novel, chance readings and patient research, amanuenses, printers, postal delays, writing instruments, economic conditions, and many other factors that inflected them on a daily basis, in small ways or crucial matters? At any rate, Joyce's long and patient struggle with the elusive and constantly changing image of the intended work, which forced him to revise and revise again until a result was achieved that could not have been envisaged at the start of the process, should make us admire all the more the books that exacted such efforts from their creator, lured him into unchartered territories and never left him alone till an unprecedented level of complexity was reached.

When we walk in the redwood forests, on the West Coast of America, we sometimes find a row of identical centuries-old trees growing in a straight line. These files of perfectly aligned giants are a powerful fuel to the imagination. We wonder if they are the remnants of a Cyclopean alley planted by an unknown ancient civilization, or even if they could be a signal left by visiting aliens for the benefit of future generations. It is inevitable that such wonders should suggest a deliberate human or preterhuman planning will, an implied author, as it were. But botanists tell us a different story. Many centuries ago, a redwood fell on the ground, and, as it decayed, new shoots sprouted along its trunk, giving birth to a perfectly straight row of future giants. What is the relevance of this tale of decomposition and germination and self-perpetuation? In the case of *Ulysses* and *Finnegans Wake,* we know that there was a planning mind, but it does not coincide with the authorial figure implied by the final work and it was never in a position to foresee the final result of its plan, the message that would be addressed to future generations of readers, or the image of the creator that would be projected, because its plans were constantly thwarted and enhanced, restricted and enlarged, by the circumstances of composition and the range of possibilities and impossibilities that they revealed. In the workshop of Joyce, we have encountered very little creation *ex nihilo* and no "full grown beauty [. . .] springing up with all its parts absolute": the process of decontextualization and recontextualization of preexisting material that we saw at work at different levels is perhaps an equivalent of the process of decomposition and germination of the redwoods.[4] When confronted with its monumental result, it can be found terribly disappointing or extremely fascinating. Disappointing if we think that returning to the origin should reveal a hidden meaning that the final work failed to manifest, but fascinating as a testimony of the resourcefulness of creative energy. The purpose of this book has been to share this fascination, communicate some of the thrill that can be felt when we are able to catch a glimpse of the mechanics of invention and encourage the reader to become personally acquainted with Joyce's manuscripts, those magic surfaces that have in store more wonders than the Mirus Bazaar, more awe than the Clongowes square ditch and Father Conmee's study combined, more excitement than Mrs. Cohen's establishment and much more fecundity than the Porters' bedroom.

Notes

Introduction: Writers Writing

1. In so doing, it encounters, and often overlaps with textual criticism, a discipline that uses some of the same documents but starts from an opposite direction: the study of textual *repetition* and its failures. Since invention and repetition are dialectically linked and cannot be studied separately, the two disciplines necessarily meet. I have emphasized the difference between them in "Production, Invention and Reproduction: Genetic criticism vs. Textual Criticism," in *Reimagining Textuality: Textual Studies in the Late Age of Print,* ed. N. Fraistat and E. Bergmann Loizeaux (Madison: University of Wisconsin Press, 2002). In "Genetic Criticism with Textual Criticism: From Variant to Variation" (*Variants* 12–13, 2016), I have tried to show on what basis they can collaborate.

2. The genetic approach has indeed been applied successfully to Joyce before genetic criticism existed as a discipline in its modern form. See note 34 below. In particular, *The Art of James Joyce,* by A. Walton Litz (New York: Oxford University Press, 1961/1964) remains entirely valid and inspiring. Recently, several exciting books have studied various aspects of Joyce's creation from this point of view, such as Finn Fordham's *Lots of Fun at Finnegans Wake: Unravelling Universals* (Oxford: Oxford University Press, 2007*),* Luca Crispi's *Joyce's Creative Process and the Construction of Characters in Ulysses: Becoming the Blooms* (Oxford: Oxford University Press, 2015) and Dirk Van Hulle's *James Joyce's Work in Progress: Pre-Book Publications of Finnegans Wake* (London: Routledge, 2016).

3. Alexandre Dumas, "Comment je devins auteur dramatique," *La Revue des Deux Mondes* 4 (1833) (my translation).

4. To take up the title of Jack Stillinger's illuminating book: *Multiple Authorship and the Myth of the Solitary Genius* (New York: Oxford University Press, 1994).

5. Frédéric Lefèvre, *Entretiens avec Paul Valéry* (Paris: Le Livre, 1926), 107–8 (my translation).

6. In this respect, *Genetic Joyce* could be seen as a distant and attenuated echo of *Poststructuralist Joyce,* the anthology that Derek Attridge and myself published thirty-eight years ago (Cambridge: Cambridge University Press, 1984). On the links between poststructuralism and genetic criticism, see Daniel Ferrer and Michael Groden's introduction to *Genetic Criticism: Texts and Avant-textes,* ed. Jed Deppman, Daniel Ferrer, and Michael Groden (Philadelphia: Pennsylvania University Press, 2004).

7. T. S. Eliot, letter to John Quinn, September 21, 1922, quoted in *The Waste Land: A Facsimile and Transcript of the Original Drafts Including the Annotations of Ezra* Pound, ed. Valerie Eliot (London: Faber and Faber, 1971), xx.

8. See Olivier Lumbroso's book, *Zola autodidacte: Genèse des œuvres et apprentissages de l'écrivain en régime naturaliste* (Genève: Droz, 2013).

9. In *Le Temps retrouvé,* Proust compares writers who change their plans in the course of writing to generals who adapt their goals according to their success in different parts of the frontline and transform a mere diversion into the main assault. See *À la Recherche du temps perdu III* (Paris: Gallimard, 1954), 981.

10. Virginia Woolf's reading notebook titled "Modern Novels (Joyce)." A transcription has been published by Suzette Henke in *The Gender of Modernism,* ed. Bonnie Kime Scott (Bloomington: Indiana University Press, 1990), 642–45. See chapter 8, this volume.

11. Ezra Pound's letter of February 21, 1918. *Pound/the Little Review: The Letters of Ezra Pound to Margaret Anderson,* ed. Thomas L. Scott, Melvin J. Friedman, with the assistance of Jackson R. Bryer (New York: New Directions, 1988), 189.

12. Pierre Bourdieu, *Manet: A Symbolic Revolution,* trans. Peter Collier and Margaret Rigaud-Drayton (Cambridge: Polity, 2017), 3–4.

13. *Revue de la Bibliothèque nationale* 43, 1992, passim.

14. This is true for *Ulysses* and *Finnegans Wake.* The genesis of the early works is considerably less documented. Most of our examples will therefore be taken from the archive of the two larger books.

15. *Ulysses: A Facsimile of the Manuscript* (New York and Philadelphia: Octagon, Philip H. & A.S.W. Rosenbach Foundation, 1975).

16. *The James Joyce Archive.* General Editor Michael Groden. 63 folio vols. (New York: Garland, 1977–78). Unfortunately, most of the reproductions are in black and white.

17. See the catalogue of the auction: *James Joyce's Ulysses: The John Quinn Draft Manuscript of the "Circe" Episode, Thursday, 14 December 2000* (New York: Christie's, 2000).

18. Jon Elster, *The Cement of Society: A Survey of Social Order* (Cambridge: Cambridge University Press, 1989), 97.

19. See Gustave Flaubert's letter to Louise Colet: "When my novel is finished, in a year, I will bring you my whole manuscript, for curiosity's sake. You will see the complicated machinery it takes for me to make a sentence" (my translation) ["Quand mon roman sera fini, dans un an, je t'apporterai mon manuscrit complet, par curiosité. Tu verras par quelle mécanique compliquée j'arrive à faire une phrase" (April 15, 1852). *Correspondance,* vol. 2 (Paris: Fasquelle, 1894), 88].

Chapter 1. Time-Bound Transactions and Contextual Transgressions

1. Gathering 30 according to the *James Joyce Archive* numbering. *JJA* 26:171–86.

2. See in particular Bernard Cerquiligni, *Éloge de la variante: Histoire critique de la philologie* (Paris: Seuil, 1989), translated as *In Praise of the Variant: A Critical History of Philology* (Baltimore, Md.: Johns Hopkins University Press, 1999).

3. Eugene Jolas, "Remembering James Joyce," *Modernism/Modernity* 5, no. 2 (1998): 11.

4. The editorial problem raised by this writing event has no satisfactory solution. The 1984 edition, answering Joyce's fervent prayer to the printers, incorporated the additions where he had wanted them to go, in the Messianic scene (*U* 15.1914–17; 15.1944–45). But this reinsertion created an interesting but completely unintended echo with the very similar passage at the end of the chapter (*U* 15.4506–9) and more discreetly at *U* 15.4698–4718 (the Alleluia). In the 1986 edition, this last echo was perpetuated, but in the case of Don Patrizio's apostrophe, the editors considered that the mid-January 1922 insertion canceled the indication on the mid-December 1921 proofs, so that only the second passage was kept (*U* 15.4506–9). Another, drastic, solution would have been to reinstate the passage in the Messianic scene and to excise the other one, on the grounds that it was only inserted at the end of the chapter as a second-best choice. This would not be a worse compromise than the other solutions, except that we would lose the changes introduced in the second incarnation of the piece.

5. The Messianic scene of "Circe" is the result of the progressive transformation of two lines of dialogue into a twenty-page long scene, a remarkable instance of expansion, even for a writer like Joyce who works mostly by accretion. There is no way to know if this would ever have stopped or how much more the scene could have grown in the absence of the birthday deadline.

6. See page "79a)" of the Rosenbach manuscript for the episode.

7. This is a simplification. The writer can also be on the receiving end of instructions addressed by a mentor or a publisher, for instance. And there is a wide array of cases of collaboration, in which the instructions are mutual (See *The Myth of the Solitary Genius,* and *Genesis* 41, "Créer à plusieurs mains," 2015).

8. *Letters* I 253.

9. Thus *variants* can be said to interpret the text in the same way as musical (or pictorial) *variations* interpret the text according to Nelson Goodman ("Variations on Variation—or Picasso Back to Bach," in Nelson Goodman and Catherine Elgin, *Reconceptions in Philosophy and Other Arts and Sciences* (Indianapolis, Ind.: Hackett, 1988). I have developed this idea, with examples relating to Joyce, in "Genetic Criticism with Textual Criticism: From Variant to Variation," *Variants* 12–13, 2016, available online.

Chapter 2. Multiple Determinations

1. The words of the English version of Lionel's aria are actually "Not one ray of hope is gleaming." Bloom has noticed earlier that Simon was "Singing wrong words" (*U* 11.696).

2. The fair copy of this episode has been lost, but it can be reconstructed with the help of the typescript and the Rosenbach manuscript. See chapter 5, this volume.

3. Michael Groden, *Ulysses in Progress* (Princeton, N.J.: Princeton University Press, 1977), 13. Each of these stages is very diverse, so we could say that there are in fact a much greater number of different projects, but one can indeed see two major shifts.

4. It is probably also the case of the *Portrait,* although we know comparatively little about its genesis. Hans Walter Gabler has demonstrated that the last chapters (chapter 4 and the first pages of chapter 5) are the oldest in the manuscript, which proves that the earlier chapters have been rewritten in the perspective of the recent developments. "The Seven Lost Years of *A*

Portrait of the Artist as a Young Man," in *Approaches to Joyce's Portrait,* ed. Bernard Benstock and Thomas F. Staley (Pittsburgh, Penn.: University of Pittsburgh Press, 1976).

5. Joyce claimed that he had written the "Nostos" episodes very early, but, as late as July 1920, he said that their style was "quite plain" (*Letters* I 143). If these early drafts did exist, they must have been very different from the final chapters as we know them.

6. This proliferation of versions attracted early attention. Even before the manuscripts became available, critics such as Leon Edel and Edmund Wilson discussed the evolution of the chapter based on the successive prepublications. It was later studied by Fred H. Higginson, A. Walton Litz, and Claude Jacquet, among others.

7. When Joyce uses this note in *A Portrait of the Artist as a Young Man* (see Luca Crispi, "The Afterlives of Joyce's 'Alphabetical Notebook' from *A Portrait* to *Ulysses* (1910–20)," *Genetic Joyce Studies* 20 [2020]), it is presented as a subjective experience of Stephen and the nostalgic disappointment is even more perceptible: "The instant of inspiration seemed now to be reflected from all sides at once from a multitude of cloudy circumstance of what had happened or of what might have happened. The instant flashed forth like a point of light and now from cloud on cloud of vague circumstance confused form was veiling softly its afterglow." (New York: Vintage International, 1993), V.1538–42 (*JJA* 10:1057–9).

8. Frank Budgen, *James Joyce and the Making of Ulysses* (Oxford: Oxford University Press, 1972), 173–74.

9. *Letters* I 205. See also *Letters* I 128, "The elements needed will only fuse after a prolonged existence together," and the unpublished letter quoted by Ellmann, "the ingredients will not fuse until they have reached a certain temperature"; Richard Ellmann, *James Joyce* (New York: Oxford University Press, 1982), 416.

10. In notebook VI.B.14, p. 32. See *The "Finnegans Wake" Notebooks at Buffalo: VI.B.14,* ed. Vincent Deane, Daniel Ferrer, and Geert Lernout (Turnhout: Brepols, 2002), 65.

11. Stefan Zygmunt Czarnowski, *Le Culte des héros et ses conditions sociales: Saint Patrick, héros national de l'Irlande* (Paris: Félix Alcan, 1919), 32n2. The source was identified by Geert Lernout. See *The "Finnegans Wake" Notebooks at Buffalo: VI.B.14,* 273.

12. See chapter 7, this volume.

13. Jacques Derrida, *Margins of Philosophy,* trans. Alan Bass (Brighton, U.K.: Harvester, 1982), 320.

Chapter 3. From Tristan to *Finnegan:* Decontextualization and Recontextualization in the Transition from *Ulysses* to *Finnegans Wake*

1. My account relies on previous scholarship, in particular on David Hayman, *A First-Draft Version of "Finnegans Wake"* (Austin: University of Texas Press, 1963); David Hayman, *The "Wake" in Transit* (Ithaca, N.Y.: Cornell University Press, 1990); Danis Rose, "A Nice Beginning: On the *Ulysses/Finnegans Wake* Interface," *European Joyce Studies* 2 (1990): 165–73; Danis Rose, "The Beginning of All Thisorder of Work in Progress," *James Joyce Quarterly* 28, no. 4 (Summer 1990): 957–65; Danis Rose, *The Textual Diaries of James Joyce* (Dublin: Lilliput, 1995); Luca Crispi, Sam Slote, and Dirk Van Hulle, introduction to *How Joyce Wrote "Finnegans Wake": A Chapter-by-Chapter Genetic Guide,* edited by Luca Crispi and Sam Slote

(Madison: University of Wisconsin Press, 2007), 3–48; Jed Deppman, "A Chapter in Composition: *Chapter II.4*," in *How Joyce Wrote "Finnegans Wake*," 304–46; Vincent Deane, introduction to *The "Finnegans Wake" Notebooks at Buffalo: VI.B.10,* and introduction to *The "Finnegans Wake" Notebooks at Buffalo: VI.B.3,* edited by Vincent Deane, Daniel Ferrer, and Geert Lernout (Turnhout, Belgium: Brepols, 2001); as well as Jorn Barger's website Robotwisdom, which is unfortunately no longer available online.

2. A version of the talk was published in the *Nouvelle Revue Française* XVIII (April 1922): 385–405, and part of it was translated for the first issue of the *Criterion* (see note 12 below).

3. Aramis [pseud.], "The Scandal of Ulysses," *The Sporting Times* 34 (April 1, 1922): 4; also see Robert Deming, *James Joyce: The Critical Heritage* (London: Routledge & Kegan Paul, 1970), 192.

4. If we are to believe "Domini Canis" [Shane Leslie] in his review of *Ulysses* in the *Dublin Review,* clxxi, September 1922, 112–19; also see Deming, *James Joyce,* 201.

5. T. S. Eliot, "'*Ulysses*,' Order and Myth," *Dial* 75 (November 1923): 480–83; also see Deming, *James Joyce,* 270.

6. Reported in Woolf's diary on September 26, 1922. See Virginia Woolf, *A Writer's Diary,* ed. Leonard Woolf (London: Hogarth, 1972), 30.

7. Woolf, *A Writer's Diary,* September 26, 1920, 28.

8. See Burton Rascoe, *A Bookman's Daybook* (New York: Horace and Liveright, 1929), 27.

9. William Carlos Williams, "A Note on the Recent Work of James Joyce," *transition* 8 (November 1927): 149.

10. Ellmann, *James Joyce,* 540.

11. Ellmann, *James Joyce,* 537.

12. T. Sturge Moore, "The Story of Tristram and Isolt in Modern Poetry, Part I, Narrative Versions," *Criterion* 1, no. 1 (October 1922): 34–49.

13. Moore spells her name "Isolt." Among several possible variant spellings, I use the Wagnerian "Isolde" because it is the form Joyce always chooses when he writes the name in full, which he rarely does. On the other hand, he uses Tristram as well as Tristan.

14. "The Waste Land," *Criterion* 1, no. 1 (October 1922): 51.

15. See chapter 3 of Hayman, *The "Wake" in Transit,* and Jean-Michel Rabaté, *Joyce upon the Void: The Genesis of Doubt* (London: Macmillan, 1991). See also chapter 6, this volume, in the "Lacedemon" notes, the diagram of deceived husbands and unfaithful wives.

16. See Joyce, *Buffalo "Finnegans Wake" Notebooks:* VI.B.10, 15.

17. See the page headed "Homer" in NLI MS 36,639/3, p. [13v].

18. Once again we see that Joyce reads too quickly: he does not seem to realize that Isolde of the White Hands is the same as Isolde of Brittany. See Hayman, *The "Wake" in Transit,* 58.

19. It is even possible that a whole notebook is missing in between, as suggested by Danis Rose in *The Textual Diaries of James Joyce,* 25.

20. On the first surviving page of Buffalo notebook VI.B.3, Joyce wrote: "to circulate / (Trist) / Trist—Go away from / me you—/ (she goes) O come back." Taken by themselves, these notes are rather enigmatic, but in Joyce's first version of the kiss of Tristan and Isolde, they will be developed into a parody of the quarrel between the lovers in the first act of Wagner's opera:

—Go away from me instantly you thing she roared. Curse your stinking putrid soul & all belonged to you scum. Forget me not!

—Perfect, you bloody bitch, he said.

He took leave of her and circulated as bidden. She let out a whistle before many instants had passed. Hearing his name called he most sagaciously ceased to walk about and turned, his look now charged with purpose.

—No, come back, she cried. How sweetly you have responded to me.

I so want you! (BL MS 47480, f. 267v; *JJA* 56: 7).

Note that, compared with the original VI.B.3 fragment, the protagonists have changed places.

21. BL MS 47480, f. 267; *JJA* 55: 446a.

22. NLI MS 41,818, p. [1r]–[1v] and BL MS 47480, f. 267v; Buffalo MS VI.B.3, pp. 42–45; NLI MS 41,818, p. [2r]–[2v]; BL MS 47488, f. 24v.

23. James Joyce, *Pomes Penyeach* (Paris: Shakespeare and Company, 1927).

24. Partial publication in *Poetry* 10, no. 2 (May 1917): 74.

25. See Hayman, *The "Wake" in Transit*, 90 and 96–98, and Rose, "The Beginning of All Thisorder of Work in Progress," 61–62.

26. The first draft of "Cyclops" is also written around an apparently unrelated poem by Verlaine (Buffalo V.A.8-2, *JJA* 14:86), but the poem is carefully boxed in to separate it from the draft. They seem to be unconnected.

27. NLI MS 41,818, p. [1r].

28. "Cissy told him too that billy winks was coming and that baby was to go deedaw and baby looked just too ducky, laughing up out of his gleeful eyes, and Cissy poked him like that out of fun in his wee fat tummy" (*U* 13.609).

29. "—The Church differentiates between the good which this man seeks and the good which I seek. There is a *bonum simpliciter*. The men you mention seek a good of that kind because they are impelled by passions which are direct even if they are menial: lust, ambition, gluttony. I seek a *bonum arduum*"; James Joyce, *Stephen Hero* (New York: New Directions, 1963), 179–80.

30. BL MSS 47481, f. 94, *JJA* 56: 2–3.

31. This is probably the reason why Joyce worked more intensely on this piece than on any of the other early sketches that were written at about the same time.

32. Since it was transcribed and published by Thomas Connolly under the name *Scribbledehobble; The Ur-Workbook for "Finnegans Wake"* (Evanston, Ill.: Northwestern University Press, 1961). It is also known as Buffalo Notebook VI.A according to Peter Spielberg's classification. On this notebook, see also the first section of chapter 7, this volume.

33. For instance, the fragment "blackedged expression" is stored in the "Eumaeus" section (VI.A, p. 801; *Scribbledehobble*, 147) before it is inserted in the first description of Tristan quoted above. The words "rather gathered" substituted to "knew" and the words "full well" added in the sentence "For now she knew ^+rather gathered+^ ^+from his persiflage+^ ^+^+full well+^ that he was a loveslave for life+^," had been arranged respectively under the "Eolus" and the "Nausicaa" section. (VI.A, p. 511; *Scribbledehobble*, 95, and VI.A, p. 681;

Scribbledehobble, 113) Isolde's solid appetite is based on a note in the *"Exiles,* Act I" section: "Sotty (Is) wants a good dinner: cervoise" (VI.A, p. 271; *Scribbledehobble, 76*).

34. NLI, MS 41.818.

35. *Poetry* 10, no. 2 (May 1917): 72.

36. Reproduced in facsimile in Richard Ellmann's *James Joyce* (New York: Oxford University Press, 1982) as plates XV and XVI. In the same way as the parodic reference to the unpublished *Stephen Hero,* this allusion was absolutely imperceptible to an external reader.

37. BL MSS 47481, ff. 2–4; *JJA* 56: 26–35.

38. Vol. I, No 4. See *JJA* 56: 91–133.

39. See Jed Deppman, "A Chapter in Composition: *Chapter* II.4," 304–46.

40. See Daniel Ferrer, "La toque de Clementis : Rétroaction et rémanence dans les processus génétiques," *Genesis* 6 (1994); English translation in *Yale French Studies* 89 (1996).

Chapter 4. The Spatial Dynamics of Invention (*Nebeneinander* and *Nacheinander*)

1. "I composed some wondrous devices for Shaun d during the night and wrote them out in the dark only to discover that I had made a mosaic on top of other notes so I am now going to bring my astronomical telescope into play" (*Letters* I 234).

2. Actually, they are often trapezoidal, since the margin widens toward the bottom and the text block consequently narrows.

3. Sometimes, however, a blank is left, destined to be filled later. For a description of the very complex progression of the first draft of *Finnegans Wake* III.4, see Hayman, *A First-Draft Version of Finnegans Wake,* 37–39.

4. Buffalo V.A.5, the second part of the second extant draft of "Sirens." This draft proves that Joyce's writing habits are not always consistent. It is written on two copybooks. The one containing the first part (now in the NLI) is written on rectos and versos continuously while the second (in the Buffalo collection) is written on rectos only.

5. Joyce numbered it "33)," in sequence with "32)," the facing verso.

6. The "letters read out in court" passage on the bottom of the right-hand page of the manuscript is probably derived from the "Breach of promise action in Kilkenny" reported on the third column of page 3.

7. Our illustration comes from "the last *pink* edition" of the *Evening Telegraph.* The color of the paper is also an indication of the freshness of the news, but it is a purely arbitrary indication, more like the date printed on top of the page than like the indexical faint ink of the "very latest" column. I am using here the image of the newspaper reconstructed by the Split Pea Press, courtesy of Ian Gunn.

8. As a discipline, genetic criticism belongs to what Carlo Ginzburg has called the "indexical paradigm"; see Ginzburg, "Clues: Roots of a Scientific Paradigm," *Theory and Society* 7, no. 3 (1979): 273–88.

9. There are areas of uncertainty (for instance, it is possible that the sequence labeled "18" came earlier), but they are relatively few.

10. In "Epiphanic 'Proteus'" (*Genetic Joyce Studies* 5, Spring 2005, http://www.geneticjoy-

cestudies.org/), Sam Slote shows that the identification between the shifting sands and language was reinforced when Joyce redrafted the passage.

11. See also Daniel Ferrer and Jean-Michel Rabaté, "Paragraphs in expansion," tr. Jed Deppman in *Genetic Criticism: Texts and Avant-textes.*

12. There is actually a remainder that cannot be analyzed into any of these components: the *gh* sound, expressive of the mouthing of the syllables by the young poet, tasting them, almost French kissing the word. The version that is finally actualized into the main text is the only variant that does not have a "g" in it, as if Joyce, at this stage, felt compelled to get rid of this corporal dimension of the word that was obscuring the superimposed meanings.

13. See the examples from "Sirens" analyzed in chapter 2. Joyce also introduced a portmanteau ("underdarkneath") in Stephen's reflections on his own poem in "Aeolus" (*U* 7.723).

14. Joseph Frank, "Spatial Form in Modern Literature" (1945), in *The Idea of Spatial Form* (New Brunswick, N.J.: Rutgers University Press, 1991), 20–21.

15. Jacques Derrida, "Two Words for Joyce: He War," in *Poststructuralist Joyce: Essays from the French,* ed. Derek Attridge and Daniel Ferrer (Cambridge: Cambridge University Press, 1984), 147.

16. Michael Groden, "Joyce at Work on 'Cyclops': Toward a Biography of *Ulysses,*" *James Joyce Quarterly* 44, no. 2 (Winter 2007). See also Luca Crispi, the "Scenes and Fragmentary Texts for 'Cyclops': June 1919" section in "A First Foray into the National Library of Ireland's Joyce Manuscripts: Bloomsday 2011," *Genetic Joyce Studies* 11 (2011).

17. "Thanking you for the hospitality"—*U* 3.405.

18. Part of the first draft of "Cyclops" is written on the margin of a poem by Verlaine. As far as we can tell, this seems to be purely fortuitous, but it marks, nevertheless, a kind of acknowledged allegiance to French Symbolism.

Chapter 5. "Sirens": Hesitations and Tipping Points

1. Joyce usually paginated his manuscripts with a pencil. The number is followed by a closing bracket, thus: "1)". Whenever I refer to Joyce's own pagination, I will make use of this format.

2. See my preliminary description in "What Song the Sirens Sang . . . Is No Longer Beyond All Conjecture: A Preliminary Description of the New 'Proteus' and 'Sirens' Manuscripts," *JJQ* 39, no. 1 (Fall 2001), and Luca Crispi's thorough analysis in "A First Foray into the National Library of Ireland's Joyce Manuscripts: Bloomsday 2011."

3. It is available online on the site of the National Library of Ireland.

4. It is interesting that in some marginal additions, the name has already been changed to "Miss Douce." This suggests that Joyce returned to that draft at a later period. In the part of the Rosenbach manuscript of "Wandering Rocks" that was dictated by Joyce to Frank Budgen, the name appears as "Miss Deuce," but this probably reflects Joyce's way of pronouncing *Douce.* When he recovered from his eye operation and could read again, Joyce corrected it to "Miss Douce."

5. The only striking (but nevertheless minor) departure in the first pages is the color of Lady Dudley's dress: it is pink instead of green, the *eau de nil,* so important in establishing the aquatic atmosphere of the chapter as we know it, is replaced by (or rather, eventually replaces)

crushed strawberries. In the Linati Scheme, the color assigned to the episode was still "coral." *Eau-de-Nil* is inserted on the second draft, next to the crushed strawberries.

6. See André Topia, "'Sirens': The Emblematic Vibration," and Derek Attridge, "Syntax and the Subject in 'Sirens,'" in *James Joyce: The Centennial Symposium*, ed. M. Beja, Ph. Herring, M. Harmon, and D. Norris (Champaign: Illinois University Press, 1986). Another interlinear correction on the first page ascribes Miss Douce's laughter to her wet lips.

7. Rodney Owen, in *James Joyce and the Beginnings of Ulysses* (Ann Arbor, Mich.: UMI Research, 1983, 65–68) surmised that part of "Sirens" was based on a very early version, and Luca Crispi writes that "the appearance of two entries from the 'Alphabetical Notebook' raises the possibility that [Joyce] had written one or more versions of at least [Simon Dedalus's visit to the barroom in the Ormond Hotel] at some stage between 1910 and 1914, specifically for *A Portrait*, though he subsequently did not use the text in that book." ("The Afterlives of Joyce's 'Alphabetical Notebook' from *A Portrait* to *Ulysses* (1910–20)").

8. "Major Powell—in my book Major Tweedy, Mrs Bloom's father," *Letters* I 198 (Letter to Mrs William Murray, December 21, 1922). In this letter, Joyce mentions a questionnaire about Major Powell that he had asked his aunt Josephine to answer.

9. He is looking more specifically at her eyes. The considerable importance of eyes, mirrors, and gazes, so striking in a chapter dedicated to music, sound, and echoes (see Daniel Ferrer, "Echo or Narcissus," *James Joyce: The Centennial Symposium*, 73–74) is already noticeable in this first draft. It is also remarkable that the celebrated ending of the episodes comes about as the result of a vacant gaze: Bloom is looking away from the "frowsy whore" and pretends to be absorbed in the contemplation of a shop window (not yet named as Lionel Mark's). It is only in an interlinear addition, expanded in the margin, that Emmet's last words come to occupy that window.

10. Two pages earlier in this first draft, Miss Douce's "Sonnez la cloche" also anticipated Gerty's subjugation of the "male gaze" but appropriately transposed on the auditory plane.

11. All the later details are already present: the polished knob, the firm baton emerging out of the sliding ring of the gently touching fingers (cf. *U* 11.1111–17).

12. The climax is more openly present in the first draft than in the published chapter where the gushing overflow is blended with the musical description (*U* 11.705–9).

13. One of them, numbered "20)" is extant (NLI MS 36,639/7/B). Since in the notebook the last page of the draft is paginated "18)," we know that a "19)" must be missing, but it is quite possible that there were more pages.

14. Michael Groden remarks: "We might conjecture that Joyce began with the opinionated, bigoted narrator and then gradually developed the series of parodies as a complement to, and a check on, the authority of the naturalistic description. But the opposite was the case: Joyce created the parodies first, the barroom scene came soon after, and the narrative voice developed last" (*Ulysses in Progress*, 124). At the level of the genesis of the whole book, it seems that a version of the barroom scene was invented first (the "Sirens" episode in its primitive form). Within that frame, some elements of the Unknown Narrator's voice were tried out, long before the defining characteristic of "Cyclops" (the contrasting heroic parodies).

15. In the "Fugue" article that was Joyce's source for the *Fuga per canonem* notes (see note 114 below), episodes are not defined. It is simply said that they are "usually founded on the main subject and counter-subject," p. 118. In Joyce's notes, they appear to be central to the

contrapuntal web, instead of being simply a transitional stage. The Homeric resonance of the term *Episode* must also have interested Joyce.

16. *Letters* I 129.

17. See Susan Brown, "The Mystery of the *Fuga Per Canonem* Solved," *Genetic Joyce Studies* 7 (Spring 2007). The search was particularly difficult and Susan Brown's discovery was particularly ingenious, because the notes were taken in Italian from an English text.

18. See Brown, "The Mystery of the *Fuga Per Canonem* Solved."

19. The margin of uncertainty comes from the fact that Joyce made changes, voluntary or involuntary, when he copied the Rosenbach manuscript and that the typist made some more reading or typing mistakes as he created the typescript.

20. See Jean-Michel Rabaté, "The Silence of the Sirens," in *James Joyce: The Centennial Symposium.*

21. In "Penelope," we will discover Molly's side of the story and find out that the cause of her look is not at all what Bloom thinks it is.

22. Except the availability of space on the page, but of course the expansion can continue on successive versions. It is for this reason that Joyce demanded multiple sets of proofs.

23. The basis for this cluster is found in two marginal additions to page "10)" of the first draft: "She viewed herself sideways. Mirror there. Molly always does before she answers the door a knock. Titivate herself." And "She knows I'm looking, knows without looking. Molly (has) devil of a quick eye to notice if anyone is looking at her. All women."

24. In "Scylla and Charybdis," this snatch of interior monologue is preceded by a (rhetorical) question addressed by Stephen to his audience: "But all those twenty years what do you suppose poor Penelope in Stratford was doing behind the diamond panes?" The name Penelope refers ironically to unfaithful Ann Hathaway but also, inevitably in the context of *Ulysses*, to Molly.

25. We have no way to tell if the text in italics, a late addition on top of the page, is a variation or a variant, a repetition or a reformulation meant to replace the version below.

26. We can see that Joyce attempts a closer integration, by adding "He walks" at the beginning of Stephen's words and then treating "Shakespeare that is" as an insertion after it, but this leads nowhere.

27. In the Rosenbach manuscript the final "O rocks" is missing, but the word "asses" (probably forgotten by the typist after "braying") is present.

28. At this point of the draft (but this is also true in the final text), the reference to the box remains unspecified. We have to reach our passage to know that it refers to a (theatre) box for a performance of *Trilby*. It is only in "Penelope" that the reader of the final text learns that the Blooms were present in order to see the famous actor Beerbohm Tree, although he was mentioned (with a question mark) in the very first draft quoted above.

29. On the inner cover of the notebook that contains the first part of the second draft, next to the *Fuga per canonem* list, Joyce had inscribed, in ink, the words "Music hath charms./ Snakes, bird/ tune canary," which were later crossed out in red crayon. It is likely that this note generated not the first occurrence of the Congreve quotation, in the main text, but the second one: "Music hath charms Owls and birds," an addition also inscribed in ink, meant to be inserted just before "Way to catch rattlesnakes." The note clearly associates music's charms with animals (even if canaries hardly qualify as "savage beasts").

30. The same paragraph offers us another curious example of memory of the context (less remarkable however, because in that case the deferral does not cause any change and because the memorial process is less impalpable) and of return of the recycled element in the same place. On the typescript, a third addition to this passage comes from the "Sirens" section of another notebook, NLI MS 36,639/5/B: "remind him of Home sweet home." It is inserted after "Shah of Persia liked that best," referring to the noise of the tuning orchestra. The source for the whole Shah of Persia scene is to be found in a fragment on the supplementary sheet to the first draft numbered "20)":

Tuning up. Queer. Shah of Persia at the ^+Antient+^ concert ^+in London+^ said he liked that best. Reminds him of home sweet home probably. Dulcimers. ^+Lumtee-tumtoo+^. Trousered girls sitting crosslegged. Wiped his nose in a window curtain. So Wonder what else he did. All depends on the custom.

Practically all the elements are already present. It was then transcribed on the verso of page "26)" of the second draft as

Tuning up. ^+Tootling, psa, psa, prr: psipsa+^ Shah of Persia liked that better ^+best+^ of all. Also wiped his nose in curtain. Custom of his country.

"Reminds him of home sweet home" was not used there. It has disappeared from this draft, and it will also be absent from the fair copy, as far as we can reconstruct it, and from the typed text. It was probably considered to be superfluous because "Custom of his country" expressed the same idea. The removal must have been deliberate, since Joyce made a note of this discarded element in the "Sirens" section of notebook NLI MS 36,639/5/B, which means that he intended to use it in the same episode. We can see that he finally inserted it in the very same place from which it had been removed. Perhaps Joyce regretted the allusion to Bloom's own frame of mind when everything tends to remind him of his home and of what was happening there, but it is likely that, in 1921, it was the reference to a song ("Home Sweet Home" by John Howard Payne and Henry Rowley Bishop, 1823) that was the decisive factor, since at that time he had undertaken to saturate the text with musical allusions and in particular with references to songs.

31. In the same way, unused elements from the workshop of previous works were incorporated into *Ulysses*.

Chapter 6. The Reading Notes I: *Ars Excerpendi*

1. The notes for *Exiles*, written a few years before the "Proteus" draft, show that Joyce shared this preoccupation with Stephen : "Her age: 28. Robert likens her to the moon because of her dress. Her age is the completion of a lunar rhythm. Cf. Oriani on menstrual flow—la malattia sacra che in un ritmo lunare prepara la donna per il sacrificio" (*E* 164).

2. See Daniel Ferrer, "Towards a Marginalist Economy of Textual Genesis," *Variants* 2/3 "Reading Notes" (2004).

3. The annotations relative to Dante, recorded by Joyce when he was a student at University College and now in the NLI (MS 36,639/1), are of a different nature: they are not meant to be extracts taken *from* the *Divine Comedy* but explanations (probably dictated by a professor or taken from a commentary) added *to* it in order to facilitate its reading. On the other hand,

Buffalo Notebook VIII.B, which was used a few years later (in Trieste) is also a gathering of long extracts. The document called "Literary extracts" by the NLI (MS 36,639/2/B), which probably dates from the summer of 1924, seems to indicate a return to the early habit of copying very substantial passages at the same time as he was cutting off very limited samples in his *Finnegans Wake* notebooks, but it is possible that it represents something quite different: Joyce's habit of committing to memory long stretches of text (see letter to Harriet Shaw Weaver of June 24, 1924, *Letters* I 216). The copying of the text would be part of the process of memorizing.

4. For a thorough presentation, see Luca Crispi, "A Commentary on James Joyce's National Library of Ireland 'Early Commonplace Book':1903–1912(MS 36,639/02/A)," *Genetic Joyce Studies* 9 (2009).

5. Luca Crispi, referring to page [17v] of the notebook, remarks, "This list of shorthand topics, fragmentary phrases and short sentences, most of which are quotations, are the first indication of Joyce's mature system of note-taking for use in his writings. It would become his preferred method of assembling material for possible use in his work for the rest of his creative life, from *Stephen Hero* to *Ulysses* and *Finnegans Wake*." ("A Commentary on James Joyce's National Library of Ireland 'Early Commonplace Book,'" 20). He also remarks that here Joyce seems to inaugurate his method of crossing out the notes that he incorporates in his drafts.

6. See Sam Slote, "The Economy of Joyce's Notetaking," in *New Quotatoes: Joycean Exogenesis in the Digital Age*, ed. Ronan Crowley and Dirk van Hulle (Leiden: Brill, 2016), 169: "If money is a promise of payment (an indication of a debt paid), then a notebook entry is a promise, made in advance, to make a text, a pledge that a text might be made from this scrap (or might not since promises can be broken). [. . .] Just as the text of *Finnegans Wake* is indebted to all the things that Joyce read (and didn't, such as *Huckleberry Finn*), notebook entries are 'I.O.U's towards a text."

7. The phrase in "Cyclops" (*U* 12.24) first appears in the *Dubliners* section of this notebook.

8. Robert Scholes remarks, "Joyce's practice with Aristotle and Aquinas was not to work out their theories but to borrow single phrases which caught his fancy and work out his own interpretations of the possibilities inherent in those phrases" (*Workshop of Dedalus* [Evanston, Ill.: Northwestern University Press, 1965], 52). This is an early form of Joyce's creative process based on decontextualization and recontextualization.

9. *A Portrait of the Artist as a Young Man*, 169.

10. Compare Stephen's remark in *Ulysses*: "Remember your epiphanies written on green oval leaves, deeply deep, copies to be sent if you died to all the great libraries of the world, including Alexandria" (*U* 3.141–42). Getting into these great repositories of world literature was another way of dignifying his writing by association.

11. Although it should be mentioned that the five pages of notes at the end of the manuscript of the 1904 "Portrait" are destination oriented.

12. For a description and analysis of this notebook, see *Workshop of Dedalus* and Crispi, "The Afterlives of Joyce's 'Alphabetical Notebook' from *A Portrait* to *Ulysses* (1910–20)."

13. For a description and analysis of this notebook, see Wim Van Mierlo, "The Subject

Notebook: A Nexus in the Composition History of Ulysse—-A Preliminary Analysis," *Genetic Joyce Studies* (2007).

14. The notesheets kept at the British Library are devoted to a single episode each, so they do not reveal anything about the plan of the book. They do not concern the early episodes and clearly belong to a later period.

15. I gave a summary description of this page in "What Song the Sirens Sang . . . Is No Longer Beyond All Conjecture: A Preliminary Description of the New 'Proteus' and 'Sirens' Manuscripts," *James Joyce Quarterly* 36, no. 1 (2001), republished with a corrective note in *James Joyce Quarterly* 50, no. 1–2 (2012–2013). I offered an interpretation in "An Unwritten Chapter of *Ulysses*? Joyce's Notes for a 'Lacedemon' Episode," in *James Joyce: Whence, Whither and How; Studies in Honour of Carla Vaglio*, ed. Giuseppina Cortese, Giuliana Ferreccio, M. Teresa Giaveri, and Teresa Prudente (Alessandria: Edizioni dell'Orso, 2015).

16. I thank Luca Crispi for his help with this document. It is important but difficult to determine the sequence of the different inscriptions on the page. It seems likely that the line of separation drawn with a ruler across the page and the two perpendicular lines delimiting a box in the right bottom corner have been added after the text had been written. Graphic clues suggest that Joyce numbered the notes as he was inscribing them (first level of numbering: 1 through 24 followed by 1 through 17). Obviously the second level of numbering (1 through 6 in larger numerals) came later and the blue crayon markings were added at a still later stage.

17. I am referring to Butcher and Lang's translation for reasons that will soon become clear. The page numbers refer to the 1879 edition of the *Odyssey of Homer Done into English Prose*, by S. H. Butcher and A. Lang (London: Macmillan). There are several editions, with minor variants of translation, but I have not been able to determine precisely which one Joyce used for these notes.

18. John Simpson, "They Simply Fade Away: News on the Life and Death of an Old Soldier—Joseph Casey," *JJON* (*James Joyce Online Notes* 2 (2012): http://www.jjon.org/jioyce-s-people/joseph-casey.

19. It is likely that this extension was prompted by the note numbered 6 in the list below: "Menelaus eats his bit? tanist."

20. For a review of the question, see Keri Elizabeth Ames, "Joyce's Aesthetic of the Double Negation and His Encounter with Homer's *Odyssey*," in *Beckett, Joyce and the Art of the Negative, European Joyce Studies* 16, ed. C. Jaurretche (Amsterdam: Rodopi, 2005), 15–48.

21. In spite of Hugh Kenner's prescription that "to appreciate the Homeric parallels in *Ulysses*, the first thing to do is to forget the Butcher and Lang version" ("Joyce's Ulysses: Homer and Hamlet," *Essays in Criticism* 2, no. 1 [January 1952]: 85).

22. At least I have not been able to find them. It is possible that they are transformed beyond recognition.

23. In chapter 5 of this volume, we saw that the continuous "Sirens" draft is interrupted after ten pages and is followed by a series of unrelated fragmentary scenes, preparing for a subsequent draft. Since the last page of the notebook was already occupied by the "Lacedemon" notes, loose leaves (one of which is extant) were used for further fragments.

24. Can it be a pure coincidence that in the summer of 1921, at proof stage, "shepherd of men" (so similar to note "8. Shepherd of the People)" was inserted there, just after "Arthur

Griffith" (see *JJA* 22:145)? The problem is that it returns not as an Homeric allusion but as an etymology of *Pimander* (*Poimandres*), deriving from a Hermetic source (see NLI notebook MS 36,639/4). It may be a case of "memory of the context" similar to what we have seen in "Sirens." The insertion appears rather incongruous in this place and disappears at the next proof stage.

25. Presumably preserved because it happened to be written in the same notebook as two important drafts.

26. See Ellmann, *James Joyce*, 355; Litz, *The Art of James Joyce*, 132–38; Scholes and Kain, *The Workshop of Dedalus*, 106–8.

27. It would have been narratologically coherent to start another sequence of numbers or to close the box at the point where the story of Menelaus's adventures with Proteus ends, but Joyce did not. The notes go on beyond that point, but they do not slavishly follow the course of the Homeric text. Joyce continued to take notes about the events in Lacedaemon and, when necessary, jumped to Book XV in order to conclude.

28. Letter to Carlo Linati, September 21, 1920, *Letters* I 147.

29. Budgen, *James Joyce and the Making of Ulysses*, 352.

30. See Luca Crispi, "The Notescape of *Ulysses*," in *New Quotatoes*, 76.

31. Frank Budgen, *James Joyce and the Making of Ulysses*, 176–77.

32. It is also confirmed by the lost notebook VI.D.7 that Danis Rose and John O'Hanlon have been able to reconstruct on the base of a partial amanuensis transcription. We will discuss this notebook in the next chapter.

33. Victor Bérard, *Les Phéniciens et l'Odyssée* (Paris: Librairie Armand Colin, 1902); W. H. Roscher, *Ausführliches Lexicon der griechischen und römischen Mythologie* (Leipzig: Teubner, 1884–1937), and also the Butcher and Lang translation of the *Odyssey*, but Joyce culled from it only a list of names.

34. If only because the many untraced entries in the extant second-order notebooks imply a corresponding number of first-order entries.

35. I thank Luca Crispi, who gave me access to a still unpublished study of this notesheet.

Chapter 7. The Reading Notes II: "With Some Reserve"

1. It was the subtitle of Thomas Connolly's edition of *Scribbledehobble* (op. cit.).

2. To make things more complicated, four different handwritings, autograph and allograph, can be distinguished in this notebook, indicating different periods of usage. In this section, we are discussing only the chronologically first stratum.

3. See also Stephen's association of the various stages of his trajectory through Dublin with specific cultural memories (*A Portrait of the Artist as a Young Man*, 168–69). The fact that, in *Ulysses*, he has to make a deliberate effort to make the same connexions ("he thought to think of Ibsen" *U* 16.52) shows that it is not a casual association but a premeditated retrieval system.

4. Jacques Derrida speaks of Joyce's hypermnesia "which *a priori* indebts you, and in advance inscribes you in the book you are reading" ("Two Words for Joyce," in *Poststructuralist Joyce*, 147). I suggest that one of the reasons for this hypermnesia is the memory of the (multiple) context(s), which is the counterpart of the "iterability" of writing (see quotation at the end of chapter 2).

5. Gilles Deleuze and Félix Guattari, *A Thousand Plateaus: Capitalism and Schizophrenia*, trans. Brian Massumi (London: Athlone, 1988), 474.

6. Sigmund Freud, *The Origins of Psychoanalysis*, ed. Marie Bonaparte (New York: Basic, 1954), 232.

7. *Letters* I 128.

8. See Durkheim's analysis of the "contagiousness of the sacred" (Emile Durkheim, *Les Formes élémentaires de la vie religieuse*, Paris: Presses Universitaires de France, 1985, 457).

9. See Roland McHugh, *The Sigla of Finnegans Wake* (Austin: University of Texas Press, 1976).

10. Some of the stories included in this book were published earlier in *Three Stories* (published in Paris in 1923 by Robert McAlmon at the Contact Publishing Co. and printed by Maurice Darantiere), in *in our time* (published in Paris in 1924 at the Three Mountain Press and "for sale at shakespeare & company, in the rue de l'Odéon"), and in various reviews, including the *Little Review* and *This Quarter*. However, Joyce's notes unmistakably come from the 1925 collection: several of them derive from a story ("The Battler") that was first published there. The edition came out on October 5, 1925, which would be a little late for the beginning of notebook VI.B.19, but, given Hemingway's admiration for Joyce (in an unpublished early version of *In Our Time* there was an analysis of *Ulysses* concluding that Mrs. Bloom "was the greatest in the world," quoted in Carlos Baker, *Ernest Hemingway: A Life Story* [New York: Charles Scriber's sons, 1969], 131–32) and their developing friendship, it is quite possible that Joyce received an advance copy or even that he read it in manuscript or in proof.

11. "One had pointed out Ezra Pound to them in a café and they had watched James Joyce eating in the Trianon and almost been introduced to a man named Leo Stein," *In Our Time*, 112.

12. In the source, on page 49, we find the word "Yup." This triggers a series of variations on the notebook page.

13. Except for a few cases where Joyce seems to have forgotten to cross out an item.

14. Translated by A. and J. Strachey. This is not the place to insist on the importance of these notes for the history of ideas (they are the only documented extended contact of Joyce with the text of Freud), or on the crucial part they have played in the development of chapter 4 of Book III of *Finnegans Wake*. They are scattered in four different notebooks, reflecting Joyce's idiosyncratic method of note-taking. Joyce seems to have started reading the book sometime in the beginning of 1925, taking notes from "Little Hans" ("Analysis of a Phobia in a Five-Year-Old Boy"), the second case history in the book, first in VI.D.3, for a few pages (as far as we can tell from VI.C.2: 142–43, corresponding to *Collected Papers III*: 151–58), then more extensively in VI.B.19, probably in the second quarter of 1925, starting again at the beginning of the case and going to the end (VI.B.19: 17–48, corresponding to *Collected Papers III*: 150–278). He then started taking notes in the same notebooks from the fifth case, "The Wolfman" (VI.B.19: 68 [or 57] to 84, corresponding to *Collected Papers III*: 477–566). For some reason, he then changed notebooks, using VI.B.9, and went back to the fourth case study that he had skipped, "President Schreber" ("Psychoanalytic Notes on an Autobiographic Account of a Case of Paranoia (Dementia Paranoides)") taking notes from it (VI.B.9: 22–25, corresponding to *Collected Papers III*: 391–418) before returning to the "Wolfman" for two pages, stopping with the note "X look for D / in sky" (VI.B.9: 39, corresponding to the

words "When he died he looked for him in the sky" [*Collected Papers III*:566]). At an indeterminate time, he took a few notes from the same case study on notebook VI.D.1 (as far as we can judge from VI.C.3: 178–79, retracing his steps to *Collected Papers III*: 562). See Daniel Ferrer, "La scène primitive de l'écriture: Une lecture joycienne de Freud," in *Genèse de Babel: James Joyce et la création de Finnegans Wake*, ed. Claude Jacquet (Paris: CNRS, 1985); Daniel Ferrer, "The Freudful Couchmare of Shaun d: Joyce's Notes on Freud and the Composition of Chapter XVI of *Finnegans Wake*," *JJQ* 22, no. 4 (Summer 1985); Wim Van Mierlo, "The Freudful Couchmare Revisited: Contextualizing Joyce and the New Psychology," *Joyce Studies Annual* 8 (1997); and Daniel Ferrer, "III.4: Wondrous Devices in the Dark," in *How Joyce Wrote Finnegans Wake: A Chapter-by-Chapter Genetic Guide*, ed. Luca Crispi and Sam Slote (Madison: University of Wisconsin Press, 2007).

15. *Collected Papers III* ("Wolfman"), 502.

16. Identified by Vincent Deane. See notebook VI.B.6, 38(i) and page 32 of the edition of *The "Finnegans Wake" Notebooks at Buffalo*, vol VI.B.6, ed. Vincent Deane, Daniel Ferrer, and Geert Lernout (Turnhout: Brepols, 2002).

17. *The "Finnegans Wake" Notebooks at Buffalo*, Notebook VI.B.14, 12–13.

18. For the late-twentieth-century reader, this kind of printed matter had paradoxically become rarer, or at least more difficult to locate and identify, than the most esoteric of classics. But today, the policies of systematic digitization and the power of the search engines have made them universally available, within a textual democracy that *Finnegans Wake* has, in some ways, anticipated in its leveling effect on culture.

19. *The Making of Ulysses*, p. 315.

20. The fascination of Miss Douce's smacking garter in "Sirens" is undoubtedly fetishistic, but interestingly, and appropriately for this musical episode, the metonymic connection is not visual but sonorous.

21. Other words of the play, like "moon" and "roses," are treated similarly.

22. Ernest Hemingway, *Death in the Afternoon* (New York: Scribner and Son, 1932), 192.

23. See the note under "Leopold" in the very early Subject Notebook: "angry with those who do not hunt Mollie."

24. Or requested. See the letter to Frank Budgen dated Michaelmas 1920, in which Joyce begs for a "catchword" that would "set [him] off" (*Letters* I 147), or the suggestion made to Harriet Shaw Weaver that she "might 'order' a piece" (*Letters* I 245) and that Joyce would write according to her specifications (the result eventually provided the beginning of *Finnegans Wake*).

25. This is the title of James Atherton's book: *The Books at the Wake: A Study of Literary Allusions in James Joyce's Finnegans Wake* (Carbondale: Southern Illinois University Press, 1959).

26. Whether the statement reported by Ellmann (*James Joyce*, 521) is authentic or not, it gives a striking image of this strategy of deferment.

27. We have the notebooks that made the discovery possible, after much searching. It is possible that Joyce entertained the idea that this private reservation could one day become public. Early in the *Exiles* notes, Joyce refers to Flaubert's preparatory scenarios for *Madame Bovary* that had recently been published in the Conard edition of 1910: "Since the publication of the lost pages of Madame Bovary the centre of sympathy appears to have been esthetically shifted from the lover or fancyman to the husband or cuckold." We can see that Joyce takes

in consideration the posthumous publication of the avant-texte, which, coming unto the public scene, shifts the internal balance of the work, displacing its aesthetic effects to result in a new center. But it seems likely that if he had thought that his notebooks would reveal *the key* to *Finnegans Wake*, Joyce would have burned them, for that would mean the end of his "immortality."

28. Michael Riffaterre, "Un faux problème: l'érosion intertextuelle," in *Le Signe et le texte: Études sur l'écriture au 16e siècle en France*, ed. Lawrence D. Kritzman (Lexington, Ky.: French Forum, 1990).

29. Michael Riffaterre, "L'intertexte inconnu," *Littérature* 2, no. 41 (1981) and "La trace de l'intertexte," *La Pensée* 215 (1980).

30. Stanislaus Joyce, *My Brother's Keeper*, ed. Richard Ellmann (New York: Viking, 1958), 124.

31. It should be noted, however, that the agrammaticality of *Finnegans Wake* is rarely syntactical. Most of the sentences in the book are grammatical, in the sense that their syntax is perfectly correct.

32. Danis Rose, *James Joyce's The Index Manuscript: Finnegans Wake Holograph Workbook VI.B.46* (Colchester: A Wake Newslitter, 1978), XIII.

33. Typescript for chapter 7 of Book I of *Finnegans Wake* (British Library MS 47474–42, JJA 47:434).

34. Presumably, the change occurred on the missing proofs for *This Quarter*.

35. See Vincent Deane's introduction to volume VI.B.5 of *The Finnegans Wake Notebooks at Buffalo*, op. cit., 8–10.

36. Besides these notes in notebook VI.B.5 (terse, as usual), Joyce also copied long passages from Chateaubriand (and from other authors represented in this notebook, like Paul Valéry) on separate sheets. See note 131 above.

37. But also with heterogeneous elements that happened to be next to them on the notebook page. For a tabulation of the use of a notebook in a particular passage at different genetic levels, see Finn Fordham, "The Transfer from Notebooks to Drafts in 'Work in Progress,'" *Genetic Joyce Studies* 3 (Spring 2003).

38. Although he did use some notesheets to regroup them for use in particular destinations.

39. On p. 4 of notebook VI.B.14.

40. On p. 161 of notebook VI.B.22.

41. See Danis Rose's preface to the Raphael transcriptions in *JJA* 41, p. XII.

42. James Joyce, *The Lost Notebook*, edited by Danis Rose and John O'Hanlon (Edinburgh: Split Pea, 1989).

43. However, for unknown reasons, Raphael's transcription of this notebook was never used by Joyce.

44. Heinrich Baumann, *Londinismen (Slang und Cant) Wörterbuch der Londoner Volkssprache* (Berlin: Langenscheidt, 1903).

45. Robbert-Jan Henkes and Mikio Fuse have generalized and systematized Rose and O'Hanlon's restorative method: other "D" notebooks are being reconstructed with the help of ad hoc databases. See Robbert-Jan Henkes and Mikio Fuse, "Inside D1," *Genetic Joyce Studies* 12 (Spring 2012).

46. For critics like Albert Boime (*The Academy and French Painting in the Nineteenth*

Century [London: Phaidon, 1971]), and before him Joseph Sloane (*French Painting between the Past and the Present; Artists, Critics, and Traditions from 1848 to 1870* [Princeton, N.J.: Princeton University Press, 1951]), the revolution introduced by Manet and the Impressionists was simply that they presented as works of art something that the Academic painters considered as mere sketches. This is a gross simplification, but we could say that modernism does bring to the finished work some of the indeterminacy that is in evidence in genetic material.

Chapter 8. Virginia Woolf's Notes on *Ulysses:* A Conversational Reading

1. Virginia Woolf, "Modern Fiction," in *The Essays of Virginia Woolf, vol. IV: 1925–1928,* ed. Andrew McNeillie (London: Hogarth, 1994), 161.

2. Joyce's notes were taken early in 1924, months before the publication of Virginia Woolf's *The Common Reader,* in which "Modern Fiction," the revised version of "Modern Novels," appeared. It is possible that Joyce's attention had been brought to the anonymous *TLS* article of 1919 by the *Little Review*: a large extract from it, including the two phrases noted by Joyce, had been published (with the inaccurate indication that it came from "the *London Times*") in the "Reader Critic" section of its September-December 1920 issue (vol. VII, 3), the issue in which the first part of "Oxen of the Sun" was published.

3. See *The Finnegans Wake Notebooks at Buffalo: Notebook VI.B.6,* ed. Vincent Deane, Daniel Ferrer, and Geert Lernout (Turnhout: Brepols, 2002), 132–37.

4. See Daniel Ferrer, "Combien d'enfants avait Lady Gervaise: Le style de l'invention dans les ébauches de Zola," in *Zola Genèse de l'œuvre,* ed. J.-P. Leduc-Adine (Paris: CNRS Éditions, 2002).

5. In 1919, Woolf published *Night and Day,* which was received as a very traditional novel. Reviewing it in the *Athenaeum,* Katherine Mansfield wrote, "We had thought that this world had vanished for ever, that it was impossible to find on the great ocean of literature a ship that was unaware of what had been happening. Yet here is *Night and Day* [. . .] a novel in the tradition of the English novel. In the midst of our admiration it makes us feel old and chill. We had never thought to look upon its like again!" Quoted in Hermione Lee, *Virginia Woolf* (London: Vintage, 1997), 386. On December 9, 1919, Woolf expressed her distress at being categorized as "Jane Austen over again" (*A Writer's Diary: Being Extracts from the Diary of Virginia Woolf,* ed. Leonard Woolf [London: Hogarth, 1972], 22).

6. In "Phases of Fiction," Virginia Woolf relays a similar complaint: "Writers are heard to complain that influences—education, heredity, theory—are given weight of which they themselves are unconscious in the act of creation. Is the author in question the son of an architect or a brick-layer? Was he educated at home or at the university? Does he come before or after Thomas Hardy? Yet no one of these things is in his mind, perhaps, as he writes" (*The Essays of Virginia Woolf,* vol. 5, ed. Stuart N. Clarke [London: Hogarth, 2010], 41).

7. Woolf borrowed the issues from a friend (Mary Hutchinson) and she returned them in May 1919. Is it significant that she had mislaid one of the episodes? See letter number 1046a, in *The Letters of Virginia Woolf,* vol. 6, ed. Nigel Nicholson (London: Hogarth, 1980), 496.

8. *A Writer's Diary,* 349. This is Woolf's phrase about Joyce's books on Wednesday, January 15, 1941, when she realized that death had concluded their rivalry.

9. In her diary, Virginia Woolf unashamedly describes the *TLS* as Her Master's Voice:

"How pleased I used to be when L. called me 'You're wanted by the Major Journal!' and I ran down to the telephone to take my almost weekly orders at Hogarth House!" (*A Writer's Diary*, 293). This was indeed a call to be answered as a worthy, if slightly rebellious, daughter of Sir Leslie Stephen. She resigned herself uncomfortably to the gentle but firm censorship of the "Major Journal" (*A Writer's Diary*, 41). See also Eric Sandberg, "A Certain Phantom: Virginia Woolf's Early Journalism, Censorship, and the Angel in the House," *Virginia Woolf Miscellany* 76 (2009): 12–13.

10. The notes are part of a notebook, now at the Berg Foundation, classified as notebook XXXI in Brenda Silver's *Virginia Woolf's Reading Notebooks* (Princeton, N.J.: Princeton University Press, 1983). They have been published by Suzette Henke as "Modern Novels (Joyce)," in *The Gender of Modernism: A Critical Anthology*. Virginia Woolf's writing, in her reading notes, is extremely difficult to decipher. I suggest the following emendations to Henke's excellent transcription:

Page 642 of Henke's transcription:

for "plunge in!" read "'plunge in.'"

for "The ordinary life reaches then the extraordinary" read "The ordinary life richer than the extraordinary."

For "Minor [. . .] minds lack quality—and as you get nothing but minor minds!" read "Their minds lack quality—and as you get nothing but their minds!"

Page 643

For "The inner thought" read "In inner thought."

for "The—thrush—throstle—" read "tre—thrust—throstle—." (Woolf notes an alliteration in a Joycean paragraph)

for "how a hare does jump" read "how a horse does jump."

Page 644

for "mainly an excuse for writing" read "merely an excuse for writing."

for "(which makes us [?urgent])" perhaps read "(which makes us regress)."

for "of any like art" read "of any live art."

for "provincial and temporary" read "provisional and temporary."

for "new versions of beauty" read "new visions of beauty."

for "We see stories where people did not see them in the past . . ." read "We see stories where people did not see them in the past. *Gusev*" (Chekhov's paradigmatic short story)

Page 645

for "It's possible that the novel to us is what the drama was to the Greeks" read "It's possible that the novel to us is what the drama was to the E[lisabethans]."

for "by no means are of finality" read "by no means aim at finality."

for "Yet it seems just possible" read "Yet it seems quite possible."

Henceforth, I will be referring to this edition as *MNJ* followed by a page number.

11. The last part of the notebook is devoted to *The Life and Letters of William Thomson, Archbishop of York . . .* , but the presence of those notes in this particular copybook seems to be fortuitous: apparently the remaining blank pages were used a few weeks later, so we can consider that it doesn't affect the confrontation between Joyce and Woolf.

12. D. W. Winnicott, "Transitional Objects and Transitional Phenomena," in *Through Paediatrics to Psycho-Analysis* (London: Hogarth, 1982), 224.

13. Virginia Woolf, "Reviewing," in *The Crowded Dance of Modern Life*, ed. Rachel Bowlby (Harmondsworth: Penguin, 1993), 160.

14. As noted by Rachel Bowlby in her edition of this essay, *The Crowded Dance of Modern Life*, 183.

15. Woolf did read some more of *Ulysses* when it was published in 1922: *Mrs Dalloway* clearly shows the influence of a later chapter ("Wandering Rocks"). But according to James Heffernan's careful weighing of the evidence, she never completely finished the book ("Tracking a Reader: What Did Virginia Woolf Really Think of *Ulysses?*" in *Parallaxes: Virginia Woolf Meets James Joyce*, ed. Marco Canani and Sara Sullam [Newcastle upon Tyne: Cambridge Scholar Publishing, 2013]). She never commented on it publicly in detail or said anything about its technical innovations beyond writing that "*Ulysses* was a memorable catastrophe—immense in daring, terrific in disaster" ("How It Strikes a Contemporary," in *The Crowded Dance of Modern Life*, 27).

16. Review published in the *Times Literary Supplement,* February 13, 1919.

17. *Essays* 2, 33.

18. *A Writer's Diary*, 293.

19. *A Writer's Diary*, 8.

20. In the published essay, where Bennett and Wells are joined by Galsworthy, this status still appears very clearly: "Mr Wells, Mr Bennett, and Mr Galsworthy have excited so many hopes and disappointed them so persistently that our gratitude largely takes the form of thanking them for having shown us what they might have done but have not done."

21. See the already quoted diary entry of March 5, 1919.

22. The famous Russian Formalist introduced the concept in 1917 in the essay "Art as Technique," which became the first chapter of his *Theory of Prose*, published in 1925.

23. This is not Woolf's first contact with *Ulysses*. A year before, she and Leonard Woolf had been asked by Harriet Shaw Weaver if they would publish the book at their Hogarth Press. She was given the typescript of the first four episodes to read, but her reaction shows that she did not read it with great benevolence or care: "We've been asked to print Mr. Joyce's new novel, every printer in London and most of the provinces having refused. First there's a dog that p's—then there's a man that forths, and one can be monotonous even on that subject—moreover, I don't believe that his method, which is highly developed, means much more than cutting out the explanations and putting in the thoughts between dashes" (Letter 924 to Lytton Strachey, March 24, 1919). One year before, she had bought *A Portrait of the Artist as a Young Man* but did not receive it more favorably: "As for Mr Joyce, I can't see what he's after, though having spent 5/- on him, I did my level best, and was only beaten by the unutterable boredom" (Letter 852 to Clive Bell, July 24, 1917).

24. *The Diary of Virginia Woolf,* volume 1: *1915–1919*, ed. Anne Olivier Bell (London: Hogarth, 1977), 315.

25. Bennett, Wells, James, Hardy, Sterne, Gertrude Stein, Conrad, Byron, Johnson and Chekhov in Woolf's notes and Fielding, Austen, Thackeray, Wells, Galsworthy, Bennett, Hardy, Conrad, Hudson, Sterne, Chekhov and Meredith in the published article, as opposed to J. D. Beresford, the Goncourts, Marguerite Audoux, Rémy de Gourmont in Sinclair's article.

26. Three years later, when the book had just been published, she was still in the same

disposition. She writes: "I should be reading *Ulysses,* and fabricating my case for and against" (August 16, 1922, *A Writer's Diary*, 46), but clearly she is looking mostly for damning evidence.

27. If chronology did not make it impossible, we might believe that Sinclair was answering Woolf's review: "I have heard other novelists say that [Richardson's novels] have no art and no method and no form, and that it is this formlessness that annoys them. They say that they have no beginning and no middle and no end, and that to have form a novel must have an end and a beginning and a middle" ("The Novels of Dorothy Richardson," *Little Review* 5, no. 12 [1918]: 5).

28. "Its very close. rather exquisite—but how without blood & flesh & brains? [. . .] Minor minds lack quality—& as you get nothing but their minds! . . . But the worst of Joyce &c[ompany]: is their egotism—no generosity or comprehensiveness. Also seems to be written for a set in a back street. What does this come from? Always a mark of the second rate. Indifference to public opinion—desire to shock—need of dwelling so much on indecency. [. . .] Would my objections apply to T[ristram] S[handy]? . . . T.S. has a warmer temperature than Ulysses" (*MNJ* 643).

29. This probably refers to Richardson. See Woolf's diary a few months later: "I suppose the danger is the damned egotistical self; which ruins Joyce and Richardson to my mind: is one pliant and rich enough to provide a wall for the book from oneself without its becoming, as in Joyce and Richardson, narrowing and restricting?" (Monday, January 26, 1920, *A Writer's Diary*, 22). Woolf's meaning is not easy to grasp. Providing "a wall for the book from oneself" is necessary, but the solution offered by Joyce and Richardson is "narrowing and restricting" and leads back to the "damned egotistical self." In the terms of Sinclair's review, one should refuse to "be the wise, all-knowing author," but one must not be content to "be Miriam Henderson." If Woolf had gone beyond the first chapters of *Ulysses*, she would have been forced to reformulate her objection against Joyce, but her struggle against the "strange, [. . .] diabolical power which words possess [. . .] to suggest the writer [. . .] without the writer's will; often against his will" ("Craftmanship," in *The Essays of Virginia Woolf*. Volume VI: *1933–1941*, ed. Stuart Clarke [London: Hogarth Press, 2011], 94) was kept up until the very end. See Daniel Ferrer, *Virginia Woolf and the Madness of Language* (London: Routledge, 1990, repr. 2018).

30. It is easy to get carried away. For instance, one might be tempted to say that the famous third paragraph of *Mrs Dalloway* ("What a lark! What a plunge! For so it had always seemed to her, when, with a little squeak of the hinges, which she could hear now, she had burst open the French windows and plunged at Bourton into the open air. How fresh, how calm, stiller than this of course, the air was in the early morning . . .") is a distant reminiscence of Sinclair's article, with its insistence on the necessity of plunging (the word is repeated eight times in the space of a few lines), perhaps in conjunction with this quotation: "Deeper down was something cool and fresh—endless—an endless garden." Or even that the ecstasy that concludes the same novel ("what is this ecstasy"), derives from Sinclair's remark, "What really matters is a state of mind, the interest or the ecstasy with which we close with life." Until further evidence turns out (but this is not very likely), such speculations cannot be proven.

31. *New York Times*, "Latest Works of Fiction" [Review of *Jacob's Room*], March 4, 1923.

Conclusion

1. Charles Lamb, "Oxford in the Vacation," *London Magazine* 2, no. 10 (October 1820): 367.

2. See Woolf's early opinion, in her *Ulysses* reading notes, that when "everything can go in," such "jumble," "without coherence," can only be "interesting perhaps to doctors" (*MNJ* 642). See chapter 8, this volume.

3. Christine Froula has analyzed the significance of the contrasting attitudes of Lamb and Woolf: for Lamb, textual authority "is—or rather must seem—timeless, inalterable, 'absolute.' A poem transcends its historical beginnings." In its final form, it "is a prelapsarian Eden wherein *critique génétique* is as unthinkable as the mortal violation of poetry's sacred borders by the snaky, erring traces of fallible intention preserved in the abhorrent holograph." On the other hand, "Woolf's desire to see the manuscript—her desire to eat of the Tree of Knowledge of Good and Evil Texts [. . .] implicitly conceives poetic authority antithetically[:] human, historical, contingent, social"; Froula, "Modernism, Genetic Texts and Literary Authority in Virginia Woolf's Portraits of the Artist as the Audience," *Romantic Review* 86, no. 3 (1995): 514–15.

4. Samuel Beckett describes "Work in Progress" as a cycle of "endless verbal germination, maturation, putrefaction." "Dante . . . Bruno. Vico. . Joyce," in *Finnegans Wake: A Symposium—Our Exagmination Round His Incamination of Work in Progress* (Paris: Shakespeare & Co., 1929), 15. Joyce himself speaks of "letter from litter" (*FW* 615.01) and "decomposition for the verypetpurpose of recombination" (*FW* 614.34–35).

Works Cited

Ames, Keri Elizabeth. "Joyce's Aesthetic of the Double Negation and His Encounter with Homer's *Odyssey*." In *Beckett, Joyce and the Art of the Negative, European Joyce Studies* 16. Ed. C. Jaurretche. Amsterdam: Rodopi, 2005.

Anonymous. "Latest Works of Fiction." *New York Times* (March 4, 1923).

Aramis [pseud.]. "The Scandal of Ulysses." *The Sporting Times* 34 (April 1, 1922).

Atherton, James. *The Books at the Wake: A Study of Literary Allusions in James Joyce's Finnegans Wake.* Carbondale: Southern Illinois University Press, 1959.

Attridge, Derek, and Daniel Ferrer. *Poststructuralist Joyce.* Cambridge: Cambridge University Press, 1984.

Attridge, Derek. "Syntax and the Subject in 'Sirens.'" In *James Joyce: The Centennial Symposium,* ed. M. Beja, Ph. Herring, M. Harmon, and D. Norris. Chicago: Illinois University Press, 1986.

Baker, Carlos. *Ernest Hemingway: A Life Story.* New York: Charles Scribner's Sons, 1969.

Baumann, Heinrich. *Londinismen (Slang und Cant) Wörterbuch der Londoner Volkssprache.* Berlin: Langenscheidt, 1903.

Beckett, Samuel. "Dante . . . Bruno. Vico. . Joyce." In *Finnegans Wake: A Symposium; Our Exagmination Round His Incamination of Work in Progress.* Paris: Shakespeare & Co., 1929.

Bérard, Victor. *Les Phéniciens et l'Odyssée.* Paris: Librairie Armand Colin, 1902.

Boime, Albert. *The Academy and French Painting in the Nineteenth Century.* London: Phaidon, 1971.

Bourdieu, Pierre. *Manet: A Symbolic Revolution.* Trans. Peter Collier and Margaret Rigaud-Drayton. Cambridge: Polity, 2017.

Brown, Susan. "The Mystery of the *Fuga Per Canonem* Solved." *Genetic Joyce Studies* 7 (Spring 2007).

Budgen, Frank. *James Joyce and the Making of Ulysses.* Oxford: Oxford University Press, 1972.

Butcher, S. H., and A. Lang. *The Odyssey Of Homer Done into English Prose.* London: Macmillan, 1879.

Cerquiligni, Bernard. *In Praise of the Variant: A Critical History of Philology.* Baltimore: Johns Hopkins University Press, 1999.

Crispi, Luca. "A Commentary on James Joyce's National Library of Ireland 'Early Commonplace Book': 1903–1912(MS 36,639/02/A)." *Genetic Joyce Studies* 9 (2009).

———. "A First Foray into the National Library of Ireland's Joyce Manuscripts: Bloomsday 2011." *Genetic Joyce Studies* 11 (2011).

———. "The Notescape of *Ulysses*." In *New Quotatoes: Joycean Exogenesis in the Digital Age*, ed. Dirk Van Hulle and Ronan Crowley. Leide: Rodopi, 2016.

———. *Joyce's Creative Process and the Construction of Characters in Ulysses: Becoming the Blooms*. Oxford: Oxford University Press, 2015.

———. "The Afterlives of Joyce's 'Alphabetical Notebook' from *A Portrait* to *Ulysses* (1910–20)." *Genetic Joyce Studies* 20 (2020).

Crispi, Luca, Sam Slote, and Dirk Van Hulle. "Introduction." In *How Joyce Wrote "Finnegans Wake": A Chapter-by-Chapter Genetic Guide*, ed. Luca Crispi and Sam Slote. Madison: University of Wisconsin Press, 2007.

Czarnowski, Stefan Zygmunt. *Le Culte des héros et ses conditions sociales: Saint Patrick, héros national de l'Irlande*. Paris: Félix Alcan, 1919.

Deane, Vincent. Introduction. In *The "Finnegans Wake" Notebooks at Buffalo: VI.B.10*, ed. Vincent Deane, Daniel Ferrer, and Geert Lernout. Turnhout, Belgium: Brepols, 2001.

Deane, Vincent. Introduction. In *The "Finnegans Wake" Notebooks at Buffalo: VI.B.3*, ed. Vincent Deane, Daniel Ferrer, and Geert Lernout. Turnhout, Belgium: Brepols, 2001.

Deleuze, Gilles, and Félix Guattari. *A Thousand Plateaus: Capitalism and Schizophrenia*, trans. Brian Massumi. London: Athlone, 1988.

Deming, Robert. *James Joyce: The Critical Heritage*. London: Routledge and Kegan Paul; New York: Barnes and Noble, 1970.

Deppman, Jed. "A Chapter in Composition: *Chapter II.4*." In *How Joyce Wrote "Finnegans Wake": A Chapter-by-Chapter Genetic Guide*, ed. Luca Crispi and Sam Slote. Madison: University of Wisconsin Press, 2007.

Derrida, Jacques. *Margins of Philosophy*, trans. Alan Bass. Brighton, U.K.: Harvester, 1982.

———. "Two Words for Joyce: He War." In *Poststructuralist Joyce: Essays from the French*, trans. Geoff Bennington, ed. Derek Attridge and Daniel Ferrer. Cambridge: Cambridge University Press, 1984.

Domini Canis [Shane Leslie]. Review of *Ulysses*. *Dublin Review* 171 (September 1922).

Dumas, Alexandre. "Comment je devins auteur dramatique." *La Revue des Deux Mondes* 4 (1833).

Durkheim, Émile. *Les Formes élémentaires de la vie religieuse*. Paris: Presses Universitaires de France, 1985.

Eliot, T. S. "The Waste Land." *Criterion* 1, no. 1 (October 1922).

———. "'Ulysses,' Order and Myth." *Dial* 75 (November 1923).

———. *The Waste Land: A Facsimile and Transcript of the Original Drafts Including the Annotations of Ezra* Pound. Ed. Valerie Eliot. London: Faber and Faber, 1971.

Ellmann, Richard. *James Joyce*. New York: Oxford University Press, 1982.

Elster, Jon. *The Cement of Society: A Survey of Social Order*. Cambridge: Cambridge University Press, 1989.

Ferrer, Daniel. "La scène primitive de l'écriture: Une lecture joycienne de Freud." In *Genèse de Babel: James Joyce et la création de Finnegans Wake*, ed. Claude Jacquet. Paris: CNRS, 1985.

———. "The Freudful Couchmare of Shaun d: Joyce's Notes on Freud and the Composition of Chapter XVI of *Finnegans Wake*." *JJQ* 22, no. 4 (Summer 1985).

————. "Echo or Narcissus." In *James Joyce: The Centennial Symposium,* ed. M. Beja, Ph. Herring, M. Harmon, and D. Norris. Chicago: Illinois University Press, 1986.

————. "La toque de Clementis: Rétroaction et rémanence dans les processus génétiques." *Genesis* 6 (1994); English translation by Marlena Corcoran in *Yale French Studies* 89 (1996).

————. "What Song the Sirens Sang . . . Is No Longer Beyond All Conjecture: A Preliminary Description of the New 'Proteus' and 'Sirens' Manuscripts." *James Joyce Quarterly* 39, no. 1 (Fall 2001).

————. "Production, Invention and Reproduction: Genetic criticism vs. Textual Criticism." In *Reimagining Textuality: Textual Studies in the Late Age of Print,* ed. N. Fraistat and E. Bergmann Loizeaux. Madison: Wisconsin University Press, 2002.

————. "Combien d'enfants avait Lady Gervaise: Le style de l'invention dans les ébauches de Zola." In *Zola Genèse de l'œuvre,* ed. J.-P. Leduc-Adine. Paris: CNRS Éditions, 2002.

————. "Towards a Marginalist Economy of Textual Genesis." *Variants* 2–3 "Reading Notes" (2004).

————. "III.4: Wondrous Devices in the Dark." In *How Joyce Wrote Finnegans Wake: A Chapter-by-Chapter Genetic Guide,* ed. Luca Crispi and Sam Slote. Madison: University of Wisconsin Press, 2007.

————. "An Unwritten Chapter of Ulysses? Joyce's Notes for a 'Lacedemon' Episode." In *James Joyce: Whence, Whither and How: Studies in Honour of Carla Vaglio,* ed. Giuseppina Cortese, Giuliana Ferreccio, M. Teresa Giaveri, and Teresa Prudente. Alessandria: Edizioni dell'Orso, 2015.

————. "Genetic Criticism with Textual Criticism: From Variant to Variation." *Variants* 12–13 (2016).

Ferrer, Daniel, and Michael Groden. "Introduction." In *Genetic Criticism: Texts and Avant-textes,* ed. Jed Deppman, Daniel Ferrer, and Michael Groden. Philadelphia: Pennsylvania University Press, 2004.

Ferrer, Daniel, and Jean-Michel Rabaté. "Paragraphs in Expansion." Trans. Jed Deppman. In *Genetic Criticism: Texts and Avant-textes,* ed. Jed Deppman, Daniel Ferrer, and Michael Groden. Philadelphia: Pennsylvania University Press, 2004.

Flaubert, Gustave. *Correspondance,* vol. 2. Paris: Fasquelle, 1894.

Fordham, Finn. "The Transfer from Notebooks to Drafts in 'Work in Progress.'" *Genetic Joyce Studies* 3 (Spring 2003).

————. *Lots of Fun at Finnegans Wake: Unravelling Universals.* Oxford: Oxford University Press, 2007.

Frank, Joseph. "Spatial Form in Modern Literature." In *The Idea of Spatial Form,* ed. Joseph Frank. New Brunswick: Rutgers University Press, 1991.

Freud, Sigmund. *The Origins of Psychoanalysis.* Ed. Marie Bonaparte. New York: Basic, 1954.

Froula, Christine. "Modernism, Genetic Texts and Literary Authority in Virginia Woolf's Portraits of the Artist as the Audience." *Romanic Review* 86, no. 3 (1995).

Gabler, Hans Walter. "The Seven Lost Years of A Portrait of the Artist as a Young Man." In *Approaches to Joyce's Portrait,* ed. Bernard Benstock and Thomas F. Staley. Pittsburgh: University of Pittsburgh Press, 1976.

Genesis 41, "Créer à plusieurs mains" (2015).

Ginzburg, Carlo. "Clues: Roots of a Scientific Paradigm." *Theory and Society* 7, no. 3 (1979).

Goodman, Nelson. "Variations on Variation: Or Picasso Back to Bach." In *Reconceptions in Philosophy and other Arts and Sciences,* ed. Nelson Goodman and Catherine Elgin. Indianapolis: Hackett, 1988.

Groden, Michael. *Ulysses in Progress.* Princeton, N.J.: Princeton University Press, 1977.

———. "Joyce at Work on 'Cyclops': Toward a Biography of *Ulysses*." *James Joyce Quarterly* 44, no. 2 (Winter 2007).

Hayman, David. *A First-Draft Version of "Finnegans Wake."* Austin: University of Texas Press, 1963.

———. *The "Wake" in Transit.* Ithaca, N.Y.: Cornell University Press, 1990.

Heffernan, James. "Tracking a Reader: What Did Virginia Woolf Really Think of *Ulysses?*" In *Parallaxes: Virginia Woolf Meets James Joyce,* ed. Marco Canani and Sara Sullam. Newcastle upon Tyne: Cambridge Scholar Publishing, 2013.

Hemingway, Ernest. *Death in the Afternoon.* New York: Scribner and Son, 1932.

Henkes, Robbert-Jan, and Mikio Fuse. "Inside D1." *Genetic Joyce Studies* 12 (Spring 2012).

James Joyce's Ulysses: The John Quinn Draft Manuscript of the 'Circe' Episode, Thursday, 14 December 2000. New York: Christie's, 2000.

Jolas, Eugene. "Remembering James Joyce." *Modernism/Modernity* 5, no. 2 (1998).

Joyce, James. *Pomes Penyeach.* Paris: Shakespeare and Company, 1927.

———. *Scribbledehobble: The Ur-workbook for "Finnegans Wake."* Ed. Thomas Connolly. Evanston, Ill.: Northwestern University Press, 1961.

———. *Stephen Hero.* New York: A New Directions Book, 1963.

———. *The Lost Notebook.* Ed. Danis Rose and John O'Hanlon. Edinburgh: Split Pea, 1989.

———. *A Portrait of the Artist as a Young Man.* New York: Vintage International, 1993.

———. *The "Finnegans Wake" Notebooks at Buffalo: VI.B.14.* Ed. Vincent Deane, Daniel Ferrer, and Geert Lernout. Turnhout: Brepols, 2002.

Joyce, Stanislaus. *My Brother's Keeper.* Ed. Richard Ellmann. New York: Viking, 1958.

Kenner, Hugh. "Joyce's *Ulysses:* Homer and Hamlet." *Essays in Criticism* 2, no. 1 (January 1952).

Lamb, Charles. "Oxford in the Vacation." *London Magazine* 2, no. 10 (October 1820).

Lee, Hermione. *Virginia Woolf.* London: Vintage, 1997.

Lefèvre, Frédéric. *Entretiens avec Paul Valéry.* Paris: Le Livre, 1926.

Lernout, Geert. *James Joyce, Reader.* Dublin: National Library of Ireland, 2004.

Litz, A. Walton. *The Art of James Joyce: Method and Design in Ulysses and Finnegans Wake.* New York: Oxford University Press, 1961/1964.

Lumbroso, Olivier. *Zola autodidacte: Genèse des œuvres et apprentissages de l'écrivain en régime naturaliste.* Genève: Droz, 2013.

McHugh, Roland. *The Sigla of Finnegans Wake.* Austin: University of Texas Press, 1976.

Owen, Rodney. *James Joyce and the Beginnings of Ulysses.* Ann Arbor, Mich.: UMI Research Press, 1983.

Pound, Ezra. *Pound/the Little Review: The Letters of Ezra Pound to Margaret Anderson.* Ed. Thomas L. Scott, Melvin J. Friedman, Jackson R. Bryer. New York: New Directions, 1988.

Proust, Marcel. *À la Recherche du temps perdu* vol. III. Paris: Gallimard, 1954.

Rabaté, Jean-Michel. "The Silence of the Sirens." In *James Joyce: The Centennial Symposium,* ed. M. Beja, Ph. Herring, M. Harmon, and D. Norris. Chicago: Illinois University Press, 1986.

———. *Joyce upon the Void: The Genesis of Doubt*. London: Macmillan, 1991.
Rascoe, Burton. *A Bookman's Daybook*. New York: Horace and Liveright, 1929.
Riffaterre, Michael. "La trace de l'intertexte." *La Pensée* 215 (1980).
———. "L'intertexte inconnu." *Littérature* 2, no. 41 (1981).
———. "Un faux problème: L'érosion intertextuelle." In *Le Signe et le texte: Études sur l'écriture au 16e siècle en France,* ed. Lawrence D . Kritzman. Lexington, Ky.: French Forum, 1990.
Roscher, W. H. *Ausführliches Lexicon der griechischen und römischen Mythologie*. Leipzig: Teubner, 1884–1937.
Rose, Danis. *James Joyce's The Index Manuscript: Finnegans Wake Holograph Workbook VI.B.46*. Colchester: A Wake Newslitter, 1978.
———. "A Nice Beginning: On the *Ulysses/Finnegans Wake* Interface." *European Joyce Studies* 2 (1990).
———. "The Beginning of All Thisorder of Work in Progress." *James Joyce Quarterly* 28, no. 4 (Summer 1990).
———. *The Textual Diaries of James Joyce*. Dublin: Lilliput, 1995.
Sandberg, Eric. "A Certain Phantom: Virginia Woolf's Early Journalism, Censorship, and the Angel in the House." *Virginia Woolf Miscellany* 76 (2009).
Scholes, Robert, and Richard Kain. *The Workshop of Dedalus*. Evanston, Ill.: Northwestern University Press, 1965.
Silver, Brenda. *Virginia Woolf's Reading Notebooks*. Princeton, N.J.: Princeton University Press, 1983.
Simpson, John. "They Simply Fade Away: News on the Life and Death of an Old Soldier—Joseph Casey." *James Joyce Online Notes* 2 (2012).
Sinclair, May. "The Novels of Dorothy Richardson." *Little Review* V, no. 12 (1918).
Sloane, Joseph. *French Painting between the Past and the Present: Artists, Critics, and Traditions from 1848 to 1870*. Princeton, N.J.: Princeton University Press, 1951.
Slote, Sam. "Epiphanic 'Proteus.'" *Genetic Joyce Studies* 5 (2005).
———. "The Economy of Joyce's Notetaking." In *New Quotatoes: Joycean Exogenesis in the Digital Age,* ed. Ronan Crowley and Dirk van Hulle. Leiden: Brill, 2016.
Stillinger, Jack. *Multiple Authorship and the Myth of the Solitary Genius*. New York: Oxford University Press, 1994.
Sturge Moore, T. "The Story of Tristram and Isolt in Modern Poetry, Part I, Narrative Versions." *Criterion* 1, no. 1 (October 1922).
Topia, André. "'Sirens': The Emblematic Vibration." In *James Joyce: The Centennial Symposium,* ed. M. Beja, Ph. Herring, M. Harmon, and D. Norris. Chicago: Illinois University Press, 1986.
Van Hulle, Dirk. *James Joyce's Work in Progress: Pre-Book Publications of Finnegans Wake*. London: Routledge, 2016.
Van Mierlo, Wim. "The Freudful Couchmare Revisited: Contextualizing Joyce and the New Psychology." *Joyce Studies Annual* 8 (1997).
———. "The Subject Notebook: A Nexus in the Composition History of Ulysses—A Preliminary Analysis." *Genetic Joyce Studies* 7 (2007).
Williams, William Carlos. "A Note on the Recent Work of James Joyce." *transition* 8 (November 1927).

Winnicott, D. W. "Transitional Objects and Transitional Phenomena." In *Through Paediatrics to Psycho-Analysis*. London: Hogarth, 1982.

Woolf, Virginia. *A Writer's Diary: Being Extracts from the Diary of Virginia Woolf*. Ed. Leonard Woolf. London: Hogarth, 1972.

———. *The Diary of Virginia Woolf*. Volume 1: *1915–1919*. Ed. Anne Olivier Bell. London: Hogarth, 1977.

———. *The Letters of Virginia Woolf*, vol. 6. Ed. Nigel Nicholson. London: Hogarth, 1980.

———. "Modern Novels (Joyce)." In *The Gender of Modernism*, transcr. Suzette Henke, ed. Bonnie Kime Scott. Bloomington: Indiana University Press, 1990.

———. "How It Strikes a Contemporary." In *The Crowded Dance of Modern Life*, ed. Rachel Bowlby. Harmondsworth: Penguin, 1993.

———. "Reviewing." In *The Crowded Dance of Modern Life*, ed. Rachel Bowlby. Harmondsworth: Penguin, 1993.

———. "Modern Fiction." In *The Essays of Virginia Woolf*, vol. IV: *1925–1928*, ed. Andrew McNeillie. London: Hogarth, 1994.

———. "Phases of Fiction." In *The Essays of Virginia Woolf*, vol. V: *1929–1932*, ed. Stuart N. Clarke. London: Hogarth, 2017.

Illustration Credits

British Library, London, UK© British Library/Bridgeman Images
Figures 2.7, 3.2, 3.4, 3.5, 3.6, 5.2, 7.4

Harry Ransom Center
Figures 1.2b, 1.7

Houghton Library, Harvard University
Figure 2.2: MS Eng 160.4, (96)
Figure 2.3: MS Eng 160.4, (39)

James Joyce Estate
Figures 1.1, 1.2a, 1.2b, 1.3, 1.4, 1.5, 1.7, 2.2, 2.3, 2.4, 2.5, 2.6, 2.7, 3.1, 3.2, 3.3, 3.4, 3.5, 3.6, 4.1, 4.2, 4.3, 4.6, 5.2, 6.3, 7.1, 7.2, 7.3, 7.4, 8.1

National Library of Ireland
Figures 2.1, 6.2

The New York Public Library
Figure 8.3

The Poetry Collection of the University Libraries, University at Buffalo, The State University of New York
Figures 1.1, 1.2a, 1.3, 1.4, 1.5, 2.4, 2.5, 2.6, 3.1, 3.3, 4.1, 4.2, 4.3, 4.6, 6.3, 7.1, 7.2, 7.3, 8.1

The Society of Authors as the Literary Representative of the Estate of Virginia Woolf
Figure 8.3

Index

DANIEL FERRER is director of research emeritus at the Institut des Textes et Manuscrits Modernes, in Paris. He has written on Woolf, Faulkner, Poe, Stendhal, Balzac, Flaubert, Zola, Proust, Barthes and Hélène Cixous and on painting, digital humanities and film theory. He has published extensively on Joyce and on genetic criticism.

The Florida James Joyce Series

James Joyce's Painful Case, by Cóilín Owens (2008; first paperback edition, 2017)

Cannibal Joyce, by Thomas Jackson Rice (2008)

Manuscript Genetics, Joyce's Know-How, Beckett's Nohow, by Dirk Van Hulle (2008)

Catholic Nostalgia in Joyce and Company, by Mary Lowe-Evans (2008)

A Guide through "Finnegans Wake," by Edmund Lloyd Epstein (2009)

Bloomsday 100: Essays on "Ulysses," edited by Morris Beja and Anne Fogarty (2009)

Joyce, Medicine, and Modernity, by Vike Martina Plock (2010; first paperback edition, 2012)

Who's Afraid of James Joyce?, by Karen R. Lawrence (2010; first paperback edition, 2012)

"Ulysses" in Focus: Genetic, Textual, and Personal Views, by Michael Groden (2010; first paperback edition, 2012)

Foundational Essays in James Joyce Studies, edited by Michael Patrick Gillespie (2011; first paperback edition, 2017)

Empire and Pilgrimage in Conrad and Joyce, by Agata Szczeszak-Brewer (2011; first paperback edition, 2017)

The Poetry of James Joyce Reconsidered, edited by Marc C. Conner (2012; first paperback edition, 2015)

The German Joyce, by Robert K. Weninger (2012; first paperback edition, 2016)

Joyce and Militarism, by Greg Winston (2012; first paperback edition, 2015)

Renascent Joyce, edited by Daniel Ferrer, Sam Slote, and André Topia (2013; first paperback edition, 2014)

Before Daybreak: "After the Race" and the Origins of Joyce's Art, by Cóilín Owens (2013; first paperback edition, 2015)

Modernists at Odds: Reconsidering Joyce and Lawrence, edited by Matthew J. Kochis and Heather L. Lusty (2015; first paperback edition, 2020)

James Joyce and the Exilic Imagination, by Michael Patrick Gillespie (2015)

The Ecology of "Finnegans Wake," by Alison Lacivita (2015; first paperback edition, 2021)

Joyce's Allmaziful Pluralities: Polyvocal Explorations of "Finnegans Wake," edited by Kimberly J. Devlin and Christine Smedley (2015; first paperback edition, 2018)

Exiles: A Critical Edition, by James Joyce, edited by A. Nicholas Fargnoli and Michael Patrick Gillespie (2016; first paperback edition, 2019)

Up to Maughty London: Joyce's Cultural Capital in the Imperial Metropolis, by Eleni Loukopoulou (2017)

Joyce and the Law, edited by Jonathan Goldman (2017; first paperback edition, 2020)

At Fault: Joyce and the Crisis of the Modern University, by Sebastian D. G. Knowles (2018; first paperback edition, 2021)

"Ulysses" Unbound: A Reader's Companion to James Joyce's "Ulysses," Third Edition, by Terence Killeen (2018)

Joyce and Geometry, by Ciaran McMorran (2020)

Panepiphanal World: James Joyce's Epiphanies, by Sangam MacDuff (2020)

Language as Prayer in "Finnegans Wake," by Colleen Jaurretche (2020)

Rewriting Joyce's Europe: The Politics of Language and Visual Design, by Tekla Mecsnóber (2021)

Joyce Writing Disability, edited by Jeremy Colangelo (2022)

Joyce, Aristotle, and Aquinas, by Fran O'Rourke (2022)

Time and Identity in "Ulysses" and the "Odyssey," by Stephanie Nelson (2022)

Joyce without Borders: Circulations, Sciences, Media, and Mortal Flesh, edited by James T. Ramey and Norman Cheadle (2022)

An Irish-Jewish Politician, Joyce's Dublin, and "Ulysses": The Life and Times of Albert L. Altman, by Neil R. Davison (2022)

Beating the Bounds: Excess and Restraint in Joyce's Later Works, by Roy Benjamin (2023)

Genetic Joyce: Manuscripts and the Dynamics of Creation, by Daniel Ferrer (2023)